TRAVELING AUTEURS

New Directions in National Cinemas

Robert Rushing, editor

TRAVELING AUTEURS

The Geopolitics of Postwar Italian Cinema

LUCA CAMINATI

INDIANA UNIVERSITY PRESS

This book is a publication of

Indiana University Press
Office of Scholarly Publishing
Herman B Wells Library 350
1320 East 10th Street
Bloomington, Indiana 47405 USA

iupress.org

© 2024 by Luca Caminati
All rights reserved

No part of this book may be reproduced or utilized in any form or by any means, electronic or mechanical, including photocopying and recording, or by any information storage and retrieval system, without permission in writing from the publisher. The paper used in this publication meets the minimum requirements of the American National Standard for Information Sciences— Permanence of Paper for Printed Library Materials, ANSI Z39.48–1992.

Manufactured in the United States of America

First printing 2024

Cataloging information is available from the Library of Congress.

ISBN 978-0-253-06954-2 (hardback)
ISBN 978-0-253-06955-9 (paperback)
ISBN 978-0-253-06956-6 (e-book)

Contents

Acknowledgments   *vii*

1. Italian Cinema Travel   1
2. Rossellini in India, or the Home Abroad   23
3. Pasolini in Africa and the Middle East and Back   68
4. Antonioni in China, Mao in Milan   109

Bibliography   *165*
Index   *187*

Acknowledgments

This book started with a trip to India in 1999 with Carlo Antonelli and Emanuela De Cecco. In its current form, this book would simply not exist without the many people who shared materials in different languages and helped me make sense of them. My colleague and friend, Ishita Tiwari, advised me on Indian cinema and culture, and Priya Jaikumar and Maja Figge helped immensely in shaping my chapter on Rossellini. Renzo Rossellini and Gabriella Boccardo have given me access to their memories and their archives, and Adriano Aprà did not mind me bumming his cigarettes on the terrace of the American Academy in Rome when we first met in 2010. Margherita Moro gave me access to material that she is currently researching on Rossellini's unfinished films, and she generously shared them with me. I have to thank Xin Zhou, our graduate student at Concordia, for his help in scouting Chinese archives in search of traces of Antonioni and Jie Li at Harvard University for reading an earlier version of this work and providing invaluable help. Claudia Weill, the phenomenal filmmaker, gave me a copy of her memorable film on Shirley MacLaine in China; Henri Roanne shared with me his beautiful film *Chine*; Regina Longo, media archivist at Brown University, helped me with some invaluable archival tips; and A. Mackenzie Roberts at the Nixon Presidential Library in Yerba Buena, granted me access to the ABC version of Antonioni's film. Ayreen Anastas provided me a copy to her films on Palestine and beyond. With them, I want to thank the Social Sciences and Humanities Research Council (SSHRC) for their generous grants over the past ten years. I am also grateful to the Cinematek Royal Film Archive of Belgium

viii ACKNOWLEDGMENTS

in Brussels, the Danish Film Institute in Copenhagen, Laura Ceccarelli at the Centro Sperimentale di Cinematografia in Rome, and the Centro Studi-Archivio Pier Paolo Pasolini in Bologna and its indomitable director, Roberto Chiesi, each for providing me with invaluable material. I also would like to thank Paola Scarnati and the staff of Archivio Audiovisivo del Movimento Operaio e Democratico (AAMOD) in Rome for their help and support in researching primary sources. Thanks to AAMOD, the world is a better place.

I am grateful to the many insightful readers of the various drafts and sections for their feedback and support: Michael Cramer, Giuseppe Fidotta, Margherita Moro, and Luca Peretti who read early drafts of this work, and the doctoral students in the seminars I taught in the Film and Moving Image Studies program at Concordia University, who were terrific interlocutors on many of this book's topics and helped me reframe some of the issues that are central to it. I am also immensely thankful to the anonymous readers of the manuscript for their suggestions and insightful comments.

Zoë Laks helped enormously with the editing of this entire volume and its preparation for submission, and Egor Shmonin assisted with preparing the images. I thank Robert Rushing, former editor of the New Directions in National Cinemas series at Indiana University Press, for his support and Allison Chaplin and the rest of the Indiana University Press team for patiently navigating the whole project.

This project also wouldn't have been possible without all the care, support, and camaraderie from friends and colleagues. At Concordia, this includes Joshua Neves, Marc Steinberg, and Haidee Wasson, with whom I shared lunches and aperitifs. On the World Wide Web, that would be Gerry Milligan, with whom I have shared aspirational fashion debates since graduate school. This book took shape in many conversations both in the old country and on Turtle Island: with Marco Bertozzi, James Leo Cahill, Marco Dalla Gassa, Shelleen Greene, Vetri Nathan, Alan O'Leary, Federico Rahola, and Gavin Walker. Help and advice has come at different stages from Charles Acland, Dudley Andrew, Paolo Caredda, Francesco Casetti, Andrea Ciccarelli, Anna Daneri, Fabio De Luca, Kay Dickinson, Tarek Elhaik, Fabrizio Gallanti, Damiano Garofalo, Anna Giaufret, Luca Guadagnino, Bishnupriya Ghosh, Peter Limbrick, Andrea Lissoni, Armando Maggi, Silvestra Mariniello, Joshua Malitsky, Mariano Mestman, Ara Merjian, Sandro Mezzadra, Fiamma Montezemolo, Willy Montini, Viva Paci, Dileep Padgaonkar, Julie Paquette,

ACKNOWLEDGMENTS

Shahin Parhami, Ivelise Perniola, Francesco Pitassio, Marina Pugliese, Elena Razlogova, Mauro Resmini, Phil Rosen, Colleen Ryan, Bhaskar Sarkar, Viviane Saglier, Antonella Sisto, Luisa Stagi, and Rhiannon Welch.

And I am always grateful to Masha for being my interlocutor, my greatest champion, my love, and my home and to Vini—for being the one and only *babaluba*.

TRAVELING AUTEURS

1

Italian Cinema Travel

[This is a call] . . . for critical intellectuals in the former and current colonies of the third world to once again deepen and widen decolonization movements, especially in the domains of culture, the psyche, and knowledge production. It further calls for critical intellectuals in countries that were or are imperialist to undertake a deimperialization movement by reexamining their own imperialist histories and the harmful impacts those histories have had on the world. Dialectical interaction between these two processes is a precondition for reconciliation between the colonizer and the colonized, and only after such a reconciliation has been accomplished will it be possible for both groups to move together toward global democracy.[1]

Solidarity

In the 1970 film directed by Citto Maselli, *Lettera aperta a un giornale della sera* (*Open Letter to the Evening News*), a group of leftist intellectual men at a cocktail party in Rome decide to write to a national newspaper to announce their decision to volunteer for and personally engage in the fight against American imperialism in Vietnam. The move is supposed to be a provocation or joke of sorts, but the letter ends up being published, and Jean-Paul Sartre immediately issues a statement from Paris in support of this newly formed culture brigade with a passion for lounging, smoking, and womanizing. The men are compelled to take up arms in order not to lose their *revolucionareidad* (revolutionary credibility), which the Cubans at that time defined as the spirit and attitude of a true comrade.[2] In the end, the Vietnamese liaison who was supposed to escort them to the front line never materializes, and these "radicals" go back to their Roman penthouses. *Lettera aperta* fits well within Maselli's career, one made up of over-the-top satires of the Italian Left's aspirations that often parodied the style and motifs of 1970s Italian political films by directors such as Marco Bellocchio, Elio Petri, Gillo Pontecorvo, Francesco Rosi, Ettore Scola, and Lina Wertmüller, to name but a few.[3] Despite its humor and obvious sarcastic intentions, *Lettera aperta* can be read as an interesting repository of tensions around politically committed filmmaking, and it is symptomatic of the Italian engagement with Third World struggles, where contradictory imperatives often clash—as in this case—within the same text. Above all, the film mocks both the posturing of the political filmmaking scene of the time and the seriousness of many leftist intellectuals' intentions vis-à-vis their actual political activism. At the same time, however, the film is deadly serious in representing the global network of solidarity and the importance of Third World issues of anticolonialism in the international community, something signaled by the mention of Sartre, the best-known intellectual ally of liberation struggles. Maselli's critique of political cinema demonstrates how pervasive this type of militant audiovisual language had become by 1970, so much so that it became open to parody by both the liberal Right and the fragmented Left that were then extant in Italy.[4]

Kristin Ross has pointed out a similar situation in the French context when "in the years immediately preceding 1968, as the war accelerated in Vietnam, and especially after December 1966 with the American bombing of Hanoi, it was the North Vietnamese peasant, and not the auto worker at Billancourt, who had become, for many French militants, the figure of the working class."[5] The Third World liberation fighter became a sort of "transitional figure, the relay between the . . . colonial other . . . and the French worker during '68."[6] The notion of the *relay* is developed in the cinematic cultural context of the distribution and dissemination of films in midcentury Iran by Kaveh Askari, who claims that this term "evokes circulation but with an emphasis on sequence, interruption, and incremental agency over top-down or seamless transparency."[7] This lack of a top-down approach to issues concerning the Global South well describes the confusing interactions and dealings that animated the reception and understanding of issues concerning liberation movements.[8] Ross's and Askari's notions of the *transitional figure* and the *relay* refigure neatly into the contemporaneous Italian context and probably also apply to large portions of the West at the time, where activists were embracing a Third-Worldist position out of a combination of solidarity and, at times, misguided political exoticism, or what Jacopo Galimberti wittingly calls "militant orientalism."[9]

What was becoming apparent in the late 1950s and early 1960s was that the liberation movements of Africa and Asia, the new democratic and socialist movement in postpartition India, and the communist revolution in China offered radical new alternatives to the status quo. These events generated a network of international solidarity, which—while centered politically on South-South connections (as in the case of the Bandung Conference in 1955 in Indonesia and the subsequent foundation of the Non-Aligned Movement [NAM], in 1961 in Belgrade and eventually the *Tricontinental* conference in 1966 in Cuba)—had significant appeal for leftist European and American intellectuals. Disillusioned with both Stalinist communism and postwar capitalism, they sought alternative paths to modernization and socialism, inspired by decolonial and postcolonial formations emerging from the Middle East, Africa, and Asia. The impact of the thought of Third-Worldist intellectuals and leaders—from Frantz Fanon to Che Guevara and their Western allies Jean-Paul Sartre and Black Panther Eldridge Cleaver, to name just a few of the most iconic figures of this period—generated a cadre of fellow travelers in the West.[10] The years of colonial upheaval and the accession to political subjectivity by "the wretched of the earth" resonated widely in the Global North.[11]

In the Italian context, as Neelam Srivastava highlighted in her groundbreaking analysis of Italy's relationship to anticolonialism, "Italy's imperial ambitions played a fundamental, though overlooked, role in the development of an oppositional discourse to Western imperialism more broadly."[12] In fact, "Italian colonialism influenced the articulation of anti-colonial discourse precisely because it was so belated; the fascist regime's illegal invasion of Ethiopia occurred in 1935, when anti-imperialist movements and alliances were flourishing across the globe, and Western public opinion was beginning to seriously question the values underpinning the imperial project. Empire, in other words, was in crisis."[13] Moreover, we must remember that it is in the 1930s, thanks to Antonio Gramsci and the Italian Communist Party (PCI), that a specifically Italian version of anticolonialism was formed that brought together "global solidarity with the oppressed, and with migrant labor worldwide, because Italians had experienced first-hand discrimination and oppression both as emigrants and within their own country."[14] Placing the roots of Italian anticolonialism into the heart of the fascist regime points to a longer diachronic connection of the Italian Left to an evolving Global

South, complicated as it was by the massive migration of the Italian labor force to northern Europe and the Americas.

Over the past decades, scholars have begun to rediscover the political, ideological, and artistic potentialities that animated these alternative political movements and their impact on the metropolitan colonial centers.[15] The repercussions of midcentury liberation movements in the Global South have been mostly erased from the Italian cultural landscape, and even though France has traditionally been at the center of these narratives, the work of Luca Peretti, Neelam Srivastava, and Mariano Mestman demonstrate that Italy has in fact been an important point of connection between European and Third-Worldist circles.[16] This historiographical rediscovery goes hand in hand with the uncovering of Italy's colonial past, whose erasure up to recent times has marred both academia and Italian society at large. In the field of Italian film studies, it is only in recent years that colonial cinema, that is to say, films shot in the Italian colonies during the occupation, resurfaced in state and private archives and were restored, made available, cataloged, and studied by a new generation of scholars of Italian colonial cinema.[17] This new interest in imperial media productions has generated in turn a renewed interest from cultural studies scholars who are looking at the "imperial debris" (to borrow the apt term of Ann Laura Stoler), the remnants of the Italian colonial past in both high and low cultural artifacts, images, and films.[18] As part of this larger intellectual project, scholars of Italian film and media are now interested in reconstructing the historical landscape of postwar Italy beyond the accepted narratives of neorealism and art cinema, by either focusing on understudied formations (industrial and ephemeral cinemas, amateur, activists, etc.) or looking at larger geopolitical intersections that brought Italian filmmakers, artists, and intellectuals in contact with larger movements of the Global South. As Italy witnesses a drastic geopolitical shift toward the postcolonial world order, these alternative circuits are now being reinvestigated because of their underexamined historical import, as well as anticipations and models for current antiracist and other global solidarity movements. This book is both part of and in conversation with these developments.

The Traveling Auteur

The main focus of this book is nonfiction and narrative documentary films made in the Middle East, Africa, and Asia by three canonical Italian filmmakers—Roberto Rossellini, Pier Paolo Pasolini, and Michelangelo Antonioni—, films that I analyze within the political complexity of their times. With this perspective in mind, I approach these traveling auteurs as actors in a geopolitical network of artists and activists involved as direct witnesses to one of the most momentous political changes of the twentieth century: the anticolonial struggles and the birth of the postcolonial world in the Global South, the reaffirmation of the NAM, and the consolidation of socialist China. I see their films as cultural objects reflecting and shaped by the Italian debates on decolonization, third worldism, and the NAM. I also investigate their afterlife at home and abroad: the resonance that these films had in the countries where they were actually shot and their reception and legacy in the Italian mediasphere. These nonfiction films in their formal diversity—which range from made-for-television reportages to narrative nonfiction—became a form of personal and political investigation of the postcolony beyond the simple repletion of colonial clichés.[19] In different ways, Rossellini, Pasolini, and Antonioni are fully aware of this visual burden, and all struggle to address and overcome it in their work without mimicking their colonial forebears, as many travel writers and filmmakers do even today.[20]

In undertaking this project of analysis of Italian filmmakers working in the Global South, I seek to "provincialize" Italian cinema studies (invoking the concept coined by Dipesh Chakrabarty) by decentering and relocating these major Italian auteurs within broader geopolitical trends, in an attempt to move away from a temporal totality and pluralize the canonical history of Italian cinema.[21] While more recently film historians have challenged a traditional Eurocentric teleological development of Italian cinema, little has been done to rethink it spatially and geopolitically. That is, I aim to use geography and politics to gauge how Italian cinema has reacted to the world outside. The notion of World Cinema, then, is used upside down here, so to speak: not as a way to include and incorporate non-Western films into an otherwise Western-centered narrative geography but as a way to look at Italian films as "worldly," that is to say, from a geopolitical perspective put forth by Masha Salazkina as "point[ing] towards an exploration of the uneven and heterogeneous processes that constitute the relations across, between, and within cinematic cultures globally."[22]

As Italy underwent accelerated modernization, many of its intellectuals recognized the challenges the country faced to be not so dissimilar from the postcolonial world at large. With its underdeveloped agrarian regions, its relative tardiness in becoming a unified state, its endemic political clientelism, and the media-led supplanting of its rural ethos by an urban, capitalist one, the dynamics of Italian progress provided lines of shared vision between the Italian intellectuals and those of the Third World.[23] Specifically, in their work, these postwar Italian filmmakers explored the cultural processes of marginalization that further developed in postwar modernizing Italy. For Marxists like Pasolini, the postcolonial world order offered a whole new path of revolutionary hope. Likewise, India offered to Rossellini a mirror to look at Italy's postwar reconstruction efforts, and China in turn offered an absolute political alterity to Antonioni and his crew. The work of these directors presents an ambitious attempt to negotiate the aesthetic ideologies of postwar European art cinema with the postcolonial world that was in the making at the time. Each looked at India, China, and African countries like Uganda and Tanzania as alternative places to Western modernity. My film corpus, then, samples the work of these Italian artists as they dealt with the global landscape of the Cold War period, following their (sometimes-ambivalent) political and aesthetic engagement with Third World politics and offering a reevaluation of the tensions and contradictions that characterized the relationship between the European Left and the emerging postcolonial / Third World ideologies. As nonfiction, or in the case of Rossellini, weak narrative fictions, these films not only record specific manifestations of the political sensibilities of the twentieth century but also test the limits of auteurism by extending and expanding the understanding of cinematic styles associated with art cinema to other modes of filmmaking (documentary) and media (television).[24]

The geopolitical atlas of those years was, from a revolutionary standpoint, exhilarating.[25] What these new geopolitical alliances had in common was the attempt to build trans-solidarity beyond race, nation-state, and language. Exemplary in this sense is the Cuban magazine *Tricontinental*, founded in 1967 as the official outlet of the Organization of Solidarity with the People of Asia, Africa and Latin America (OSPAAAL). As highlighted by Anne Garland Mahler in her book *From the Tricontinental to the Global South* (2018), this group, more than others, aimed at transcending nation and race to create a true *communitas*, "a community of feeling, an affective community of solidarity that transcends national and regional geography and whose affinities are not based on location, language, or blood."[26] The impact, and particularly the echo, of the new NAM (officialized in Belgrade in 1961) and the liberation struggles that were taking place all over the colonized world had an outsize impact on the Western Left. All the movements that coalesced around the ideology of 1968 and that had such a vast influence on the artistic and more specifically filmic production of the times had to deal, in one way or another, with this new geopolitical configuration.

This was very much true in Italy, where pockets of film culture were imbued with Third-Worldist awareness. We can detect in some cultural hot spots a shift in the Italian cinematic culture of the 1960s, from the valorization of traditional social(ist) realist aesthetics, emblematized by neorealism, to an emerging form of militant criticism triggered by new political cinemas. The Mostra Internazionale del Nuovo Cinema di in Pesaro, established by Lino Micciché and Bruno Torri in 1964, played a particularly crucial role in the dissemination of new cinemas from revolutionary hot spots, especially in the Americas. With politicized publics eager for new militant cinema, the event catered to audiences whose enthusiasm had initially been fostered by the Mostra Internazionale del Cinema Libero in Porretta Terme (the Porretta Terme Free Cinema Festival) and the Festival del Cinema Latino-Americano (the Latin American Film Festival) in Santa Margherita Ligure and Sestri Levante.[27]

While none of my chosen traveling auteurs were directly involved in these revolutionary struggles, these new geopolitical openings resonated in their decision to embark on these non-Western projects in addition to percolating in the leftist culture at large.[28] It's difficult to imagine the trips of Rossellini, Pasolini, and Antonioni outside of this new political framework, one that was generated by fractures and fissures in the Cold War regime. We are also confronted with an interesting dialectical phenomenon. On the one hand, realism (and neorealism more specifically) offered a model for progressive cinemas in Asia and Latin America, as analyzed by Lucia Nagib, who goes as far as claiming that realist cinema is indeed the most visible and common feature of World Cinema.[29] The dissemination and prestige of Italian postwar cinema reached far and wide across screens on both sides of the Iron Curtain and throughout Latin America and India.[30] On the other hand, the "actual existing neorealists" (ultimately, each of my chosen auteurs planted their roots solidly in the neorealist movement) turned to the non-West for inspiration, not just in terms of different and exotic content for their subjects but in search of aesthetic freedom and inspiration triggered by a new interest in hot spots of political change. This book, then, retells the story of neorealism and of Italian auteurs, who are usually understood to be part of art cinema (rather than any sort of militant cinema). In my analysis, I frame them in their attempt at mediating between their neorealist origins, art cinema's present, and the horizon of Third-Worldist and Global South cinemas of the 1960s.

Cinema and Travel

Cinema and travel have a long-shared history—film production, distribution, and exhibition have always been international and transnational, and films have always relied on and borrowed from travel's experiences and infrastructures for its orientalist representations.[31] Thus, in addition to textually based analyses of films, this project addresses their production, critical reception, and afterlives in and outside of Europe and North America using fieldwork methods and archival research. To quote James Clifford, this is "work entering a very large domain of comparative cultural studies: the diverse, interconnected histories of travel and displacement in the late twentieth century." Taking a hint from Clifford, I ask myself, "How [does] cultural analysis constitut[e] its objects ... in spatial terms and through specific spatial practices of research?"[32] In this book, I use *travel* as a method of analysis of both filmmaking practices, in what I define as "travel essay films," and personal and political encounters in the age of mass travel.[33] The early travel "pioneers," with or without a camera, have been replaced by the "bohemian bourgeois"—masses of tourists, who replicate and amplify consolidated tropes of exotic locations and display "a fascination for the 'real life' of others."[34] Clifford's engagement and critique of consolidated anthropological practices rooted in colonial ideologies resonated with these late midcentury travels, as they look at the world with a new political lens.

Borrowing from Pratt, I model these films as "zones of contact" in a transnational network of artists and filmmakers, a framework that allows us to analyze the relationships between film cultures, political entanglements, and travel.[35] Zones of contact are, according to Pratt's original formulation, "social spaces where cultures meet, clash, and grapple with each other, often in contexts of highly asymmetrical relations of power, such as colonialism, slavery, or their aftermaths as they are lived out in many parts of the world today ... the space of colonial encounters, the space in which peoples geographically and historically separated come into contact with each other and establish ongoing relations, usually involving conditions of coercion, radical inequality, and intractable conflict."[36] James Clifford, in his essay

"Museums as Contact Zones," uses this concept to activate museums as "sites of historical negotiations, occasions for an ongoing contact." The audio-visual material I am dealing with displays many of the elements identified by Clifford, as they are cultural products trapped in a negotiation of power and privilege impossible to otherwise untangle. In fact, attempts at claiming either solidarity or innocence as a mode of approaching these spaces through film seem to confirm the double bind that runs through the process of filming the "Orient"—a double articulation of political engagement and exoticism that will run throughout the course of this work, serving to unmask how the process is caught up in the very imperial project of global power even as it tries to dismantle it.[37] In short, I follow Edward Said's advice in his "Traveling Theory" when he invites scholars "to map the territory covered by all the techniques of dissemination, communication, and interpretation."[38] I take this as a starting point to think of these films and filmmakers as more than both European auteurs and white men in the "Orient" and instead envision them as subjects at the intersection of larger political events. The performances of affinities, alliances, and solidarities, as well as the cleavages and contradictions that traversed the postcolonial and socialist projects these filmmakers were traveling through, will be part of a wider picture in which they are agents and subjects alike.

In this book, I am interested in a cinematic geography understood as "an international construct established through travel," as Kay Dickinson puts it in *Arab Cinema Travels*, in referring to that invented geography known as the Arab World.[39] In my work, I am interested in using the notion of travel to deploy "the actual experience of moving through, as well as perceiving and reconfiguring, space."[40] That space I am referring to is one of transnational solidarity, of dialogue between the bipolar geopolitics of the time: a "third space" of possibilities that, as we know, was and is highly contested.[41] In short, I want to use *travel as method* so as to posit travel both as a subject of research and as a heuristic that allows investigation into uncharted geographies. It is for this reason that I would like to add to the gallery compiled by Tzvetan Todorov in *On Human Diversity* of the modern traveler (as "the impressionist, the allegorist and the disenchanted"), the concept of the *political traveler* in the age of decolonization.[42] I borrow from Maureen Moynagh's recent work on political tourism, by engaging with that category of traveler "who seeks to participate in or manifest solidarity with a political struggle taking place 'elsewhere' in the world . . . [who] practise[s] a kind of 'world citizenship' that is about imagining a different kind of belonging, a different kind of human relationship, and a different practice of the self than are typically afforded through exclusively national, ethnic, or gendered forms of belonging."[43] More precisely, in the decolonial world, this political traveler engages, in the words of Leela Gandhi, in "minor narratives of crosscultural collaboration between oppressors and oppressed" across the North-South geopolitical divide.[44] Moreover, the encounter with the Middle East, Africa, and Asia brings these directors in contact with fellow *tiermondiste* intellectuals and artists of their times and places them in real or imaginary dialogue with other *auteurs* (such as Santiago Álvarez, Youssef Chahine, Julio García Espinosa, Med Hondo, Joris Ivens and Marceline Loridan, William Klein, Louis Malle, Chris Marker, Sarah Maldoror, Gillo Pontecorvo, Jean Renoir, Agnès Varda, René Vautier, and more recently Trinh T. Minh-ha and Portuguese filmmakers Miguel Gomes and Filipa César, among others) whose work similarly seeks to investigate the connections between geopolitical intimacies on a global scale. As such, this project traces part of a larger network of artists and intellectuals who share a transnational history of geopolitically engaged cinema, a network with wide-ranging ramifications in the contemporary everyday world.

The Travel Cinema Spectrum

The Italian film culture of the '60s and '70s offers a wide variety of travel films with very different scopes, intentions, and results. On the one hand, there are the *auteur documentaries* that this book directly engages with, along with other similar authorial, art film–influenced productions. On the other side of this "travel film spectrum," we find the notorious *Mondo* films, originated by quasi-anthropologists and gonzo reporters Franco Prosperi and Gualtiero Jacopetti (who were, by the way, each part of left-wing intellectual circles— Jacopetti specifically was a *partigiano*, a resistance fighter during World War II). Their first feature, the 1962 *Mondo Cane* (*A Dog's World*, directed by Cavara, Jacopetti, and Prosperi) introduced the world to the *shockumentary*, originally a marginal phenomenon in the standard history of Italian cinema, which in recent years has been fully rediscovered and repurposed for a more comprehensive and meaningful understanding of national cinema.[45] Films like *Mondo Cane* and those made in its wake were exploitation "fake documentaries" (highly staged and choreographed nonfiction) that offered voyeuristic commentary on cultural practices and taboo subjects in both "modern/First" and "primitive/Third" worlds. As Alan O'Leary has recently pointed out, these exploitation films were in dialogue, rather than at odds, with most cinematic productions of the time. For example, "the sensational aspects of the films . . . [and] the ironic tone" were representative of the Italian comedy of those same years, which were known for their "employment of found footage and associative structure . . . recall[ing] experimental film; the[ir] restaging (sometimes frank, sometimes dissembled) of 'real' events or practices . . . characteristic of postmodern filmmaking; and the[ir] voyeurism anticipat[ing] reality television."[46] This dialogue between high and low cultural products at the core of the *Mondo* films' aesthetics and politics is symptomatic of a more fluid relationship between genres than many scholars would like to admit. The shockumentary as a contact film genre borrowed from the debates in visual anthropology, travel film ethics and style, exposés, and reportage popularized by the then nascent television, as well as popular genres of mass entertainment. But more than anything else, it weaponized already pervasive clichéd and fossilized racial imaginaries that originated in orientalist representations, which translated into the 1960s "travel film" as a combination of global "exotica" and a "rearticulation of the colonial archive."[47]

What Antonioni, Pasolini, and Rossellini as well as Prosperi and Jacopetti have in common is a shared zeitgeist and a shared filmmaking toolbox. This matter-of-fact attitude toward the "travel spectrum" allows us (as Marco Dalla Gassa and Gaia Giuliani have already demonstrated in their recent groundbreaking work) to level the playing field by avoiding strict auterist readings of celebrated filmmakers and instead opens up a new world of potential narratives both historically and ideologically vis-à-vis Italian cinema and media.[48] This is true as well of the intimacy of auteurs and popular filmmakers with a shared colonialist outlook that runs through the entire Italian political spectrum of the time (and beyond), a consequence of the unchallenged colonial history and the *italiani brava gente* myth that remains pervasive in Italian culture.[49] In short, the double articulation of exoticism and solidarity that we see at the political and ideological level in these films is replicated in their stylistics, as populist and accessible mainstream documentary techniques are mixed with more experimental moments.

The Postcolonial Uncanny

Edward Said defines the Orient as "almost a European invention, [which] had been since antiquity a place of romance, exotic beings, haunting memories and landscapes, remarkable experiences."[50] This invention that through repetition and replenishment has perpetuated itself and percolated in Western culture is still very much part of our contemporary visual landscape. From the end of the eighteenth century until now, the multiplication of racial clichés has, if anything, strengthened. Television first and the World Wide Web today has filled screens with exoticized and racialized images, where the Other is still a figure of anxiety.[51] As in an unmodifiable recipe, all the stories, films, memoirs, YouTube vloggers, and podcasts still project an Orient made of tigers, gurus, sacred rivers, funeral pyres, colorful women, scrawny elders, dwarves, trained monkeys, and breathtaking landscapes and, at the center, standing tall, the impassive traveler, his gendered, colonial, domineering gaze as the fulcrum. This is what Ariella Azoulay in her 2019 book, *Potential History: Unlearning Imperialism*, defines as the key imperial figure of "the discoverer and its homologues in the quest for knowledge—the inquisitive mind, the art connoisseur, the philosopher," whose "status, authority, and legitimacy" cannot be doubted.[52] This "discoverer," owner of the "imperial eyes" theorized by Pratt, has shaped the Western approach to representation of any non-Western alterity.[53] Even the filmmakers I am engaging with are part of this orientalist discourse: often sporting a Safari jacket, as with Rossellini in India; or cruising for sex like Pasolini; or taking a hieratic detached position like Antonioni—each interface with the Orient alongside all the concern and anxiety that this signifier has acquired in the Italian and Western imaginary. It evokes, it seems to me, that "uncanny" phenomenon analyzed by Sigmund Freud in his 1917 essay "Die Unheimlich." As Freud explains, *Unheimlich* is that which is familiar and should not be, that which should remain repressed and yet resurfaces at a conscious level. Homi Bhabha, when translating the concept of *Unheimlich* into English, uses the term *unhomeliness*: literally not feeling at home (different from "homeless": without a home), along with a feeling of unease, of being disoriented.[54] What Bhabha points to geographically is not just the encounter with the absolute alterity of uninhabited spaces—the wilderness, the desert, or the arctics—but the encounter with *the postcolonial space*.[55] Those who have traveled into the postcolony can immediately acknowledge that the lengthy and significant force of colonial domination has produced remains of the empire that catches the traveler's eye at every turn, between hotels, roads, country clubs, and resorts, all enveloped in an "unsettling" space.[56] Western travelers find themselves interacting with this new world through either mystical fusion or a normalizing and stereotyping process of anxiety in an attempt to compensate for this postcolonial Unheimlich.[57]

This anxiety of the white man traveler in postcolonial spaces has been theorized as the ultimate orientalist experience, from Said's *Orientalism* to Mary Louise Pratt's *Imperial Eyes*, Karen Caplan's *Questions of Travel*, Alison Griffiths's *Wondrous Difference*, and Fatimah Tobing Rony's *The Third Eye*, just to mention the best-known theoretical engagements with this issue.[58] While I acknowledge and accept these readings, I am interested here in turning the term *travel* into an actual instrument that can be used to fix, rig, or sabotage the chain of clichés that animate orientalist discourses. I want to look at travels that are, although inevitably participating in the orientalist/ tourist gaze, problematic enough not to fit in the mold and offer a way out, so to speak, of the orientalist quicksand that traps the Western traveler every time they try to represent the Other. Each of my chosen traveling filmmakers is in fact involved in a double articulation of solidarity and orientalism, two registers that a symptomatic reading of their work makes emblematically and embarrassingly clear.

Traveling Auteurs

My *Traveling Auteurs* are not heroes of the revolution. I have no intention of looking at them as the new Lord Byron fighting for the freedom of the oppressed or as Westerners to whom every artistic freedom is afforded. In a recent razor-sharp analysis of racial issues in Italian media, Gaia Giuliani cut to the heart of the matter when, in her discussion of Italian filmmakers abroad, she points to the position of privilege, actual and rhetorical, that they embody and how their narrative sexualization of black and brown bodies, specifically in the case of Pasolini, is one of domination and mastery. Following Giuliani's lead, this book will not celebrate white men's burdens or their accomplishments—it will, though, point to issues of "trans-affective solidarity" that motivated these men, and more importantly, the films they ended up making.[59]

Each chapter of this book focuses on a series of distinct case studies while offering a broad survey of Italian political travelers/filmmakers to provide both a synchronic and a diachronic understanding of these processes. Chapter 2, and the starting chronological point for this overview of these filmmakers' engagements with the post-Bandung world, reviews Rossellini's films shot in India between 1957 and 1958, which include a feature film, *India: Matri Bhumi* (1959), and two documentaries developed for Italian and French national television. Respectively titled *L'India vista da Rossellini* (1959) and *J'ai fait un beau voyage* (1958), they consist of ten episodes of approximately 25 minutes each, in which Rossellini blends expository documentary, political commentary, and personal travel observations. It is in these personal inserts, diary entries, visual vignettes, quips, and narrative asides—in short, in this "personal camera" mode (to use Rascaroli's term)—that Rossellini lays out the irresolvable aesthetic, political, and ideological conundrums that the Western artist faces when traveling outside of the known.[60] Rossellini arrived in India upon direct invitation from prime minister Jawaharlal Nehru, an admirer of his postwar films, who felt the need to invite the neorealist master to document the immense modernizing effort of his nation. Nehru wanted to have a European name brand as spokesperson for himself and his Congress Party, and who better than Rossellini, whose cinema deployed a rhetoric of the "rebirth of a nation" in his home country? Indeed, Rossellini, it has to be said, went above and beyond the call of duty, building an ode to India's unprecedented scale of modernization, as I discuss in depth in chapter 2. Rossellini managed to write a personal diary and made an essay film about his encounter with the vastness and irreducibility of the Indian subcontinent. While some of this material looks cute and a bit passé to our own contemporary postmodern and postcolonial perspective, Rossellini's India project sits as a major achievement in expressing the spirit of the Bandung Man, that spirit of possibility of a third way out of Cold War dynamics.[61]

Quite startlingly, these films do not engage with the affect of authenticity, the desire to show one's own innocence and good intentions so typical of the orientalist traveler; rather, they take the viewers through an investigation of real events (politics, society, economics) as seen through the authorial lens of Rossellini's narrative world to which his audience is accustomed. They treat the exploration of the lives and problems of the common people trapped within overwhelming historical events (*Rome, Open City*, 1945); the analysis of social classes (*Europa '51*, 1952); the renegotiation of individual identities within society (*Francesco, giullare di Dio* [*The Flowers of Saint Francis*], 1950); the study of individuals' psychological reactions to trauma (*Stromboli*, 1950); and the dissection of love and relationships (*Voyage to Italy*, 1954). These narrative themes, rather than being a drag on the actual engagement with the postcolonial environment and politics of India, guide Rossellini in orienting himself in this new reality, and in turn it helps "me" (white Western viewer trained on postwar art cinema) to follow the history of a new country.

In chapter 3, I look at Pasolini's medium-length films shot in Africa and the Middle East between 1967 and 1970. A survey of his opus reveals an inextinguishable passion for what he stubbornly called Terzo Mondo (Third World), rejecting the teleological notion implied by the term *developing countries* as the recapitulation of a unilateral imperialist ideology, instead making the most of the planetary aspects of the revolutionary project of the socialist postcolonial nations.[62] Pasolini's engagement finds expression in numerous films, reportages, and poems that deal with non-Western subjects or that have a non-Western location. In this study, I focus on *Sopralluoghi in Palestina per il vangelo secondo Matteo* (*Location Hunting in Palestine*, 1964), *Le mura di Sana'a* (*The Walls of Sana'a*, 1971–73), and *Appunti per un'Orestiade africana* (*Notes Toward an African Orestes*, 1969). Pasolini brings to his political travel filmmaking a Marxist awareness of the Global South as well as an original approach to this subject matter, that of the *appunti* (notes). These *appunti* are essay travel films that blend vérité-style shooting with reenactment, found-footage inserts, nondiegetic sound interventions, and the whole toolbox of modernist midcentury experimental cinema. Through this very specific essayistic film style, very much indebted to the travel writing tradition that "accommodates the private diary, the essay, the short story, the prose poem, the rough note and polished table talk with indiscriminate hospitality," Pasolini enacts and projects his agenda as a queer Marxist European intellectual in search of Orestes in Tanzania and Uganda, of Sana'a's unique decay, of Jesus in Palestine, and, as the ultimate unifying impulse behind these interests, of the black and brown bodies that trigger his sexual and political desires.[63]

In the chapter 4, I engage with Antonioni in China. His *Chung Kuo, Cina* (1972) is probably the best known of the films I discuss in this book, for reasons beyond the actual film—a review in a Chinese newspaper triggered a worldwide witch hunt against Antonioni that had ramifications in Italian and wider world politics. In my writing I first and foremost reposition the film within its proper original environment—its production history, its geography, and its stylistics—to bring the film into dialogue with both Italian and Chinese contemporary media landscapes. I am interested in comparing this film, which was perceived by the Chinese authorities and reviewers as a foreign object that invaded their cultural space, to the contemporaneous visual culture of the Cultural Revolution. I also aim to position the film in relation to Antonioni's career as a documentary filmmaker and to the Italian mediascape. In so doing, I am trying to understand both synchronically and diachronically the Chinese and Western reception of the film.

Every chapter of this book also explores the social as well as the cultural afterlife of these films and filmmakers. As Pontecorvo's *The Battle of Algiers* (1966) has been for decades at the center of Algerian cultural debates, many of the films I deal with had lively legacies through which they often accrued divergent symbolic meanings.[64] My starting points and inspirations for this part of my research have been, quite interestingly, works of research creation, or critical art practices, as they are sometimes called. Exemplary in this sense is the work of Berlin-based Portuguese artist Filipa César, who, working in tandem with the Angola film archive, produced a small masterpiece of post-colonial filmmaking: her film *Spell Reel* (2017), in which images of the eroding Angola film archive are restored, repurposed, and finally screened back to the Angola audience. The film movement, back and forth into militant film history, reactivates the archives, turning pieces of debris into allies.[65]

In the case of Rossellini, I look at the Indian Films Division productions, focusing in particular on documentaries about infrastructure and dams, since this type of depiction plays a key role in all Rossellini's Indian films. As Priya Jaikumar claims, it is the "mutuality of the encounter" that unbinds certain films from orientalist tropes.[66] This mutuality is very much operational in Rossellini, both because of his use of local cast and crew (including writers and producers) and because of Rossellini's awareness of contemporary Indian filmmaking practices. Rossellini's engagement with the Indian film community will be scandalously epitomized by both his relationship with screenwriter Sonali DasGupta and his political engagement with Nehru's socialist policies. I will investigate Pasolini's African and Middle Eastern legacy by looking at *Waiting for Pasolini* (2007), a film directed by Daoud Aoulad-Syad and produced by Abderrahmane Sissako. While absolutely fictional, this film offers a glimpse on issues of labor and the impact of Western filmmakers on non-Western countries. I will also explore another short experimental film, Ayreen Anastas's *Pasolini Pa* Palestine* (2005), which remakes Pasolini's *Sopralluoghi*, translating his script into Arabic and making his film into a map for exploring contemporary Palestine. And finally, I will focus on Antonioni's film reception, since it quickly became a *cause célèbre* of supposed Chinese censorship, Western insensitivity, and, for some, an inspiration to think about Maoism. In the conclusion of chapter 4, I will look at the impact of Maoism on Italian filmmakers, focusing in particular on Marco Bellocchio's work for the group Servire il popolo (To serve the people). Assessing these Italian Maoist films allows me to look back at China, in order to figure out how Chinese Maoism was understood and translated in the Italian context.

More broadly, this book aims to challenge the understanding of national cinemas—by rewriting a small fraction of Italian cinema history and reinserting the Global South in that narrative. It also aims to expand the notion of the auteur by highlighting the impact that the different postcolonial struggles had on these filmmakers. I view Antonioni's, Pasolini's, and Rossellini's responses to the liberation and revolutionary movements in the Middle East, Africa, and Asia as integral to their whole artistic and political projects. Beyond the idea of the encounter with the Other, this actual embracing and sharing of a political project is disseminated in the afterlives of the filmmakers themselves. That is, there is a postcolonial Pasolini, Rossellini, and Antonioni, each of whom would not be understandable without these experiences. Moreover, I want to engage with European cinema at large: that is, to think European cinemas in a larger geopolitical context. This is very important if we consider the extent to which the notion of national cinema is under attack in film circles and yet how much it is replicated due to institutional constraints (the "Introduction to X Cinema" is often the only class that protects small-area and language study programs from neoliberal university deans). Rethinking the geopolitics of national cinemas, presenting a contrapuntal narrative to the very often linear teleological tale presented by many national cinemas' textbooks, rearranges that "great cultural archive" (as Said calls it in *Culture and Imperialism*), that is, that familiarity with the Western empire that doesn't make you question any sense of separation or fracture. Instead, the encounters with these "rich cultural documents," where the interaction between West and East is made evident, is a way to challenge any univocal mode of explicating both cinema and the world.[67]

The decolonizing efforts triggered by a renewed understanding of the current racial crisis are rooted in what Sandro Mezzadra and Federico Rahola define as "the postcolonial condition," as well as a renewed consciousness of people of color and Indigenous populations alike, who are eager to be heard and seen at all levels of political and cultural scenes; this wider impulse is in fact redefining the cultural landscape of "the West."[68] That is why I am interested in this book in rethinking the colonial archive through the paradigm of travel.

18 TRAVELING AUTEURS

This archive is intended here both as "an essential producer of categories, narratives, and typologies employed in the administration of the colonized"[69] and metaphorically as the repository of images, clichés, and fossilized imaginary which sits at the core of "the Italian unconscious," to quote the aptly titled Luca Guadagnino 2011 documentary *Inconscio italiano* on the forgotten colonial massacres perpetrated by Italian forces in Ethiopia. These "categories, narratives, and typologies," whose afterlives continue to nourish and regiment the Italian colonial imaginary, are in fact a direct continuation of the color line, to use the salient definition crafted by W. E. B. Du Bois to explain the geography of the colony. This color line now runs deep in the Italian imaginary, perniciously pervading any and all folds of both high and low culture, as many scholars have recently highlighted.[70]

With this book, I join the effort of scholars such as Shelleen Greene, who analyzed the representation of blackness in postwar Italian cinema, and Neelam Srivastava, who rediscovered the anticolonial resistance in Italy and its artistic presence. These efforts, along with the research of Leonardo De Franceschi, Derek Duncan, Gaia Giuliani, Stephanie Malia Hom, Aine O' Healy, Silvana Patriarca, Luca Peretti, Sandra Ponzanesi, and other young scholars around the world who are tackling head-on the colorblindness of contemporary media and film studies, are all works that, by digging into real and ideological archives in which these clichés are solidly locked, reanimate and reactivate lost and stolen memories.[71]

As emphatically stated by Ariella Azoulay: "We have allies in the archive, even if they are often defeated in their mission, and, rather than confirming their relegation to the realm of history, we should engage with their deeds as political partners and not as objects of research."[72] It is with this attitude that I approach my traveling auteurs' often forgotten travel essay films to bring back to life a world of political and aesthetic potential for the study of both national cinema and the auteur, in order to challenge these terms, and if possible, to regenerate these obsolete parameters.

Notes

1. Chen, *Asia as Method*, vi.

2. On *revolucionareidad*, see Rozsa, "Edge." As I review this book, I received news of the death of the dear comrade Citto Maselli, "the last communist director."

3. For an overview, see Lombardi and Uva, *Italian Political Cinema*, and Uva, *L'immagine politica*. On the representation of labor in this period of Italian cinema,

see Resmini, *Italian Political Cinema*; Barattoni, *Italian Post-Neorealist Cinema*; and Pinkus, *Clocking Out*.

4. For a discussion of the anticolonial moment in Italian cinema, see Caminati, "Italian Anti-Colonial Cinema."

5. Ross, *May '68*, 170.

6. Ross continues by noting Chris Marker's engagement with this figure:

> "Having worked with a collective of filmmakers and workers to produce the *cinétract* on the Rhodiaceta strike in 1967, *A bientôt, j'espère*, Marker and his group chose to premiere the film they had been making virtually simultaneously about Vietnam, *Loin du Vietnam*, to an audience composed of Rhodiaceta workers at Besançon. . . . In both his choice of screening locale for the Vietnam film and in its actual texture—Marker incorporated clips from the earlier strike film into the footage of *Loin du Vietnam*—the context of anti-imperialism . . . was inserted directly into the context of industrial militancy in France." (Ross, 183)

7. Askari, *Relaying Cinema*.

8. For a concise discussion of the history and relevance of the term Global South, see Mahler, "Global South." For a critical stand on the term, see Palomino, "Disadvantages."

9. Galimberti, "Maoism," 219.

10. Ponzanesi and Habed, *Postcolonial Intellectuals*.

11. What Sartre, writing in 1964, called "the most significant event of the second half of this century: the birth of nationalism among the peoples of the Middle East, Asia and Africa." Quoted in Ross, *May '68*, 327; originally from Sartre, "Grenouilles," 155.

12. Srivastava, *Italian Colonialism*, 1.

13. Srivastava.

14. Srivastava, 3.

15. Among many excellent works, see Kalter, *Discovery*; Mahler, *Tricontinental*; Christiansen and Scarlett, *Third World*; and Panvini, "Third Worldism." For more works specifically on cinema and the arts, see Djagalov, *Internationalism*, and Salazkina, *Global Socialist Cinema*.

16. See Ottolini, "Giovanni Pirelli," and De Giuseppe, "'Terzo Mondo.'" See also the very astute Galimberti, "Third-Worldist Art?," on arte povera's Global South aspects.

17. Ben-Ghiat, Italian Fascism's *Empire Cinema*; Fidotta, "Ruling the Colonies"; Mancosu, *Vedere L'impero*.

18. Deplano and Pes, *Quel che resta dell'impero*; Giuliani, *Colore*; Brioni and Gulema, *Horn of Africa*; Lombardi-Diop and Romeo, eds., *L'Italia postcoloniale*.

19. For foundational work on travel as an imperial *dispositif*, see Pratt, *Imperial Eyes*, and Kaplan, *Questions of Travel*. On travel writing and its politics, see Lisle, *Travel Writing*.

20. Lisle, 3.

21. Chakrabarty, *Provincializing Europe*.

22. Andrew, "Atlas"; Salazkina, "World Cinema."

23. For example, the idea of the Italian *meridione* as a "colonized land" was already in the "Lyons Theses" developed by Antonio Gramsci and the Italian Communist Party in 1926, in thesis no. 8: "Esso dà alle popolazioni lavoratrici del Mezzogiorno una posizione analoga a quella delle popolazioni coloniali" [It (the current political situation) gives the Southern workforce a position analogous to that of the colonized people, my translation] (Gramsci, *Tesi di Lione*).

24. On modernist auteurs and television, see Cramer, *Utopian Television*.

25. On this foundational moment in Global South history, see Lee, *Bandung Moment*; Prashad, *Poorer Nations*; and Kahin, *Asian-African Conference*.

26. Mahler, *Tricontinental*, 10.

27. On Porretta Terme, see Boarini and Bonfiglioli, *Mostra*. On Pesaro, there is no comprehensive history as of yet, but one can look at Mestman, "*L'ora dei forni*."

28. Italy had an active cohort of filmmakers involved in actual solidarity politics, such as Valentino Orsini, Ansano Giannarelli, Gillo Pontecorvo, and Gianni Amico, whom I discuss at length in Caminati, "Italian Anti-Colonial Cinema."

29. Nagib, *Realist Cinema*.

30. See the essays in the collections Giovacchini and Sklar, *Global Neorealism*, and Ruberto and Wilson, *Italian Neorealism*.

31. In *Orientalism*, Edward Said argued that the travel writing of authors such as Richard F. Burton and Gustave Flaubert was central to the construction of orientalism and its discourses. Many scholars have pursued Said's initial argument by illustrating the extent to which travel writing reinforced or transgressed colonial rule, such as in Clark, *Travel Writing*. As far as cinema is concerned, in the vast literature on the subject, I suggest Peterson, *Education*; Ruoff, *Virtual Voyage*; and Dickinson, *Arab Cinema Travels*.

32. Clifford, "Traveling Cultures."

33. For the shift from traveler to tourist, see Zuelow, *Modern Tourism*; for solidarity tourism, see Moynagh, *Political Tourism*.

34. MacCannell, *Tourist*, 91. On the link between cinema and tourism, see Crouch, Jackson, and Thompson, *Converging Cultures*; Crawshaw and Urry, "Tourism"; Strain, *Public Places*; and Choe, *Tourist Distractions*.

35. Djagalov and Salazkina, "Tashkent '68." See also Pratt, *Imperial Eyes*, and Clifford, "Museums."

36. Pratt, *Imperial Eyes*, 4.

37. In this book, I also consciously shy away from the term *cosmopolitanism*. While many have argued for a more nuanced reading of this term, I fundamentally agree with Timothy Brennan's critique of this term in *At Home in the World*.

38. Said, "Traveling Theory," 247.

39. Dickinson, *Arab Cinema Travels*, 2.

40. Dickinson, 2.

41. I use this term according to Homi Bhabha's configuration, as that postcolonial space that offers new possibilities of meaning negotiation. See Rutherford, "Third Space."

42. Todorov, *Human Diversity*. Originally published as *Nous Et Les Autres: La Réflexion Française Sur La Diversité Humaine* (Paris: Seuil, 1989).

43. Moynagh, *Political Tourism*, 2.

44. Gandhi, *Affective Communities*, 6.

45. See O'Leary, "Italian Cinema," for a full reassessment of *Mondo* films within the canon of Italian cinema. Also see Goodall, "Shockumentary Evidence"; Giuliani, "Razza Cagna"; and Clò, "Mondo Exotica."

46. O'Leary, "Italian Cinema," 11.

47. See Adinolfi, *Mondo Exotica*.

48. Dalla Gassa, *Orient (to) Express*; Giuliani, *Race*.

49. This phrase can be roughly translated as "Italians are decent people," putting forward the presumed innocence and impeccable behavior of Italians in the colonial context. See the thorough work of Patriarca, *Italian Vices*, and Del Boca, *Italiani*. The moniker *italiani brava gente* was popularized by Giuseppe De Santis's 1964 eponymous film on the disastrous retreat from Russia by Italian forces during World War II.

50. Said, *Orientalism*, 5.

51. On the vast bibliography on exotic images in contemporary cinema, I recommend King, *Lost in Translation*; Huggan, *Postcolonial Exotic*; Weaver-Hightower and Hulme, *Postcolonial Film*; and Kwon, Odagiri, and Baek, *Colonial Cinema*.

52. Azoulay, *Potential History*, 53.

53. Pratt, *Imperial Eyes*.

54. Bhabha, *Location of Culture*, 22.

55. Blunt and McEwan, *Postcolonial Geographies*.

56. Bhabha, *Location of Culture*, 2.

57. For Bhabha, fetishism has the same psychological root as the racial stereotype: "The *functional* link between fixation of the fetish and the stereotype (or stereotype as fetish) is even more relevant. For fetishism is always a 'play' or vacillation between the archaic affirmation of wholeness/similarity—in Freud's terms: 'All men have penises'; in ours: 'All men have the same skin/race/culture'—and the anxiety associated with lack and difference—again, for Freud

'Some do not have penises'; for us 'Some do not have the same skin/race/culture'"
(Bhabha, 109).

58. Said, *Orientalism*; Pratt, *Imperial Eyes*; Kaplan, *Questions of Travel*; Griffiths, *Wondrous Difference*; Rony, *Third Eye*.

59. Mahler, *Tricontinental*, 10.

60. Rascaroli, *Personal Camera*. Rascaroli rightly points to the "inheritance of the decidedly auteurist and anti-mainstream, anti-establishment cinema of the new waves, and of European and North-American avant-gardes" for this mode of filmmaking. See Rascaroli, 6.

61. A poem by Pier Paolo Pasolini, "L'uomo di Bandung" (Bandung Man) was published in 1964, and is now available in English, see Pasolini, "Bandung Man" or for the Italian version, see Pasolini, "L'uomo di Bandung."

62. On the notion of the "planetary" vis-à-vis cinema, see the brilliant de Luca, *Planetary Cinema* and Elias and Moraru, *Planetary Turn*.

63. Raban, *Love & Money*, 253.

64. Bedjaoui, *Cinema*; Cortini, Peretti, and Scarnati, *Algeria*.

65. See her own essay on this project, César, "Meteorisations."

66. Jaikumar, *Where Histories Reside*, 135.

67. Said, *Culture and Imperialism*, xxi, 20.

68. Mezzadra and Rahola, "Postcolonial Condition."

69. Stoler, *Imperial Debris*, 4.

70. Grechi and Gravano's edited collection has amply proven that the current "present imperfect" still lives and is fed by a rich colonial archive, amply mobilized and unquestioned by the media. Grechi and Gravano, eds., *Presente imperfetto*.

71. See for example De Franceschi, *L'africa*; De Franceschi, *Schermo*; Duncan, "Postcolonial"; Giuliani, *Race*; Grechi, *Museo*; Hom, *Mobius Strip*; Greene, *Equivocal Subjects*; O'Healy, *Migrant Anxieties*; and Patriarca, *Race*.

72. Azoulay, *Potential History*, 199.

2

Rossellini in India, or the Home Abroad

The European who goes from Persia to India, observes . . . a prodigious contrast. Whereas in the former countries he finds himself still somewhat at home, and meets with European dispositions, human virtues and human passions—as soon as he crosses the Hindus he encounters the most repellent characteristics, pervading every single feature of society.

—G. W. Friedrich Hegel, *The Philosophy of History*

Hindostan is an Italy of Asiatic dimension, the Himalayas for the Alps, the Plains of Bengal for the Plains of Lombardy, the Deccan for the Apennines, and the Isle of Ceylon for the Island of Sicily. The same rich variety in the products of the soil, and the same dismemberment in the political configuration. Just as Italy has, from time to time, been compressed by the conqueror's sword into different national masses, so do we find Hindostan, when not under the pressure of the Mohammedan, or the Mogul, or the Briton, dissolved into as many independent and conflicting states as it numbered towns, or even villages.

—Karl Marx, "The British Rule in India"

Shooting in India turned out to be quite a logistic nightmare for Roberto Rossellini. The production process took several years and involved applying for (and receiving) all the appropriate permits, setting up a crew, almost a year of filming, and exhausting and extensive car trips up and down the subcontinent, all to record what would eventually become the French-language made-for-television reportage *J'ai fait un beau voyage* (1959), its Italian equivalent *L'India vista da Rossellini* (1959), and the full-length feature *India: Matri Bhumi* (1959). These three works aimed to be, according to their director's intentions, historically accurate depictions of Nehru's modernization process as well as portraits of a mythological and timeless India.

There are three modes of filmmaking in action in Rossellini's India Project (which I define as the three media works I mentioned, plus the large amount of paratextual material generated before, during, and after the trip): the celebratory, official portrait of India that Rossellini was called on to portray; the "orientalist sublime" with its visual clichés; and the "personal camera," a diaristic mode of taking notes with the camera. The forced modernization imposed by the India National Congress Party (or simply Congress, the ruling party in postpartition India) transpires through the majestic framing of dams, roads, bridges, and factories in a long, uninterrupted depiction of achievements in technology and engineering as well as the hard work of some of the millions of people involved in these massive endeavors. The India Project is a living monument to both Indian ingenuity and planning, very much in line with the demands of the Indian government, the de facto sponsor of the films. But this ode to modernity and modernization lives alongside a vast array of orientalist clichés that are omnipresent in the films as well as in the letters, diaries, and other material that accompany the preproduction and production phases of these films. On the one hand, Rossellini is fully aware of this literary and visual burden and often engages with it while conscious of its stereotypes; on the other, he seems to fully enjoy the pleasure of what Priya Jaikumar has defined as the "oriental sublime."[1] In between these two tall orders, we find personal inserts, diary entries, visual vignettes and quips, and narrative asides that reflect, in short, a "personal camera" mode (to use Laura Rascaroli's term) that Rossellini uses to lay out the irresolvable aesthetic, political, and ideological conundrums that the Western artist faces when traveling outside of the known home. Rascaroli rightly points to the "inheritance of the decidedly auteurist and anti-mainstream, anti-establishment cinema of the New Waves, and of European and North-American avant-gardes" for this mode of filmmaking, in which Rossellini is fully imbricated.[2]

This is the toolbox of the Italian director abroad, the traveling auteur in the land of the Other and the Elsewhere. It is an essayistic approach that wants to narrativize the postcolonial experience that will set a trend, I believe, in European approaches to filmmaking outside the West.[3] I call this irresolvable aesthetic, political, and ideological conundrum that faces the "traveling auteur" (the white male Western artist) the postcolonial uncanny (see chap. 1). The discovery of unexplored territory, both in a geographical sense (the

Indian continent) and in an artistic sense (the possibility to experiment), while removed from the bitterness that had accompanied the release of his last films in Europe, is paired in Rossellini's productions with both curiosity and a psychological disorientation that overcomes the Western traveler and narrator. The encounter with this Elsewhere generates many questions: How does one overcome the orientalist legacy of colonial literature and visual art? How can one be an *auteur* without imposing a univocal and superficial vision of the Other? The India Project reveals, in its ambiguity of genre (fiction, historical documentary, travel diary, experimental film), Rossellini's *working throughs*. Quite startlingly, these films immediately move away from the notion of "authentic experience" that is so typical of the orientalist traveler, the first and unique explorer in terra incognita, to take us through an investigation of real events (politics, society, economics) but seen through the authorial lens of Rossellini's narrative world, with which the Rossellini audience is already familiar.

During his career Rossellini engaged with the exploration of the life and problems of the common people (*Rome, Open City*, 1945), the analysis of the relationship between social classes (*Europa '51*, 1952), the renegotiation of individual identities within society (*Francesco, giullare di Dio* [The Flowers of Saint Francis], 1950), the study of individuals' psychological reactions to trauma (*Stromboli*, 1950), and the dissection of love and relationships (Viaggio in Italia, *Voyage to Italy*, 1954). These narrative themes, rather than being a drag on the actual engagement with the postcolonial environment and politics of India, help him and his viewers orient themselves in a new reality. In short, Rossellini engages with India through an approach that makes amply manifest from the onset the "art cinema" status of these products. In doing so, he makes the strange familiar, dispelling the usual orientalist trappings of the "first encounter film" (the white man's stupor in front of the unknown). The style of the filming and editing, yielding peculiar long takes; the cunning use of local and nonprofessional actors; the playful Brechtian tricks of unmasking the *dispositif* through the mixing of fiction and document; the engagement with local screenwriters and laborers; and the wish to have multiple storylines interact with the epochal events of Indian modernization all contribute to Rossellini's novel approach to India.[4]

In spite of the original plan of making an "Indian *Paisan*," all that is left of the neorealist approach is the episodic nature of the Indian films and a teleology (if not even perhaps a theology) of liberation and modernity that sees postfascist

Italy and Nehru's postpartition modernizing efforts speaking to each other in Rossellini's imagination.[5] Many of the statements by Rossellini about India must be read as reflections on two countries perceived as temporally aligned, such as when in an interview with François Tranchant and Jean-Marie Vérité in 1959 he states: "[in India,] I felt I found some familiar things . . . a bit like the paternal home you return to at Christmas. . . . I had the feeling of being in Naples once again."[6] In his *Time and the Other*, Johannes Fabian defines temporality as one of the major epistemological issues of anthropological representation; accordingly, the "denial of coevalness"—that is, the allochronism of anthropological representation—can lead to the Other not just living in a geographical alterity but being positioned somewhere behind in the chronotope of modernity.[7] While Rossellini is not shy of orientalist stereotypes in his narrative, his films are happening in a coevalness quite new in Western Indian films. This "now" manages to place most of the orientalist tropes in the background in order to focus on India's fast-paced modernization, even though it's not articulated through the kind of heavily industrial, technocratic, and muscular imaginaries of the USSR, since Rossellini's films always manage to incorporate nature.[8]

The film's working titles, *India '57* first and then *India '58*, speak well of both the auteurist direction of the project, reminding viewers of other Rossellini films where the here and now and the temporal and spatial markers at the core of the project, such as *Germania anno zero* (*Germany, Year Zero*, 1948) and *Europa '51* (*Europe '51*, 1952). They also work as a clear message to the audience of the synchronicity and actuality of what is shown. This comparative anthropology that brings India and Italy in dialogue confirms Walter Mignolo's reflections on the intellectual relations between the peripheries, which sometimes bypass the center to create new synergies.[9] This Italian-Indian nexus is very interesting geopolitically because it has the conceptual formation of a Global South connection, pointing to Italy's ambiguous status as a southern European nation-state with a complex state formation. As Marx already noted from his 1853 Western-centric framework in one of the epigraphs to this chapter, India was indeed an "Italy of Asiatic dimension" because of its fragmented political and linguistic landscape and its history of foreign domination. Because of this specific history, Italy is trapped in a double orientalist bind. On the one hand, it is grouped with southern countries as Europe's internal "Orient" (often associated with the notorious PIGS: Portugal, Ireland, Greece, and Spain). Roberto Dainotto notes that southern Europeans embraced Said's notion of orientalism as a term that enabled them to revisit and rethink their position as Europe's internal Others, while also arguing, quoting poet Giuseppe Goffredo, that the European Union "represent[ed] the South as an estranged fetish, crystallized in chronic backwardness, arrested in a ruined present."[10] On the other hand, to this European (self)-Othering, we have to add Italy's history of internal colonization, since for many historians the unification process that flattened cultural and linguistic differences and imposed a strict central government control was the equivalent of a true colonization process.[11] As Claudio Fogu distinctly put it, "what was formed by the Risorgimento was not a nation-state but an Empire State, created through the occupation of a southern kingdom that was generally conceived as African soil."[12]

It is not a surprise that Rossellini reacts to this Indian encounter with a comparison to Naples, the ultimate porous town according to Walter Benjamin's acute definition, where the southern city embodies a place of a contamination of styles, an overlapping of the private and public, and ultimately sheer chaos ("porosity is the inexhaustible law of life in this city, reappearing everywhere," as vividly described by the fearful German philosopher).[13] Naples as the internal Other of Italy, its own homemade orient (as Benjamin notes, it is its similarities to North African cities that unsettle the northern traveler), resonates with what Rossellini "feels" in India: a place very far away and also very close.[14]

It is precisely these two temporalities—a mythical, atavistic India beyond the full grasp of reasoning inherent in any orientalist representation and the allochronism of modernity and its modernization—that become for Rossellini actual hermeneutic modes through which to approach India. What recent scholarship has noted, and which hopefully this contribution will clarify, is how Rossellini, like Fritz Lang and Jean Renoir before him, inserted himself in a series of modernist entanglements that rejected the simplistic orientalist reading through the lens of colonial appropriation and pointed instead toward a cultural exchange that revalues both the works of the traveling Westerners and the cultural capital and influence of the Indian cinema industry.[15]

Entangled Modernities

Indian film personality B. D. Garga asks in his memoire: "What do Robert Flaherty, Jean Renoir, Roberto Rossellini, Herman Hesse, Steven Spielberg, Paul Scott and MM Kaye, E. M. Forster, David Lean and Richard Attenborough have in common? INDIA."[16] India is a staple of Western culture either as an orientalist trope or as an actual site of anthropological investigation, and as we have seen in Rossellini, these two loci often coexist. With independence and the rise to power of Jawaharlal Nehru in 1947, we see an intensification of filming in India as the government deployed the propaganda potential of film to promote the new state. When Nehru inherited all the instruments of propaganda put into place by the British Empire, he immediately consolidated in the Films Division of India all the preexisting Information Films of India (IFI), Indian News Parade (INP), and Army Film Center (AFC), set up during World War II as tools of imperial propaganda.[17] Moreover, the Nehru administration both formally and informally supported foreign filmmakers' ventures in the country in order to create a counternarrative to the colonial filmmakers who had shaped the aesthetic and narrative of the country in the colonial era. Richard Osborne discusses the films made in India between 1939 and 1947, before the advent of independence from colonial rule, and notes that a recurring trope in both prewar documentaries about India and ones made after World War II is that "the life of India is in the villages" and that new technologies and scientific enterprise would help provide a way forward for peasant populations.[18] These familiar tropes—the old versus the new and East meets West—were meant to be understood as directly connected to the positive influence of colonial power. But the new films promoted by Nehru stress other values, such as cooperation and education. Because of more available access to travel, the welcoming opportunities provided by the government, a rich and flourishing film industry (what film historians define as the golden age of Hindi cinema), and of course the beauty of the locale all provided an ideal environment for shooting.[19] It is for this reason that in India we see first the Swedish filmmaker Arne Sucksdorff, who broke the orientalist vein in Western representation with his films *Indian Village* (1951) and *The Wind and the River* (1953), which won best short at the Venice Film Festival, followed by Jean Renoir, Fritz Lang, Roberto Rossellini, and subsequently Louis Malle and Pier Paolo Pasolini, just to name the best-known auteurs.[20]

My interest in Rossellini in India is also triggered by the very low cultural status of these films, which were perceived as oddities at best, and politically compromised orientalist hodgepodge at worst. For example, Tom Gunning, in his expansive volume on Fritz Lang, described the Indian epic *Der Tiger von Eschnapur* (*The Tiger of Eschnapur*, 1958) and *Das indische Grabmal* (*The Indian Tomb*, 1958/59) as camp, to be enjoyed for their excess.[21] In spite of the clear orientalist nature of these films, and the "ethnic drag" of the actors (Germans or Americans in brown- or blackface), recent scholarship by Maja Figge has shown that the films were part of a larger web that made references to Lang's own oeuvre, to maharaja movies popular in Weimar cinema, and to Hollywood's orientalist adventure films and Arabian night movies and highlighted Lang's engagement with Indian commercial cinema and his exchange and cooperation with Indian filmmakers and producers.[22] Quite interestingly, both Fritz Lang and Roberto Rossellini visited the sets of K. Asif's monumental *Mughal-e-Azam* (1960), an epic historical drama set in sixteenth-century Hindustan that fully embraced what a Western audience might perceive as a mythologizing self-orientalization with loud costumes, sets, and performances but that was very much part of Indian filmmaking style.[23] Likewise, Renoir's *The River* (1956), the story of a British family relocating to India, in which the director's focus is not on Indian society but on the family's young daughter, resembles in many ways what Rossellini will do with *Voyage to Italy*: filter the experience of disorientation through feminine subjectivity (the eponymous novel from which the film draws inspiration bears the signature of Rumer Godden, a female English author who grew up in Bengal). Critics have never been benevolent toward this film: aside from a few praises on the spectacular use of color (the first Technicolor film in India), *The River* is accused of being theatrical and, most of all, of failing to suitably investigate the surrounding social context. Priya Jaikumar's revaluation of this film notices how both Renoir personally and the film itself are in dialogue with contemporaneous Indian cinema through the use of local labor. Jaikumar's "reverse ethnography" method, that is, the anthropological study of the French film crew and the labor production history it depicts, is a model that will come in handy to us as well. Against a trite postcolonial grain that condemns a priori any representation of the non-Western world as implicitly orientalist, *The River* was in dialogue with Indian cultural productions of the time, both in terms of crew and technicians on the set and through the actual political, ideological, and stylistic choices of the film.[24]

A Culture of Reality

To fully grasp Rossellini's trip to India, it is essential to expand the understanding of his work, usually delineated along the lines of neorealism and art cinema, to the tradition of nonfiction film, educational and didactic media, and their rhetorical modes of expression. I intend to do so by tracing Rossellini's early work and placing it in the context of the documentary film culture of the 1930s–40s in Italy, and, later, by highlighting his relationship to French film ethnographer Jean Rouch. By removing the notion of art cinema as a stand-alone category focused on the auteur and on fiction film as an expression of such artistic interiority, Rossellini's career can be seen as exemplary in breaking the dialectic of modernism (figured as alienated auteurism) and realism (conceived as newsreel-style, politically and socially conscious filmmaking). Rossellini did so by moving seamlessly between levels of practice that the high modernist discourse sought to keep strictly separate: fiction and nonfiction; alternations in modes of production (independent, sponsored, etc.); and media, genre, and style switching. Furthermore, he tended to blend these modes polyphonically rather than separately and through ironic distancing techniques. Rossellini not only was inspired by but also actively participated in such socially driven educational projects as various practices of visual ethnography. Rossellini's work in made-for-television didactic biopics (*La prise de pouvoir par Louis XIV*, [*The Taking of Power by Louis XIV*], 1966), journalistic interviews (*La forza e la ragione: Intervista a Salvador Allende* [*Interview with Salvador Allende*], 1971–1973), and NBC coproductions (*Idea di un isola* [*Idea of an Island*], 1967, a series of nonfictional comic sketches about Sicily), just to name a few, force us to reassess his work and the film culture that surrounded him.[25]

In a recent essay on Rossellini's made-for-television historical dramas—spanning ten years of his career, from 1966 until 1975—Michael Cramer claims that Rossellini's later works reconnect twentieth-century art with pedagogy. Taking Fredric Jameson's reflection in *Brecht and Method* on "the taboo of the didactic in art" triggered by twentieth-century modernism as his starting point, Cramer rereads these historical films in terms that place them outside the codes of art cinema and in dialogue with premodernist forms of didactic art.[26] Following Cramer's argument, I argue that Rossellini is symptomatic of a very specific type of modernist filmmaking, part of what critics have termed "the anthropological turn." Such a formation has been widely theorized by the likes of James Clifford and Hal Foster and, in relation to moving image practices, by Catherine Russell, David MacDougall, Fatimah Tobing Rony, and, more recently, Anne Grimshaw and Amanda Ravetz.[27] It is essential to remember that there were observational practices already in place in the European film circles from which both neorealism and vérité borrowed. The narrative that surrounds the anthropological turn in twentieth-century modernist art—the discovery of "the primitive," with the interest in the irrational, primordial, and sensuous aspects of modernist experimentation—is shown to have roots in ethnographic discourses (the same impulse can be traced to the emerging culture of reality in Italy in the 1930s–40s, from which neorealism emerged, and which found its culmination in the Rouchian documentary mode of the 1960s).[28] It is my contention that such a constellation of generic connections helped generate both the neorealist movement and, eventually, the postwar narrative ethnographies in which Rossellini was directly involved and of which the India Project represents a culmination.

Rossellini was typecast as the essential neorealist when his postwar films were taken up by André Bazin and the Parisian film circle as the de facto embodiment of the "*Cahiers* line." As Dudley Andrew has recently written, Bazin was looking for a cinema of authenticity based on "the camera in search of the world," and Rossellini's aesthetics provided a perfect case study.[29] Vociferously defending the newsreel-style realist cinema of Rossellini's early films—*Rome, Open City, Paisan* (*Paisà*, 1946), and *Germany, Year Zero* as well as the more complex modernist narratives of alienation in his later "Bergman period," *Stromboli, Europe '51*, and *Voyage to Italy*—Bazin and his fellow Parisian critics successfully burned a very specific idea of Rossellinian cinema into the critical mindset of the film world. Rossellini was identified as an auteur, and what this excluded were any nonfiction works. If Rossellini had died in 1954, his critical afterlife would be much the same as it is now.

It is amusing to think that Rossellini started his career as an animal documentary filmmaker with a series of short films shot in and around Rome. One of the earliest of these works, *Fantasia sottomarina* (*Undersea Fantasy*, 1938) is shot in Ladispoli, by the Roman seashore. Rossellini had a large aquarium built on the rooftop of his family house, and the resulting six-minute film presented fish "falling in love" while accompanied by a schmaltzy orchestra soundtrack. The film was produced by INCOM (Industrie Corto Metraggi), a production company formed by Luigi Freddi (already head of the Direzione Generale del Cinema) and his assistant Sandro Pallavicini.[30] Why was the fascist INCOM producing a documentary film about fish in the late thirties? Documentaries were a profitable business in Italy after the implementation of Law 1000 in April 1926, which made it compulsory to screen a newsreel or documentary film alongside every feature film.[31] Quite often these would be propagandistic or didactic shorts produced by the state-owned LUCE company (an acronym for L'unione Cinemtografica Educativa, and founded by the Duce himself in 1925).[32] Even a cursory look at Rossellini's early productions—such as these early nature films—shows evidence of an ethnographic impulse in his practice, which also manifested itself narratively in the "fascist trilogy" of the forties: *La nave bianca* (*The White Ship*, 1941), *Un pilota ritorna* (*A Pilot Returns*, 1942), and *L'uomo dalla croce* (*The Man with a Cross*, 1943). All these films show an interest beyond melodrama in everyday details of their protagonists, who are often clearly marked through a specific detail as belonging to a certain region or social class. When upper-class characters appear, it is only in service of a nationalist project of social recomposition.[33]

Indeed, critics at the time had already singled out this very particular quality in Rossellini's method, which is indicative of the ability of these early Rossellini works to stand out as hybrid products located somewhere between the LUCE newsreel—omnipresent at the time in Italian theaters—and a postcalligraphic fiction whose other visible examples at the time were De Sica's *I bambini ci guardano* (*The Children Are Watching Us*, 1943) and Visconti's *Ossessione* (*Obsession*, 1943), among others. Already in his fascist trilogy, in spite of the obvious propagandist tone, Rossellini was developing a very personal and original form of realism, which combined ethnographic instances with sociological investigation reminiscent of Robert Flaherty (whom Rossellini often mentioned as one of his major inspirations). Interestingly, these early films already have a self-reflexive sensibility in terms of both apparatus and narrative strategies, anticipating some later 1960s experiments. While Vittorio De Sica and Luchino Visconti incorporated the pressing social issues and the stylistic traits of the time (open-air shooting, long takes, nonprofessional actors, etc.) into a recognizable melodramatic narrative structure— De Sica borrowing heavily from vaudeville shows (*il varietà*) and bourgeois theater, Visconti blending operatic mise-en-scène and American film noir— Rossellini had already developed a dialectical technique that brought reality and fiction to a point of collision.

Fantasia sottomarina (1938) is only the first in a series of animal narrative documentary shorts that comprise a small but interesting corpus: *Daphne* (unfinished, 1939), *Il ruscello di Ripasottile* (*The Brook of Ripasottile*, 1940), *La vispa Teresa* (*Lively Teresa*, 1940), and *Il tacchino prepotente* (*The Bullying Turkey*, 1940), all of which can be read in relation to both Disney animations (very popular in Italy at the time) and European experiments. Moreover, they resemble the underwater experiments of Jean Painlevé, which Rossellini might have seen at the Venice Film Festival in 1935 and 1936, and they are certainly part of a larger trend of interest in scientific documentary at the time (such as Germaine Dulac's shift from surrealism to science films in that very period), along with the popularity of other French scientific filmmakers Étienne-Jules Marey's assistant Lucien Bull and microcinematographer Jean Comandon. Or, to look back at Italy, the great precursor to the cinema of the animal kingdom, Roberto Omegna, a very interesting yet understudied figure of the Italian artistic scene at the turn of the century.[34] Furthermore, both the popular Disney animation and the widespread scientific trend in European filmmaking can be understood as embedded within a broader transnational trend of narrative documentary filmmaking that ranged from Great Britain to France and Italy and back.[35]

Rossellini in Paris

Rossellini's 1954 *Voyage to Italy* was a resounding fiasco at both national and international box offices and was despised by Italian critics, who accused the master of having abandoned the surly path of neorealism in favor of bourgeois authorial aesthetics.[36] Notwithstanding the fact that Nikita Khrushchev had freed European intellectuals from the oath of allegiance to the Communist Party, liberating them from Moscow's aesthetic directives on socialist realism, Rossellini did not fit into the new mold of Lukácsian critical realism proposed by the editorial committee of *Cinema nuovo* (which finds in Luchino Visconti's 1954 *Senso* the true model of realist poetics infused with historical critique).[37] "Difesa di Rossellini" by André Bazin, also printed in *Cinema nuovo*, would not be enough to rescue this film from total failure.[38] While Bazin's appeal was not heard in Rome, Paris seemed to welcome this film with open arms.

Godard himself will write of the India Project: "Today, Roberto Rossellini has re-emerged with *India '58*, a film as great as *Que Viva Mexico!* or *Birth of a Nation* and which shows that this season in hell led to paradise, for *India '58* is as beautiful as the creation of the world."[39] But before *Cahiers du Cinéma* hailed *Voyage to Italy* as a masterpiece: Jacques Rivette wrote that with this all other films have suddenly aged by ten years, while François Truffaut noted that it was an unprecedented cinematic undertaking. What had caught the attention of these young critics is made clear in this statement by Jacques Rivette: "It's a television aesthetic, a direct one. . . . Realism is neither a writing technique nor a directing style. It is a way of thinking: a straight line is the shortest path between two points."[40] In sum, it is the simple plot, the underacting of both protagonists, Ingrid Bergman and George Sand, paired with the minimalist style of Rossellini's shooting techniques that speak to the emerging French filmmakers. Truffaut does a good job of capturing this feeling: "Directors from all over the world will stop imitating fiction, in favor of the confession and of the diary."[41] This confessional and diaristic style, already identified as *caméra-stylo* by Alexandre Astruc in his provocative 1948 essay "Birth of a New Avant-Garde: The Camera as a Pen" (used by Truffaut as the basis for his 1954 essay, "A Certain Tendency in French Cinema"), theorizes the necessity, on the director's part, to not only be a metteur en scène but to also become an author who has control over their work from beginning to end.[42] With the notion of the camera-pen—or in other words the camera's ability to perform direct writing—Astruc proposes to free the cinema from the concrete requests of tout court show business and from the intricacies of plot in order to allow the images to become a way to express one's own thoughts as flexibly and insightfully as written language.[43] Furthermore, Astruc optimistically notices how 16mm film and television will allow for a total democratization of images and how cinema will no longer be only entertainment and performance but, instead, will become a fundamental instrument for human communication, to the point that one will no longer be able to speak of "cinema" but of "cinema*s*," a concept that is used many times by Rossellini in his theorization of an expanded cinematic apparatus, now a daily reality in our digital world.[44] However, the part of Astruc's essay that is perhaps most relevant to Rossellini's method has to do with his opposition to visual metaphors. Astruc contraposes the lightness obtained through writing ideas directly onto the film to Sergei Eisenstein or Henri-Georges Clouzot's weightiness. Truffaut asserts the author's role as the cinematographic equivalent to the novelist, able to express themselves through thematic elements, through personal ways of creating characters, and, most crucially, through the movement and the exploitation of actors and objects within the time and space of a given frame. It is not by chance that it is Astruc himself, in a short essay he wrote in 1946, who notes how the narrative documentary that had developed as much in England as in France and the United States has now become the aesthetic parameter for contemporary European cinema, reconnecting the new diaristic cinema to the tradition of Alberto Cavalcanti and Robert Flaherty's school.[45]

Rossellini often mentioned his admiration for three very different film-makers, all three of whom have dealt with non-Western subjects: Robert Flaherty, Jean Renoir, and Jean Rouch. While Flaherty's mastery of narrative documentary and Renoir's staging and narrative techniques have already been part of the critical debate surrounding Rossellini, the importance of young visual anthropologist Jean Rouch hasn't yet been clearly assessed. His statement "I would have never shot *Moi un noir* (1958) if Roberto had not encouraged me to do it"[46] shows the importance of his Parisian encounter with Rossellini.[47] Their first meeting took place, so to speak, virtually. Rouch's *Au Pays des mages noirs* (1947) was screened at the Cinémathèque Française along with *Stromboli* in 1950.[48] Rouch and Rossellini were personally introduced by Enrico Fulchignoni, one of Rossellini's best friends and at the time the director of the UNESCO film division in Paris. The friendship between Rouch and Rossellini became a true collaboration, however, when they established a small study group, the Atelier Collectif de Création, patronized by future directors of the nouvelles vagues.[49]

In 1956, Rouch was already working on *Jaguar*, though it was completed and distributed only in 1971. *Jaguar* tells the story of three youth of the Nigerien savanna who leave their land in search of better fortune and adventures. The three travel together for months along the coast and through Ghanaian cities. They separate in order to work in different cities, and, last, having become jaguars (men who are experts on life and the city), they return home. The film is shot over the course of many years and without the use of synchronous sound, as this was not yet available in portable, affordable formats. Rouch convinced two of the three protagonists, Damouré Zika and Lam Ibrahim Dia (the third one was Tallou Mouzourane), to join him in Paris once the film had been edited in order to comment on the final product. The film's soundscape is made up of conversations based on the protagonists' recollections: jokes, puns, and questions and answers about what happens on screen. *Jaguar* caught Rossellini's attention right away thanks to a few technical details: it had been shot in 16mm, the actors were all nonprofessional, it was shot exclusively in Africa, and most importantly of all, it offered a mixture of fiction and document. As Rouch writes, "For me, as an ethnographer and filmmaker, there is almost no boundary between documentary film and films of fiction. The cinema, the art of the double, is already the transition from the real world to the imaginary world, and ethnography, the science of the thought system of others, is a permanent crossing point from one conceptual universe to another; acrobatic gymnastics, where losing one's footing is the least of the risks."[50]

That Rouch and Rossellini were in contact with one another was already known from what Truffaut tells us (but Truffaut, as a devout disciple, states that the young Rouch had inherited his best qualities from the master, Rossellini).[51] What is more interesting is the fact that it was Rossellini who convinced Rouch to abandon the voice-off narration in order to replace it with the actual voice of the actors (according to a statement by Alain Bergala, critic at *Cahiers du Cinéma*).[52] This stylistic change also led to an ideological change. Finally, a voice was being given to the subjects of scientific research, capsizing the consolidated hierarchical episteme of anthropology that mandated an objective distance between observer and observee. With *Jaguar*, *Moi un noir*, and later films, Rouch developed a new aptitude in his approach to the representation of alterity. Notwithstanding the critiques against his method, the impulse toward a reflexive cinema (that at times becomes tout court diaristic) and toward a more participatory form of ethnography (that will see its full blooming in the productions of meta-anthropologists Clifford Geertz and James Clifford) will free the entire anthropological discourse from the simple idea of translating the customs and ways of a culture into another culture. Reflexive cinema began working instead, toward the thick description theorized by Geertz, where the analysis of the ethnic Other and the investigative method are studied reflexively as part of the same discursive formation: the object, the analysis, and the subject of anthropological research must be observed jointly as they are contemporaneously involved in the research.[53]

From Rouch, in turn, Rossellini borrows the method of using sound without the option of live-recorded audio. From his initial idea of hearing the protagonists' voices recounting their experiences in the first person, Rossellini construes the possibility of narrating simple and predictable stories of local life. This is indeed what we see in *India: Matri Bhumi*, where the four episodes are narrated by the protagonists. Stories—for both Rouch and Rossellini—were based on field research. Even though this may be read as the voices of "natives" who "speak" Western ideas, it still replaces the omniscient narrator's "voice of god" and offers a plurality and a polyphony new to Western cinema.[54]

We could summarize the two artists' different approaches in the following way: Rouch carries out ethnological investigations using the genre of filmic fiction, while Rossellini produces filmic fiction by using the methods of ethnological investigation. And this can be explained not just by looking at their respective backgrounds but also at their preestablished objectives. Rossellini is a filmmaker whose object of analysis is human nature, while Rouch is an ethnographer who discovers the power of the camera and adapts it to his scientific needs. There was, in short, a definable "Rouchian method" that permeated the Parisian artistic community of the time, including the soon-to-be nouvelle vague directors and more radical filmmakers like Agnès Varda, Chris Marker, Alain Resnais, and others later known as Rive Gauche group.[55]

Voyage to India (December 9, 1956)

With Renoir's help, Rossellini met Jawaharlal Nehru in London in June 1955. India had been in Rossellini's mind for quite some time, at least since December 1931, when he had met Gandhi in Rome, as the Mahatma was heading back to India via Bari after talks with the British government.[56] In an interview in November 1955 for *Cinema nuovo*, Rossellini declared,

> Producers don't want me to work anymore, what I have to say is no longer of interest to them. That's why I've accepted the offer that Indian cinema made me. I was given free rein: in India, I'll be able to study the atmosphere, to analyse significant issues and highlight the ones that will allow me to valorise the magical, fakiristic and philosophical traditions and to juxtapose that tradition to new emerging voices, to the voices that are gaining authority. Ultimately, it will be the great Indian city [*città*, but probably a typo for *civiltà*, civilization], with its grandeur, with its past and its future, that will take me by the hand and write that story for which nothing has been imposed upon me.[57]

India: Matri Bhumi (literally "India Mother Earth," or the humus of the earth), the feature-length film presented at Cannes in 1959, was written by Rossellini with the decisive contribution of one Indian writer, Sonali Sen Roy DasGupta, and the French Iranian Fereydoun Hoveyda.[58] Tag Gallagher notes in his biography of Rossellini how he made systematic use of Sonali in an attempt to stay close to his subjects and unbalance the structure of the exotic film (neither Lang nor Renoir, for example, had Indian writers on their teams). Moreover, Rossellini had as his assistant directors on the set Jean Herman, a twenty-four-year old recent graduate of IDHEC (the prestigious

Institut des hautes études cinématographiques in Paris), who would eventually become a well-known writer under the nom de plume Jean Vautrin, who at the time was working as a lecturer in art history at a university in Bombay, and M. V. Krishnaswamy, a.k.a. Kittu, a young Indian Films Development (IFD) director whom Rossellini had met in Rome at the Centro Sperimentale di Cinematografia, which he was attending.[59] Kittu, born in Mysore, was essential for the completion of the film as his duty expanded over the course of the shoot. At the top of the production team sat Jehangir "Jean" Bhownagary, innovative Indian/French filmmaker, at the time Deputy Chief Producer of the IFD, which along with Rossellini's own company, Aniene Film, and the French UCG (Union Générale Cinématographique), ultimately produced the film.[60] Also working on the film were IFD cameramen Prem Vaidya and some electricians and manual workers.[61]

A lot has been written on Sonali and the scandalous nature of the relationship that developed with Rossellini, which generated an international outrage. Dileep Padgaonkar wrote an extensive account of this affair in his very thorough *Under Her Spell*.[62] What interests me here was that Sonali was a graduate of Visva-Bharati, in Santiniketan in West Bengal, a college founded by poet laureate Rabindranath Tagore under principles of community living and respect for nature. When her husband Hari San Gupta (whom Renoir had originally recommended as sound person) realized that he could not work with Rossellini because of a previous engagement, he showed Rossellini a treatment his wife, Sonali, had written. Their artistic collaboration was indeed a success, as she managed to provide Rossellini's script with a tangible Indian presence. The exact import of her contribution to the script has been confirmed by documents recently unearthed by Margherita Moro in Renzo Rossellini's archives, in particular a document in which Sonali declares that she gives up all her rights to the film, and another letter sent by Rossellini to "Sonalini" in which an amount of 8,500 rupees was agreed on in exchange.[63] Indeed, we can see important traces of contemporary Indian cinema embedded in the narrative, starting with the title of the film, which is reminiscent of the 1957 Mehboob Khan's monumental *Mother India*, an epic drama that narrates the struggle of a single mother in a rural community, to the contemporaneity of the stories (such as the case of the worker at the Hirakud Dam), to the attention to details of daily life in the countryside.

The film is roughly divided into four episodes. After a quick newsreel-style introduction, with the voice-over narrating the religious and ethnic

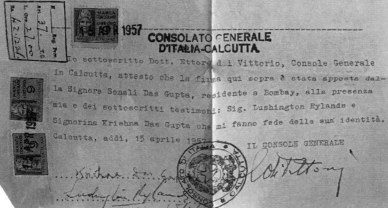

Figure 2.1. Sonali DasGupta transfers the rights of "India 1957" to Roberto Rossellini. Signed at the Italian Consulate in Calcutta on April 15, 1957 (Private Archive).

diversity of the subcontinent, the film starts with the story of a *mahout* (an elephant herder) falling in love with a young woman; the second episode describes the strife of a worker at the Hirakud Dam; in the third, an old villager tries to rescue a tiger from hunters; and in the fourth and last episode, a monkey is let loose by the death of its master. The film begins with bird's-eye-view shots of crowds in Bombay. But this aerial view rapidly transforms into a series of zoom shots that have us diving into the crowds, and, among the indistinct masses—highlighted by the commentary that narrates: "thousands, tens of thousands, hundreds of thousands, who flood the city like a river"—the camera begins to pause on specific individuals, while it identifies them by their occupation, religion, and the caste to which they belong. We then move to a handheld camera view of the streets, in yet another attempt to deepen the individual focus and identify the different components of Indian society. This movement from the top down, from the generic to the particular, is the narrative technique employed by Rossellini to usher us into the four episodes that make up the film. According to Gallagher, there were nine episodes in the original script, including one titled "Community Projects," about government engineers who help villagers reform their agriculture; "The Widow," about a woman who keeps her husband's factory going after his death despite her brother-in-law's opposition; "The Importance of Meditation," about a mountain community that detours a road so that truck traffic will not make its three hermits leave; and "The Land Donor," about a rich man who gives everything away and becomes a beggar.[64]

Cutting down to four stories was probably necessary from a production standpoint, but also the four vignettes remaining form a powerful narrative, political, and metaphorical arc. The four sections cover four geographical parts of India (North, South, East, and West); men at four stages of their lives (a young man of marriageable age, a middle-aged man with a wife and child, an aged man, and a dead man); and men engaged in four kinds of transactions with their natural and animal environments (an elephant keeper, a dam builder, a forest dweller, and a monkey trainer). This division replicates, according to Priya Jaikumar, the Vedic Hindu notion of the four *ashramas*, or stages of life (assuming a masculine subject), which move from the first stage of *brahmacharya* (as a student and unmarried man) to the second stage of grihastha (a householder), to the third stage of vanaprastha (literally, a forest dweller or retired man), and to the final stage of *sannyasa* (renunciation).

Figure 2.2. Rossellini at the Hirakud Dam. Photograph probably by Jean Herman (Fondo Rossellini, Centro Sperimentale di Cinematografia, Rome).

Each stage prescribes essential life lessons and behaviors.[65] Also, as pointed out by Alain Bergala, all four episodes deal with couples at different points of their married life (engagement, family, old age, and death).[66]

After the confusion and quick editing of the prologue set in Bombay, we find ourselves in the Khanapur forest near Mysore, in Karnataka (this is where the filming officially started on March 15, 1957), in order to follow a group of elephants as they move logs. Suddenly it is the *mahout*'s first-person account that breaks the ambient sound that was accompanying the scene (dominated by the bell that hangs around the elephants' necks). He is a young Indian elephant owner who rides the creature as part of his daily work as a lumberjack. The story is very simple, and it acquires even more of a fable-like tone in the synopsis. One morning, the *mahout* notices a crew of puppeteers entering town and falls in love with the director's daughter. The young man summons the girl's father, who is from a nearby town, and asks for her hand. Their love story is told in parallel with the elephants' mating season. At the end, both the woman and the elephant will become pregnant.

Rossellini, in an attempt to justify the simplicity of the tale, states: "In the film instead [as opposed to the TV documentaries], the subject matter is elaborated in order to be represented. I tried to express the feeling of India, the internal warmth of its people. I tried, if I may say this without fear of sounding ridiculous, to render poetically my sensations as a reporter."[67] How does one express the sensations of a reporter "poetically"? I think that slow editing style, which Rossellini had theorized as *tempi morti* (literally dead-time scenes, or waiting scenes), produce in the filmic text the necessary tension for the explosive event to follow.[68] At the same time, he highlighted the documentary aspects of his cinema: "Every solution is a result of waiting. It is waiting that allows one to live, that unleashes reality, that—after a period of preparation—provides liberation. Let's look at the tuna-fishing episode in *Stromboli* as an example of this. This is an episode that is born out of a period of waiting. A feeling of curiosity for what is to come accrues within the viewer: then it's the explosion of the fish-slaughter. Waiting is the powerful force that lies within every event in our life: this is also the case in cinema."[69]

These slow sequences in *India*, however, are no longer foreshadowing an event; instead, they become an event in their own right.[70] They are the actualization of the twofold ideology of the film: to investigate and to narrate. Rossellini explores the forms of "contemplative cinema" that from Apichatpong Weerasethakul's to Pedro Costa's films gain much success in the circles of the movie festivals of our times under the moniker of slow cinema.[71] Rossellini wants to free the spectator from the suturing system of fiction, both on a stylistic level (field/reverse shots, soundtrack, etc.) and on a content level (motivation, plot, identification with the viewer). The long breaks that leave the viewer in front of the elephants' work culminate in the most beautiful scene of the episode. After a morning of work, the elephants are brought to the river where they are washed by their *mahouts*. While in the third episode we will witness the devastating effects of industrial modernity imposed onto the premodern world of the village, the elephants' bath, with its powerful heavenly and ritualistic symbolism and with its minimal edits—no commentary, only the background noise as sound accompaniment—captures the event and provides an opportunity to explore the symbiotic relationship between man and animal. Rossellini uses these moments of pure observation to emphasize that "the live object of the realistic film is the 'world,' not the story, not the narration."[72]

Figure 2.3. Rossellini with an elephant. Photograph probably by Jean Herman (Fondo Rossellini, Centro Sperimentale di Cinematografia, Rome).

The most striking stylistic feature is the creative use of sound. While the film was shot without sync sound, with both 16 and 35mm cameras in the hands of DP Aldo Tonti, Rossellini employed a technique described in the titles as *illustrazione sonora*. This sound illustration, or sound design, was meant to provide a more realistic, live-action sound experience for the audience. It is a mix of three separate sound tracks: the live sound recorded on location during the shootings; the voice-over narrative provided in the French edition by unnamed narrators speaking French and, in the Italian version, speaking Italian with a marked Indian accent; and the musical score made up of traditional Indian music processed by musicologist Alain Daniélou, probably from his own recordings.[73] This mix of sources and techniques can be thought of as emblematic of a certain type of development of ethnographic fictional documentary. The soundscape of the film is the most memorable part of Rossellini's *India*, and this choice gives a particularly cinematic feel precisely to that same elephant bathing scene that opens the first episode. This six-minute-and-thirty-second sequence follows the work of the animals as they proceed through removing tree trunks in a patch of jungle and then take their long morning bath in the river. This piece of observational cinema, with no voice-over or nondiegetic sound, just the live soundtrack, offers another poignant entry into a blending of cinematic styles that shapes the composition of the film.

While the first episode's main theme is tradition, with the second episode, which portrays the construction of the Hirakud Dam over the Mahanadi River in the state of Odisha (filmed between April 19 and 26, 1957), Rossellini moves from the southern forests to the Eastern plains. The episode begins with the description of the last stages of the construction process. The story follows the reflections of a laborer who worked on the dam: once the structure is complete, he is forced to move with his family in search of another occupation. The first scene is filmed with a camera car passing through a long line of laborers who are preparing to abandon the dam's enormous construction site. The car's long tracking shot is actually a subjective view, from the perspective of Devi, the story's protagonist, an East Bengali refugee because of Partition. It is, indeed, his voice that begins to tell the story of the construction process: "There were thirty-five thousand of us, seven years of labor." In the French version it is the voice of Rossellini himself who dubs the character, an obvious sign of the importance of this episode and this character for the India Project. The man gets off the jeep to visit the site manager and receive his final paycheck. The remainder of the episode follows the laborer who performs one last nostalgic survey of the site. The reflections that accompany this footage explore the debate between modernization and tradition in an attempt to depict the significant changes taking place in Nehru's India. Once again, Rossellini's decision to shoot the film rigorously from a character's point of view constitutes the central issue when it comes to a postcolonial interpretation of the film. An example of this is the central scene of the episode, when Devi decides to perform a ritual bath in the waters of the new artificial lake. Treating it as if it were the shore of an ancient lake, the laborer, shot from behind in a fixed frame, enters the water to bathe.

The Orient has represented for the Western traveler the place par excellence in which to "see" in order to not be seen, to "narrate" without being narrated about, to put oneself in an artificial "beyond"—a privileged and unassailable place—from which to impose a certain vision onto the subordinate, onto the culturally or economically inferior. Rossellini is conscious of this postcolonial positionality, and he faces the difficulty of representing India with the double approach of documentary and fiction. It is interesting to note that watching the documentary *L'India vista da Rossellini* helps our understanding of certain moments of great political naivete in *India: Matri Bhumi*. An example is the episode of the dam itself: we once again see the Hirakud Dam in the eighth episode of *L'India vista da Rossellini*. Here, the viewer observes real data for almost an hour, free of plot or musical accompaniment. Rossellini's commentary is dry and limited to factual information: numbers, statistics, victim counts, financial budgets, and so on. In *India: Matri Bhumi* all this is left out. The bathing scene, a two-minute-and-thirty-second shot with no camera movements, shows Devi as he undresses, enters the water, bathes himself, prays, comes out, and gets dressed again. This manages to bring forth the individual drama of the young man once more homeless, the collective drama of the Partition and forced industrialization and, meta-cinematically, the presence of the observational camera. As Devi inscribes these words on a stone, "I, Devi Chakravarti, and my wife found asylum here when we were thrown out of East Bengal due to the separation with Pakistan," the drama of Indian recent history becomes materially visible.

N. S. Thapa's (one of Nehru's favorite filmmakers) Films Division documentary *Bhakra Nangal* (1958) celebrates the building of the eponymous dam on the Sutlej River. The twenty-minute film has a long, descriptive section acknowledging the accomplishments of local engineers and machines—but quite interestingly toward the end the laudatory tone suddenly stops. The big orchestral music leaves room for more intimate sounds as the camera focuses on individual workers. Each is allowed to introduce himself in his native tongue, and in a gesture of unity for a common cause, the diversity in physical features, dress, and languages is channeled toward the common cause of India's modernity in their short speeches. As the late fifties saw a widespread development of these kinds of massive public projects throughout the socialist world, and cinema was the natural medium to celebrate them, Nehru's obsession with hydroelectricity and dams, which he called "the new temples of India," is visible in many FDI-produced films like *Rivers in Harness* (1949)

46　　TRAVELING AUTEURS

and *Golden River* (1954). Rossellini's episode is very clearly influenced by these films, and it's easy to imagine the Hirakud Dam's episode as just an expansion of one of these short character portraits in Thapa's film, shot at the same time as Rossellini's.[74] The impact of his Indian crew in developing this episode shows one more time the engagement Rossellini's films had with contemporaneous Indian film style, themes, and methods.[75]

In the third episode (filmed from June 6 to 8 around Rourkela, not far from Hirakud), Rossellini tells the story of an old shepherd, Ashok, and his wife in a remote forest village. The arrival of a group of workers upsets a tiger, which attacks and kills a man. While the hunt for the stray tiger begins, the old man ventures into the forest on his own, in hopes of fending off the tiger and saving it from the hunters. The relationship with nature is the theme of this story, and it draws a sharp contrast to the Hirakud episode, as here the destructive aspects of modernization are openly put forward. The most interesting moment from a stylistic and ideological point of view is the actual encounter with the tiger. The edits join the old man's gaze with shots of the tiger, filmed in 16mm and not in continuity with the rest of the episode: not only the tiger and the man never appear in the same frame, but the shot/reverse-shot composition of this episode also reveals the awkward editing. The blown-up 16mm image of the tiger is discolored and blurred, the background is noticeably different than the place from which the old man is gazing. In short, it is very clear that the two scenes have been shot at different times, in different places, and with a different camera and film stock.[76] Rossellini seems to happily betray one of the fundamental rules of Bazinian cinematic realism. In fact, Bazin writes in "Montage interdit" in regard to Harry Watt's *Where No Vultures Fly* (1951)—the story of an English family that builds an animal sanctuary during World War II in Africa and a "mediocre" work in his opinion—that the film is characterized by banal parallel edits and a conventional and naive kind of suspense, until the little boy is dangerously close to a lioness.[77] "Then suddenly, to our horror, the director abandons his editing style that has kept the protagonists apart and gives us instead parents, child, and lioness all in the same full shot. This single frame in which trickery is out of the question gives immediate and retroactive authenticity to the very banal montage that has preceded it."[78] In the same essay, Bazin recalls the moment in Charles Chaplin's *The Circus* (1928) when Charlie and the lion are in the same cage. Essentially, it is through the use of depth of field and long sequence shots, through maintaining the spatiotemporal fluidity of the

ROSSELLINI IN INDIA

action that the film brings us, all at once, toward the highest point of cinematic emotion. As Serge Daney writes regarding this aspect of Bazin's theory, at the base of realism lies the ban on editing when two objects can be in the same frame and, most of all, a form of sado-aestheticism by virtue of which one must die for the sake of the image: "This is eroticism for Bazin," Daney closes sarcastically.[79] Rossellini's choice seems to offer, on the metacinematic plane, a reflection on the dispositif that is already visible in the first neorealist films and becomes even more evident during the Bergman period. It is the most symbolically charged moment of the film—the encounter with the beast, around which the entire episode is structured—that seems "detached" due to the technical discrepancy. Once again Rossellini "lowers" the event to its reality of documentary footage. Rossellini has used a similar dedramatizing technique in one of the most dramatic moments of *Rome, Open City* when the shot/countershot exchange between Pina and Francesco, right before her death, is suddenly interrupted by a third lateral shot, delinking the narrative from the visual exchange. Sure enough, Rossellini's episode ends in doubt, as we don't know what will happen to the tiger or the old man.

A monkey and its owner are on a journey from village to village. This is the fourth and last episode of the film, written by Kittu (according to Dileep Padgaonkar), and it was supposed to be shot in Bodh Gaya in the state of Bihar.[80] This is a key location for Buddhism, as here is where the Buddha is said to have achieved Enlightenment. But the scandal of Rossellini's relationship with Sonali had been made public, and the crew had to shorten their shooting time (it was shot in Mumbra, near Bombay, from May 18 to 22). The episode begins with the man's death. His monkey continues its journey and performs alone at a fair. Without anyone to take care of it, it attempts to return to its natural environment, but the wild monkeys reject it. Finally, we see it in the last sequence in a circus. Certainly, the cruelest and saddest of the film, this episode brings us back to Rossellini directing animals, as in his very early shorts. Also, exotic literature is filled with topoi of wild animals. As Isabella Pezzini notes, "the cruelty and irreducible ferociousness of the animals in these areas are obvious anthropomorphisations, and, by adjacency, often become descriptors of their human compatriots."[81] Rossellini also seems, in a way, a victim of this facile anthropomorphism.[82] As seen in the episode with the tiger, if *India: Matri Bhumi* refuses the orientalist stereotype in order to use animals as actual characters of the story, one cannot avoid noticing how the monkey is a victim of solitude and maladjustment to its surrounding society of animals and humans, exactly like the protagonists of *Stromboli* and *Europa '51*. The animals—particularly the monkey, in this story—are part of Rossellini's poetic world. The simplicity of this last, nonverbal episode wishes to have the expressive and emotional force of an evangelical parable. On which side lies freedom? Where is true life to be found? These are the questions that Rossellini poses throughout his career and that conclude the Indian adventure.

The film then closes with the same newsreel tone in which it had begun. This time, it is presented without a commentary voice but only with the sound of tablas and the initial images of Bombay. We end where we started, in the middle of the city with a handheld camera, at the end of this voyage to India.

Television in India

The two four-hour television documentaries, *L'India vista da Rossellini* and its French counterpart *J'ai fait un beau voyage*, are opportunities to create a new didactic audiovisual text. In an interestingly anticipatory move, Rossellini was already in the late fifties thinking about the possibility of the end of cinema's dominance by communicating his Indian experience in the new space of TV broadcasting. India becomes a trip in the contested future of the media. Every episode is structured around a specific theme (episode ten is about animals in India) or geographical location (episode one is entirely devoted to Bombay). Working with an open-ended script, the interviewer triggers Rossellini's responses. His live voice-over accompanies the images shot by Aldo Tonti in both 35mm and 16mm. At times, complex sociopolitical issues are thematized. For example, episode six, "The Lagoons of Malabar," gives Rossellini the chance to discuss Josué de Castro's *Geography of Hunger*, probably the study that had the strongest influence on Rossellini during this period.[83] At the time, the Brazilian de Castro was president of the Food and Agriculture Organization (FAO), a scientist of nutrition, and a key figure for Marxist intellectuals around the world. While his preliminary work has been superseded by more complex studies, his major assessment—that hunger is not a natural law but, rather, the direct product of a specific historical juncture—was a powerful influence on such contemporary economists as Amartya Sen (and filmmakers and theorists alike, such as Glauber Rocha and his "aesthetics of hunger"). In this epoch, de Castro's work had a revolutionary impact on many state policies. De Castro attacked colonialism precisely on the planning front, contesting that it forced fertile land into monocultures that permanently drained the soil. Moreover, de Castro flips the Malthusian axiom that hunger is caused by overpopulation by claiming that overpopulation is instead one of the many disastrous consequences of hunger, all solvable through technological innovation. Here there is an intellectual convergence between Rossellini's beliefs and the policy of the Indian government, which explains the invitation to make these TV documentaries. (Nehru was a strong believer in de Castro's theories.) Rossellini's film, was shot for UNESCO fifteen years later, *A Question of People* (1974), is a project that is directly connected to the issues raised in this volume. The first version of *La lotta dell'uomo per la sopravvivenza* (*Man's Struggle for Survival*, 1970) was meant to be titled "A History of Nutrition," modeled on de Castro's title. Once again according to Renzo Rossellini, the two had met in Brazil, where Jorge Amado had put them in touch with each other. De Castro's great revolution regarding nutrition is of true Copernican value.[84] As Carlo Levi writes in the insightful introduction to the Italian translation (*Geografia della fame*, 1954), for de Castro "hunger . . . is an all-human fact, connected to the conditions of a society: not brought about by natural laws, but produced by a given historical situation."[85] De Castro denounced colonial economic politics that condemned a fourth of the world to monoculture and latifundium. De Castro further proposed a theory that may seem somewhat contrived now but was well received at the time. Since populations that eat large quantities of protein tend to have lower birthrates, the scientist draws a direct parallel between protein intake and birthrates, according to which decreasing births will be enough to provide more protein to people. This is a scientific conclusion for de Castro, and it has to do with the increase of sterility in populations that are well nourished. Given that the last major famine in India occurred under the British occupation between 1943 and 1945 in Bengal, merely a decade before Rossellini's project, one might also say that, like *Germany Year Zero*, this was a reclamation project, a reminder of the vast terror of famines associated with colonial rule in an epoch when the West's memory of these events was being rapidly covered up by revisionism and denial. At times, Rossellini's enthusiasm for Nehru looks suspiciously like a revival of the unthinking adoration of Stalin within Popular Front culture, transferred to a Third World figure. Certainly, production support must have had an effect on Rossellini's admiration for Nehru. Yet, an explanation based on self-interest ignores both the historical context (there was widespread admiration for the Indian leader among European intellectuals) and the fact that Rossellini could have made other choices, rather than plunging back into the documentary field.

L'India vista da Rossellini was recorded in the RAI studios in Rome. In filmed conversation with Rossellini throughout this series was a journalist from the Communist weekly *Vie nuove*, Marco Cesarini Sforza. The production's most visible features are the profound disdain that Rossellini displayed toward the interviewer and the blatant discrepancy in character between the two. Rossellini is curious and humble in regard to the grandeur of the Indian subcontinent, yearning to understand and to help to understand. The journalist is conceited, sanctimonious, complacent with the interviewee, and ideologically a shapeless container of the orientalist trivialities circulating in Italy at the end of the 1950s. The program, which consisted of ten episodes, each about 25 minutes long (for a total of 251 minutes), was structured as an alternation between two shots: one frontal, which shows the two protagonists as they amiably converse, the other from behind, showing images of the Indian journey projected on a screen in front of the two speakers. After a short briefing on the topic at hand, the film begins. In the first episode, "India senza miti" (India without Myths), Cesarini Sforza informs us that "these are the travel journals of a traveler whose eyes are open to the reality that surrounds him," who "used the camera in the same way a specialist news reporter uses a pen," and, moreover, he proclaims that "what is narrated will not be a narration but a conversation." Rossellini adds to this that "perhaps, Salgari is the most honest, the most truthful." Emilio Salgari (1862–1911) was a very successful and popular adventure novel writer, author of more than two hundred books across various popular genres. He is mostly associated with the Tigers of the Malaysia series, and the character of Sandokan, a pirate of the South China Sea whose many adventures often take place in India, specifically in conflict with the British Empire and its puppet governors. In displaying his full awareness of the Western orientalist tradition, Rossellini faces head-on the issue of orientalist representation. By placing Salgari in a position of ideological prominence ("the most honest"), Rossellini simply means to say that Salgari did not try to be accurate in his stories; rather, he created a world from scratch, a Western projection of a decadent, idle, and sensual Orient.

But right after having accepted Salgari's exotic vision, Rossellini executes his program of social, political, and anthropological education. India is "an extraordinary country because it is undergoing a great struggle for development," and talking about himself, he declares that "[his] efforts were directed towards seeing an India that was absolutely real." "What surprised me the most about Indians"—declares Rossellini—"is their deeply rational spirit." In fact, in "India senza miti," he ambushes the viewer. The episode begins at the Banganga Tank, the sacred pool at the temple of Walkeshwar on Bombay's Malabar Hill. From here, it moves to a Parsi temple, while Rossellini explains how different religions coexist peacefully and that it is not uncommon to see members of different religions frequent one another's temples. We see images of a Catholic church being visited by Muslim and Hindu women, for instance. But suddenly, the elegiac atmosphere of religious coexistence is interrupted. The sequence begins with a group of people sitting with their legs crossed and reading attentively. The dauntless journalist with whom Rossellini converses asks: "Are they praying?" With a skillful countershot, Rossellini replies: "No, we're at a horse race!" The "sacred books" that these individuals are holding on their laps are the racetrack programs used for betting.[86] Through this scene, Rossellini attacks the self-importance and superficiality of a foolish orientalist vision. He also denounces, from a metacinematic point of view, the viewer's preconceptions and the inevitable deceptiveness of cinematic realism that makes us see cause and effect even where they are not present. This ambush frees us from the duty of having to discuss religion, and Rossellini can now take us to a game of cricket played by schoolchildren, a field hockey match in one of Bombay's parks, and street jugglers with a tamed monkey (an obvious inspiration for *India: Matri Bhumi*'s last episode). We then move on to a snake charmer (we are on Marine Drive in Bombay), but Rossellini comments, "The true spectacle was me," as the Indian kids are more interested in the Western crew and the camera equipment, once more pointing self-reflexively to the cinematic apparatus.

The second episode, "Bombay, la porta dell'India" (Bombay, the Door of India) is dedicated to ethnic-religious tolerance: "India is an enormous stomach, it has digested everything that came from outside," he proclaims. The most meaningful episode of the film is, without a doubt, the ending that focuses on the two funerals, a Muslim burial and a pyre at a Hindi funeral. It is also with a funeral pyre that Pasolini during the filming of *Appunti per un film sull'India* (*Notes for a Film on India*, 1968) decides to conclude his film. But while Pasolini overwhelms this moment with a voice-over delivering his final considerations on the Indian experience, Rossellini decides to let the viewer contemplate the images in silence.[87]

The third episode is dedicated to "Architettura e costumi di Bombay" (Bombay's Architecture and Lifestyle), where we traverse the entire city by car, but not before a Rossellinian introductory trick. In Chowpatty Beach, the images pause to show people resting just about everywhere: on sidewalks, on ledges, at the feet of the statues of British generals. Rossellini recalls how in Roman sculptures the subjects are normally represented in a state of idleness (a reference to the museum scene in *Voyage to Italy*). These gentlemen who are taking a nap on the steps of a station pique the Roman director's attention, but they also trigger the wish to observe the similarity between West and East, a common humanity that Rossellini employs in order to show that Indians, all things considered, are "just like us." Or actually, better than us: "Look at what India has done in ten years," observes Rossellini. The scenes investigate the postcolonial palimpsest: the camera switches its focus, and we see images of sailboats and a container ship at the horizon, to reaffirm the coexistence between tradition and modernity. "In India, you find the contemporaneity of history: immersed in the past but existing in the present." The images that follow are nowadays typical of a tourist visiting India, but in 1957, they were a novelty (Italy already had television for a few years, but images of alterity were still not part of everyday programming). We move from the outdoor laundry establishment of Dhobi Ghat to the porters with their loads of chafing dishes and so on. What fuels Rossellini's enthusiasm is the precision and the rationality of these immense operations, a logistic nightmare that, instead, seems to continue seamlessly. Given that the majority of this working class is illiterate, both the clothing and the meals are color coded. Rossellini proudly affirms that the deliveries always take place in a timely and faultless fashion!

In the fourth episode, we are in Versova a fishing village located North of Bombay, populated by the Marathi people. Here, we are shown how fish is used both as food and as fertilizer. This episode introduces us to a model that we will see repeated in the course of the various episodes of the documentary (and it is typical of Rossellini's didactic mission, which we will find in many of his television films), a model whose entire cycle of industrial production is studied and analyzed in detail: from the use of boats, to the methods of drying the fish, to transportation. At times, these scenes feel like infomercials promoting the politics of modernization featuring fishing.

To soften the seriousness of this topic, the fifth episode is largely dedicated to cuisine, and it begins with Rossellini himself, who reads a lentil soup recipe. For an Italian audience, whose cultural parochialism and culinary pride Rossellini knows well, he praises the wonders of Indian cuisine. The images continue, and "Verso il sud" (Heading South) takes us to a Muslim village and then continues on toward Madurai and the very baroque temple of Alagorkoil (now we are in the state of Tamil Nadu). In this episode, Rossellini takes advantage of his good knowledge of the local architecture and of the political, social, and religious history of this very lively region of India. And Rossellini never misses a chance to promote one of the ideological keynotes of this Indian journey: the tolerance and the civil coexistence of people of different languages and cultures, in a new, harmonious democracy. From the director's words, it seems evident that this is not silly cultural naivete; it is a cultural project in line with Nehru's politics of peaceful coexistence. The future of India depends also on its (true or presumed) past of tolerance and harmony, and Rossellini, with Lukácsian perspectivism, adapts to this vision.

The theoretical principles at the base of Rossellini's vision of India are to be found in two volumes that were very popular at the time. The first one is Nehru's cultural biography of his own country, *The Discovery of India*, a memoir originally published in 1946 and written in the Ahmednagar fort, where he had been imprisoned by the British from 1942 to 1945. The other is Tibor Mende's interview, *Conversations with Mr. Nehru*, published in 1956.[88] These texts (had Rossellini been more pedantic, he would have listed the volumes in the opening credits) are the protagonists of the sixth episode, "Le lagune di Malabar" (The Malabar lagoons). As usual, the unteachable Cesarini Sforza begins, in his complete historical-geographical ignorant bliss: "We've reached the South-Western coast, in Malabar. . . . Is life here any easier or is it more difficult?" Rossellini explains: "They are way poorer. But I must give historical pointers regarding the last two hundred years of Indian history. . . . The country's impoverishment is due to the commercial barriers instituted by the British in order to protect Manchester's textile industry. Artisans must return to live on land. Monocultures have developed with strict industrial objectives." "Le lagune di Malabar" follows with great attention the local fishing practices and the harvesting of coconut. Thankfully, Rossellini's face is not shown when Cesarini Sforza observes that "they climb like flies," referring to the coconut pickers, or when he describes images of young Dravidian females as "pleasingly different." The tone of the images, the long sequence pan shots that accompany the boats in the lagoon, seems to trigger a certain reverie in both narrators. We are in the state of Kerala, and the focus is on villages located within the coconut forests, on the colors of the jungle and on the vessels ("it looks like a Phoenician boat"). But finally, the technical and pragmatic aspects take the lead, and the episode continues with its wickerwork production (the English protagonist in Renoir's *The River* was a wickerwork magnate) and the matchstick factory. "A country that one can dream to go live in," concludes Rossellini, while the images show some boats that carry copra, the coconut husk.

In the seventh episode, "Kerala," we stay in Malabar, and this time, Rossellini focuses on the endemic diseases of the region and on the great steps taken by the Indian government. After having informed us of the pandemic of malaria and elephantiasis, he focuses on the now widespread vaccination programs. He discusses at length the character of the local population:

> I recently read Roger Caillois' book, *Les jeux et les hommes*.[89] Caillois divides the game into four groups: luck, ability, masquerade, and vertigo (paroxysm). There are, therefore, civilizations that are based on luck and ability (as is the case with the Mediterranean basin), or Africa which is identified with the masquerade. In India, none of these ludic moments exist, and especially absent is the notion of luck. This may be because what exists there is struggle, in their religion there is a struggle between destruction and preservation, so they have a very rational and concrete approach to life.

This kind of statement, though considered to be less scientific nowadays than a few decades ago, was widespread at the time. Among the most bizarre images of this documentary, we have those of a group of Norwegians in Kerala, within the international aid program known as the Indo-Norwegian Project, intent on helping to improve boating technologies. Rossellini, always ready to defend local wisdom and acumen, points out how the Norwegian boats are too large and become immobilized by monsoons, in distinction to the agile local vessels. Even Cesarini Sforza, after hours of reeducation by Rossellini, must admit that "India is much more rational than we had thought." Rossellini's tired reply is: "I'm glad you think I'm right." The episode ends with images of the Indian laborers in the icehouse used for the preservation of fish and run by the Norwegians wearing freezer coveralls, then a factory of cement tubes, and, last, the beautiful images of a group of pale Norwegian and Indian children who joyfully swim together in an enchanted crystalline sea.

With the eighth episode, "Hirakud, la diga sul fiume Mahanadi" (Hirakud, the Dam on the Mahanadi's River), we are fully immersed in Nehru's modernization efforts. In West Bengal, in the state of Orissa, the Mahanadi River is about to be rerouted through the walls of the Hirakud Dam. The episode begins with a camera car that slowly approaches the area where the dam is being built, followed by one of the now habitual involuntary gags: "In the centre"—Rossellini explains—"we have the peaks of the mountains that have now become islands, and they create some 'sanctuaries' for animals, especially for birds." The English "animal sanctuary" is translated into Italian as "*riserva naturale*," but Cesarini Sforza is deceived by Rossellini's use of the English expression (which he confuses with the Italian *santuario*, meaning "holy shrine") and asks: "Is this in reference to the holiness of animals?" Rossellini (by now dispirited) says, "Well, I don't know" and continues with a few more facts: "275 villages have been submersed by this lake . . . and 35,000 workers were employed. . . . The work is carried out solemnly, in silence." And Cesarini Sforza adds promptly: "[Like] silent, laborious ants. What nobility of deportment, what composure!" Long and silent pan shots of the construction are then shown, and a lateral tracking shot of the scrapyard, followed by a forward movement toward the memorial dedicated to those who lost their lives on the job, and then a backward zoom, and finally Rossellini can state: "And here is the finished work! And this is a girl from Orissa who admires the work completed by her and her workmates."

The ninth episode is entirely dedicated to the pandit Nehru, portrayed as the only true man of providence, who is bravely trying to solve the enormous problem of modernizing the largest democracy in the world. Rossellini recounts his first encounter with Gandhi: "I met Gandhi when he was in Rome on his way to a roundtable conference in London, in 1931–1932 [he was actually on his way back]. A man of action, very quick, swift as a ferret. Nehru is more of a saint; he wants to create a democracy in India." The episode opens with the title "Il pandit Nehru" (The pandit Nehru) and, this time, we see Hirakud from above, with Nehru looking down from an airplane window. Certain aspects of this episode make it seem like more of an official newsreel, with the inauguration of the dam and a military celebration. Rossellini comments: "This 13 of January, 400,000 people came from as far as two, three, four hundred miles." But the scene ends quickly, and the troupe follows the pandit to Nalanda, the Buddhist university. Nehru's meeting with the young Dalai Lama allows Rossellini to showcase his knowledge of

Buddhism: "Do you know how Buddha ended his sermons? This is my suggestion to you. Try it, and if you find it beneficial, adopt it." We then move on to the Visva-Bharati University (alma mater of Sonali DasGupta), founded by the poet Rabindranath Tagore, located north of Kolkata, and committed to the integration of Western and Eastern texts and to political and religious tolerance: "One of the textbooks is Benedetto Croce's *L'estetica*," Rossellini comments ecstatically.

The tenth episode is dedicated to a topic very dear to Rossellini, "Gli animali in India" (Animals in India). In both the television documentaries and the film *India: Matri Bhumi*, domesticated and wild animals are compared to one another and are analyzed for both their physical and social presence within the community and their symbolic value. In Rossellini's cinema, animals are introduced as beings to be observed as such (and to be loved, in true Franciscan spirit) and as metaphorical figures to be read in relation to the human society that surrounds them. This is the case with the tiger in the third episode of *India: Matri Bhumi*, as discussed, and the monkey in the fourth episode. In this tenth episode of *L'India vista da Rossellini*, there are two true Rossellinian moments. The first has to do with an elephant. The crew approaches the animal to photograph it, but the *mahout* dismounts it and makes a fuss. He takes out two artificial tusks, places them in the animal's mouth, and mounts it once again, letting the crew take photographs. For Rossellini, this "love and respect for the elephant's pride is truly moving." One of the shots becomes more engaging when we see Rossellini in colonial attire (white shirt and light-colored pants) as he enters the frame to offer food to a beggar. It is quite significant that the only authorial insertion, after a year's worth of filming and work, takes place right here, in this moment of immeasurable pain and of total consciousness of the negligibility of this specific gesture in the grand scheme of human suffering.

The episode continues with more animals. First, the jungle's street sweepers, vultures devouring a dog's carcass (Rossellini comments: "They are dreadful but so very elegant"), and then enormous bats, eagles in the Karapur jungle, a heron in flight, and Yamuna monkeys with their gray fur and black feet and faces. Then appear some images filmed with a telephoto lens, such as the tigers "peeing in order to mark their hunting territory," as well as the elephant scene that we saw in the first episode of *India: Matri Bhumi*, with the *mahouts* who wash the large animals in the river. The episode then continues with a flock of ducks crossing a railroad. The conclusion is nearing, and it is time to take stock of things:

> SFORZA: Your attitude towards India . . . has shown us the more optimistic data. What critiques can be made?
> ROSSELLINI: A sense of fulfilment for the sense of tolerance that allows them to live together.
> SFORZA: We gave them machines, but what . . . what can be exported from their way of life?
> ROSSELLINI: We haven't given them much . . . the great spirit of tolerance is part of their culture.

Rossellini here recalls how one of Krishna's principles establishes that a people's level of civility is measured by its tolerance.

The French version, *J'ai fait un beau voyage*, presents itself in the same unpleasant graphic and orientalizing style that we saw in the Italian edition (for instance, the title appears in a silly arabesque font) but with the advantage of the presence of journalist and writer Étienne Lalou in the studio. The dialogue between the two is more to the point: Lalou asks Rossellini if he is interested in magic, and Rossellini promptly answers "le magique ne m'attire pas . . . c'est la réalité qui m'intéresse" (magic does not attract me . . . it's reality that interests me). Not only the tone but also the cinematography is more interesting: we are no longer in a screening venue with a screen at the front, but face to face in a studio with the images being played with faded transitions on a television screen. Lalou shows, from the very beginning, much more substance than his Italian counterpart. After the first question, similar to the Italian version's beginning in which Rossellini wants to dispel the myth of India as a magical land, Lalou quickly moves on to more technical questions: what cinematographic tools and materials the director brought to India, and who contributed to the filming process. But most of all, Lalou has a clearer sense of pace. The questions are quick, the dialogue is fluid, and Rossellini's answers are on point. The joke about the men sitting at the racetrack is better organized and timelier from a comedic perspective. What is also interesting is the difference in the "sound illustration": on top of the tablas that also accompany the Italian version, the French soundtrack chooses sound effects more freely. In the racetrack scene, a parody of the Anglo-Indians, and in the cricket match scene, the band music ironically recalls British colonization. Technical questions allow Rossellini to praise the handheld camera, saying, "Je m'amuse beaucoup plus avec le 16mm que le 35mm," to which Lalou keenly replies, "L'antécedént de la sensibilité modern."[90] Even here, of course, the documentary is affected by the cultural atmosphere of the time. An example of this is the way in which the sacredness of cows is explained as a utilitarian phenomenon. This is typical of material anthropology, which reads every cultural event as a direct consequence of primary needs: the cow is sacred because it is useful, for example.

The second episode concentrates on laziness, and this gives Rossellini the opportunity to talk about Naples, especially the Collezione Farnese of the Museo Archeologico (Rossellini's audiences are already familiar with this room from the scene with Ingrid Bergman in *Voyage to Italy*). The third episode features a change of set, and cuisine is the topic of discussion. Lalou is the one reading the recipe, this time, and this allows Rossellini to interject with a funny joke for French audiences: "Bah, écoute, je mange des spaghetti tous les jours."[91] On a more serious note, the French version provides more space for scientific details, and Rossellini is able to discuss the need for protein in human diets, and the importance of nitrogen in fertilizing the land. The episode ends on something more upbeat with a *langoustine à la cardamome* recipe recited by Rossellini himself.

The third and fourth episodes replicate, in both their images and text, the Italian version. The fifth episode continues, in what seems like a fairly tedious tone, with stories about Indian cuisine. Rossellini explains how to prepare a lentil dish, followed by the bored gaze of the presenter, who is clearly wondering what French viewers will think of this chubby Italian man reading recipes on TV. In the following episodes, the model mimics that of the Italian version, and Rossellini simply translates everything he has already said to Italian audiences. Worthy of mention is the fact that, in the ninth episode, he at last cites Nehru's volume directly (*The Discovery of India*) and Mende's interview (*Conversations with Mr. Nehru*), which together constitute the fulcrum of Rossellini's idea of India. And finally, in the last episode, Rossellini manages to quote his favorite writer Vitaliano Brancati to critique the machismo of Italian men.

Encyclopedia

On the key role played by the Indian trip in Rossellini's modus operandi, Alain Bergala poignantly writes that Rossellini "renie son propre passé d'auteur,

ROSSELLINI IN INDIA

d'artiste, et s'apprête à fonder, sur l'expérience et la méthode d'India, rien de moins qu'une nouvelle 'vocation' du cinema: didactique, encyclopédique, universelle."[92] Sure enough, Rossellini, upon his return from India, declares:

> I have a great project for South America, Brazil and Mexico in particular. I will send groups of young people to both countries: they'll be carrying out a preliminary investigation. One of them will be a writer, one a photographer, one a sound technician, and a filmmaker will lead the group. Here's how I'll proceed: I'll create an index for each country and I will study, with my collaborators, all the problems that arise: nutrition, agriculture, farming, languages, habitat, etc. As you can see, it'll be the work of a *geographer* and an *ethnographer*, which does not limit itself to being a mere scientific study but will allow the viewers to discover something new. Art will be the point of arrival of these preliminary works. My work will consist of creating a piece that is a poetic synthesis of each country. After all, that's what neorealism is. I went overseas in search of this method, but I could use it in Europe as well. I've returned from India with a new outlook. Wouldn't it be interesting to make ethnological films on Paris or Rome? Let's look, for example, at wedding ceremonies: the ritual's value as a profound expression of mankind disappears by becoming habitual. Well, we must rediscover the rituals on which our society is founded through the new eyes of the explorer who describes the customs of a so-called primitive people.[93]

As this particular project never took off, Rossellini's remaining career will be devoted to didactic cinema, which includes made-for-television biographies of famous historical characters, as in *Socrates* (1971), and various TV mini-series, such as *Atti degli Apostoli* (1969) and *Il messia* (*The Messiah*, 1975). As this material has been recently analyzed in depth by Michael Cramer, India and the India Project stand at an interesting crossroads even beyond Rossellini's own career. Specifically, they bring me to think in larger terms of the geopolitical imaginary world of the 1960s, the role of nonaligned countries in the global sphere, and the intervention of moving images in this scenario. I would like to conclude this chapter with a quote from Dileep Padgaonkar, whose book and whose intense email exchange with me over the course of many years before his recent passing has been fundamental in the making of this chapter. In his *Under Her Spell*, he writes,

> At first sight, *India Matri Bhumi*—which I saw only in 2006—embarrassed me [to] no end. Time and again Rossellini had asserted that he had steered clear of a tourist's vision of the country. Indian exotica was not for him. Yet

here he was focusing on elephants, tigers and monkeys and making sweeping comments on the values Indians hold dear—non violence, tolerance, patience, restraint, realism and so forth. While he had avoided the clichés of the orient by western, and especially American filmmakers, he had nevertheless projected an India shorn of its intractable problems: the depredations of the caste system, the persistence of superstition, the rampant poverty and, no less significant, the penchant to indulge in horrific violence that was obvious during the Partition riots only a decade before Rossellini shot his film. . . . To an Indian who had been mesmerized by Rossellini's neorealist trilogy, *India Matri Bhumi*, therefore, appeared to be a promise woefully unfulfilled.[94]

As Padgaonkar continues in his analysis, elements of the film that I highlight in this chapter, in particular the anti-Hollywood stance of this project, convinced him to rethink his opinion, and in the end, he compares Rossellini to parallel cinema directors such as Mani Kaul (for his interest in India's *shastriya kala*, or traditional arts) and Kumar Shahani (for his essayistic style). What we gather from Rossellini's engagement with India is a complex approach to larger non-Western imaginaries, mediated through a personal authorial lens; pressure to engage with a positive vision of modernization; and the long tradition of orientalism. As with Pasolini and Antonioni after him, Rossellini generates multiple articulations of developmentalism, exoticism, and a genuine sense of wonder that cinema still can and does trigger today. In short, it is travel cinema's multiple and contradictory debts that I explored elsewhere with James Cahill that sit firmly at the core of Rossellini's and of my analysis alike.[95]

We Are All on a Spaceship

At first sight, not much has remained of this trip to India, to which Rossellini invested a couple of intense years of his life. In fact, quite the opposite happened. The afterlife of this project was exclusively to the detriment of the "cultural capital" of the director. His affair with Sonali DasGupta generated a transatlantic scandal, which became a full-on media frenzy once the couple touched down in Rome. Beyond this tabloid story, all his Indian films quickly disappeared—too tainted by biographical accidents for the contemporaries and too passé for the new generations that read into this just another orientalist approximation of a wannabe anthropologist.

Thanks to my friend Carlo Antonelli, I had the privilege of spending a week in the former villa of the Rossellinis at the Circeo on the Roman seashore. It has a swimming pool built for Ingrid and a back room for meditation arranged with Indian pillows for Sonali. And of course, buried right below in the local cemetery, there's Anna Magnani, who decided to haunt the traitor Roberto even from the afterlife. This kind of architectural materialization of Rossellini's life, I realized, is visible in his work, and the impact of "the discovery of India" played a key role. First, the didactic and the authorial became more evident in his work upon his return, for the pedagogical tendency that was already visible in his early animal shorts became, in the neorealist period, bolder after India. The same happened to his relations to the small and big screen and their different aesthetics, which blended in the post-India phase along this new prominent didactic line.[96] The legacy of India has to be found in these two new venues of investigation. First, we can see it in his new passion for the geopolitics of the world at large, a full-on geopolitical engagement with new places, people, and ideas. Thanks not in small part to the contribution of Renzo and his production company San Diego film, his work takes on an international perspective—making this second part of Rossellini's career a real voyage into the world, and often into the Third World. With this comes a new understanding for what nowadays we call the Global South as well as an attempt to expand the cultural borders and to de-westernize filmmaking.

Among the many anecdotes about the years spent in Houston, the most interesting one is when Rossellini recounts bringing a group of scholars to watch the yellow fever virus on the big screen.[97] The scientists do not recognize it: they were used to seeing the world of the very small only under specific conditions of light, magnification, and observation position. This "micro-neorealist" experiment, if we can call it that, convinced Rossellini even more of the need for a dialogue between the sciences and between the sciences and the public. It is clear that for Rossellini, exploration through film also becomes an exploration of film and the audiovisual medium more broadly.[98] Television becomes the ideal medium for reaching places and people furthest from the centers of scientific thought. One of the scientists comments during an interview, "We are all on a spaceship," and Rossellini concludes, "Science will give lead to a new type of humanism" and, we might add, to a new type of cinema in which the exploration of the world by the camera is at the heart of artistic creation.

Notes

1. Jaikumar, *Where Histories Reside*, 132.
2. Rascaroli, *Personal Camera*, 6.
3. This legacy of exchanges is being investigated by Maja Figge in a project currently titled "Entangled Modernities: Transnational Film Relations Europe and India (1947–1975)."
4. Brunette, "Brechtian." Brunette implies that the "estrangement" is caused by Rossellini's obsession with presenting "things as they are," and this "mild experimentalism" comes from his "idiosyncratic way of looking at the world."
5. Herman, "Rossellini," 8.
6. Rossellini, *Il mio metodo*, 185 (my translation).
7. Fabian, *Time and the Other*.
8. Rossellini seems to be at least aware of this issue: "Non bisogna dimenticare che esiste una grande parte del mondo ipocriticamente chiamata 'in via di sviluppo' e che è semplicemente sottosviluppata, perchè i suoi abitanti si trovano, cronologicamente, in un altro momento della storia umana. Noi siamo lì, davanti a loro, presenti e minacciosi; e loro con un' angoscia immensa, si sentono arretrati, il che non è giusto perchè possiedono una vera civiltà (e non sono sicuro che la nostra sia del tutto compiuta). Ebbene, io penso che sia molto importante fare qualcosa per il mondo intero, ossia prendendo in considerazione tutti gli spettatori possibili." (We must not forget that there is a large part of the world hypocritically called "developing" and that it is simply underdeveloped because its inhabitants are, chronologically, in another moment of human history. We are there, in front of them, present and threatening; and they, with immense anguish, feel backward, which is not right because they have a real civilization [and I'm not sure that ours is fully completed]. Well, I think it's very important to do something for the whole world, that is, taking into consideration all possible viewers.) (Rossellini, *Il mio metodo*, 18, my translation).
9. Mignolo, *Local Histories/Global Designs*.
10. Dainotto, *Europe (in Theory)*, 173. The original quote is in Giuseppe Goffredo, *Cadmos cerca Europa: Il sud fra il Mediterraneo e I' Europa* (Milan: Bollati Boringhieri, 2000), 66.
11. The complexity of Italy's current position in the aftermath of this forced unification has been succinctly drawn by Lombardi-Diop and Romeo, a context that includes the "Southern question, intranational and international mass emigrations, new mobilities, the subaltern position of Italy within the European Union, and the geopolitical dislocation of Italy as the Southern frontier of Europe" (Lombardi-Diop and Romeo, "Italy's Postcolonial 'Question'"). For a discussion on issues of internal colonialism postunification, see Dickie, *Darkest Italy*; Moe, *View from Vesuvius*; and Schneider, *Italy's "Southern Question."*

12. Fogu, *Fishing Net*, 5.

13. Benjamin, *Reflections*, 163–73. See also Glynn, "Porosity."

14. "Similarly dispersed, porous, and commingled is private life. What distinguishes Naples from other large cities is something it has in common with the African kraal: each private attitude or act is permeated by streams of communal life. To exist—for the northern European the most private of affairs—is here, as in the kraal, a collective matter" (Benjamin, *Reflections*, 171).

15. I am thinking of the work of Maja Figge, for example, who has been at work on the relationship between modernist European cinema and India with a groundbreaking project that investigates what she calls the history of "entangled modernities." She points both to the shuttling between European and Indian cultural industries beyond the usual univocal study of influence imposed on the Global South and to the actual modernity (and modernism) of the Indian art film scene. See Figge, "(Post)Koloniale."

16. Garga, *Art of Cinema*. See also film society pioneer Mulay, *Rajahs and Yogis*.

17. Deprez, "Films Division."

18. Osborne, "India on Film," 66.

19. Gokulsing and Dissanayake, *Indian Popular Cinema*.

20. Stjernholm, "Post-Independence India." Bengali documentary filmmaker and critic Ritwik Ghatak notes that "India is one of the richest countries to be exploited by the camera—and almost all of it still virgin" and brings forth Sucksdorff's Indian documentaries as example of what has been done. Ghatak, "Documentary," 58.

21. Gunning, *Fritz Lang*, 458–60.

22. Mennel, "Returning Home"; Shedde and Hediger, "Come On, Baby"; Sieg, *Ethnic Drag*; Figge, "(Post)Koloniale."

23. See Thomas, *Bombay before Bollywood*, for an accurate depiction of this period in Indian cinema. I would like to thank my colleague Ishita Tiwary for recommending this book and for her insightful comments on this chapter.

24. Jaikumar, *Where Histories Reside*. *The River* was a huge success at the Venice Film Festival (where in 1951 it shared the International Prize with Robert Bresson's *Diary of a Country Priest* and Billy Wilder's *Ace in the Hole*).

25. I discuss this more at length in Caminati, "Culture of Reality." The original English version of this TV program was titled *Roberto Rossellini's Sicily: Portrait of an Island*, broadcasted by NBC on December 29, 1968.

26. Cramer, "Rossellini's History Lessons." See also Cramer, *Utopian Television*.

27. Russell, *Experimental Ethnography*; MacDougall, *Transcultural Cinema*; Rony, *Third Eye*; Grimshaw and Ravetz, *Observational Cinema*.

28. On the traffic between European art cinema and ethnography, see Caminati, "Culture of Reality."

29. Andrew, *What Cinema Is!*, 6.

30. Rondolino, *Roberto Rossellini*, 27.

31. Bertozzi, *Storia del documentario italiano*, 61.

32. Perniola, "Documentari fuori regime," 376.

33. Hay, *Popular Film Culture*; Hay, "Placing Cinema"; and Landy, "Genre," each makes a similar point.

34. Tosi, *Cinema before Cinema*. This work was originally published in Italian in 1984 as *Il cinema prima di Lumière*.

35. I have discussed this elsewhere in Caminati, *Roberto Rossellini documentarista*.

36. Tullio Kezich calls it "inadequate, amateur," Fernando Di Giammatteo finds it unclear and pretentious, and, according to Marino Onorati, the only prospect Rossellini has left is to leave the industry and to find himself a different profession altogether. Quoted in Gallagher, *Adventures*, 459.

37. Aristarco, *Sciolti dal giuramento*. This edited collection (roughly translatable as *Free from the Oath*) included interventions from Renzo Renzi (his original piece appeared on June 10, 1956), Paolo Gobetti, Umberto Barbaro, Italo Calvino, and Vittorio Spinazzola.

38. Bazin, "Difesa."

39. Hoveyda and Rivette, "Entretien," 14, quoted in Gallagher, *Adventures*, 561.

40. Godard will write about India: "Today, Roberto Rossellini has re-emerged with *India '58*, a film as great as *Que Viva Mexico!* or *Birth of a Nation* and which shows that this season in hell led to paradise, for *India '58* is as beautiful as the creation of the world." (Godard, *Godard on Godard*, 140)

41. Truffaut, "Rossellini," 3.

42. Astruc, "Stylo"; Truffaut, "Tendance."

43. Laura Rascaroli writes that the pen metaphor had already been used by Cesare Zavattini in the journal *Cinema* (issue 92 in 1940) and can now also be found in Zavattini's *Neorealismo ecc*. Rascaroli, *Personal Camera*, 194.

44. Astruc's forethinking is highlighted in Sørensen, "Digital Video."

45. Astruc, "Renaissance," 5.

46. Jean Rouch, quoted in Gallagher, *Adventures*, 459.

47. Rouch and Rossellini, "La ricerca," 47.

48. Surugue, "Jean Rouch,"14.

49. Nijland, "Jean Rouch," 30.

50. Rouch, *Ciné-Ethnography*, 20–21.

51. François Truffaut, quoted in Verdone, *Roberto Rossellini*, 199.

52. Mundell, "Rouch." Rossellini comments on this as well: "Una delle cose che li (i distributori francesi) ha scioccati è che il film non era commentato da uno speaker: ogni storia era raccontata in prima persona e avevo trovato degli indiani che sapevano parlare francese, ma con un accento. Era importante per me riportare dall'India qualcosa di autentico. Non volevo né scandalizzare gli spettatori né esaltare l'India."

(One of the things that shocked them [the French distributors] is that the film was not commented by a speaker: every story was told in the first person, and I had found some Indians who could speak French, but with an accent. It was important for me to bring back something authentic from India. I didn't want to either shock the audience or glorify India) (Rossellini, *Il mio metodo*, 12, my translation).

53. See Geertz, *Works and Lives*, 3–30, for an analysis of the notion of thick description.

54. See Wolfe, "Historicizing," 152. Among the harshest critics of Jean Rouch's work in Africa was Ousmane Sembène. See Rouch and Sembène, "Historic Confrontation." For a more articulated critique of the distance between Jean Rouch and postindependence African filmmakers as a disservice to Rouch's collaborators hailing from West Africa, effectively effacing them from both French and African film histories, see the insightful Berthe, "Entomological Critique."

55. See Astourian, *"Moi, Un Noir"* and Eaton, *Anthropology*, 8.

56. Rossellini talks extensively about his fascination with India in Hoveyda and Rivette, "Entretien."

57. Rossellini, "Dopoguerra," 346. According to Gallagher, the original invitation had come from the film producers, the Borkar brothers. I have been unable to confirm this information. See Gallagher, *Adventures*, 580.

58. Caminati, *Roberto Rossellini documentarista*, 35–44.

59. According to Padgaonkar, Kittu was an "assistant" to Rossellini through the shooting of *Voyage to Italy* (*Under Her Spell*, 52).

60. Sutoris, *Visions*.

61. Prem Vaidya became a very active documentary photographer and filmmaker for the IFD. His diaries and good memory were instrumental for Dileep Padgaonkar in his reconstruction of the timeline and map of the shooting.

62. Padgaonkar, *Under Her Spell*. I would like to thank Dileep, who recently passed, for the help he provided over many email exchanges.

63. Margherita Moro found these two documents reproduced here in Renzo Rossellini's archive. The value of 8,500 rupees in 1957 was a considerable sum, as the average salary of a middle-class family was 200–400 rupees.

64. Gallagher, *Adventures*, 609.

65. Jaikumar, *Where Histories Reside*, 170.

66. Bourgeois, Bénoliel, and Bergala, *India*, 54.

67. Rossellini, *Il mio metodo*, 169, my translation.

68. Rascaroli and Rhodes, *Antonioni*, 9.

69. Rossellini, *Il mio metodo*, 91, my translation.

70. Hughes, "Recent Rossellini."

71. De Luca and Barradas Jorge, *Slow Cinema*.

72. Rossellini, *Il mio metodo*, 88, my translation.

73. Daniélou, *Labyrinth*.

74. These "dam films," so very typical of this historical period of electrification and modernization of the subcontinent are to be looked at in juxtaposition to, for example, the 1971 documentary by Marxist Bengal filmmaker S. Sukhdev, *A Village Smiles*, in which a new ecological consciousness points to the hardships and damage brought about by these massive land projects. See Roy, "Moving Pictures," and Salazkina, *World Socialist Cinema*.

75. Rossellini is aware of the work of the FDI, as mentioned in a letter to Enrico Fulchignoni, dated January 25, 1957, *Filmcritica* 390 (December 1988): 571, quoted in Gallagher, *Adventures*.

76. Jean Herman remembers that the tiger was shot in a zoo near Bombay, before this episode was even conceived, and amusingly defines Rossellini's style as "*refistolage* a priori" (beforehand patching up). See Bourgeois, Bénoliel, and Bergala, *India*, 36.

77. This essay appeared originally in French in Bazin's *Qu'est-ce que le cinéma?* in 1958 (117–29). It was a rewriting of two essays that appeared in *Cahiers du cinéma*, one published in 1953 with the title "Le réel et l'imaginaire," and the other in 1956 titled "Montage interdit." The essay appears in English along other essays under the title, "The Virtues and Limitations of Montage" (Bazin, *What Is Cinema*, 41–52).

78. Bazin, 49.

79. Daney, "L'Écran," 34, my translation. For more on sadism in Bazin, see Daney, "Screen of Fantasy."

80. Padgaonkar, *Under Her Spell*, 125.

81. Pezzini, "Asia teatro," 245, my translation.

82. In Bourgeois, Bénoliel, and Bergala, *India*.

83. During this period, Rossellini and Zavattini were planning to work together on a film based on de Castro's book. See Cassarini, *Miraggio*, and Moro, "Roberto Rossellini," 10–15.

84. Since our first meeting in 2010, Renzo Rossellini and Gabriella Boccardo have been nothing by supportive and enthusiastic of my work. Many information in this book comes from different conversations with them over the years.

85. Castro, *Geografia*, vi.

86. Rossellini successfully employs one of the first tricks of cinema, labeled "debunking" by Siegfried Kracauer, which he exemplifies through Charlie Chaplin's *The Immigrant* (1917) (Kracauer, *Theory*, 307).

87. Margherita Moro has unearthed two letters handwritten by Rossellini, both addressed to Nehru. One letter to introduce Pasolini, this "poet, writer and cinematographer" to the pandit, and another letter in which he accuses Pasolini of "repeating all the stereotypes" about India.

88. Nehru, *Discovery*; Mende, *Conversations*.

89. Caillois, *Jeux*; the English-language version was published as *Man, Play and Games* in 1961.

ROSSELLINI IN INDIA

90. "I have more fun with the 16mm camera than the 35mm"; "The antecedent of modern sensibility."

91. "Listen, I eat spaghetti every day."

92. "Denies its own past as an author, as an artist, and prepares to found, on the experience and method of India, nothing less than a new 'vocation' of cinema: didactic, encyclopedic, universal" (Bourgeois, Bénoliel, and Bergala, *India*, 50).

93. Rossellini, *Il mio metodo*, 189.

94. Padgaonkar, *Under Her Spell*, 212.

95. Cahill and Caminati, *Cinema of Exploration*.

96. Many of these made-for-TV biographies contain some interesting technical experiments, such as Rossellini's work on fake backgrounds using mirrors in order to re-create exotic or ancient locations. The best parts are usually the re-creation and repurposes of old machinery, as in the case of *L'età di Cosimo de Medici* (1972–73) where Renaissance science is brought back to life. See Licheri, *Rossellini*, and the insightful documentary by Jean-Luis Comolli, *La dernière utopie: La télévision selon Rossellini* (2006), which goes into detail, with help from Beppe Cino, in unmasking all of Rossellini's tricks.

97. Rossellini was in residence at Rice University in Houston, as guest of the foundation run by the De Menil family, from 1971 to 1973, working on a project titled *Science*. About two hours of footage is archived by RAI in Rome with the title *Rice University*, while the rest of the footage sits partially in the archives of Italian state television and partially in the archives of the Menil Collection (built by Italian architect Renzo Piano). Margherita Moro, PhD student at the Università di Udine, is working on this topic and already produced a wonderful documentary on this forgotten work (*The Last Utopia of Roberto Rossellini*, 2020).

98. As Hannah Landecker writes, "the microlife goes hand in hand with the history and theory of cinema" ("Microcinematography").

3

Pasolini in Africa and the Middle East and Back

In the 1964 poem "Profezia" ("Prophecy") dedicated to fellow traveler Jean-Paul Sartre, Pier Paolo Pasolini writes:

Alì dagli occhi Azzurri
uno dei tanti figli di figli,
scenderà da Algeri, su navi
a vela e a remi. Saranno
con lui migliaia di uomini
coi corpicini e gli occhi
di poveri cani dei padri
sulle barche varate nei Regni della Fame. Porteranno con sé i bambini,
e il pane e il formaggio, nelle carte gialle del Lunedì di Pasqua.
Porteranno le nonne e gli asini, sulle triremi rubate ai porti coloniali.
Sbarcheranno a Crotone o a Palmi,
a milioni, vestiti di stracci
asiatici, e di camice americane.
Subito i Calabresi diranno,
come malandrini a malandrini:
"Ecco i vecchi fratelli,
coi figli e il pane e formaggio!"
Da Crotone o Palmi saliranno
a Napoli, e da lì a Barcellona,
a Salonicco e a Marsiglia,
nelle Città della Malavita.

. . .

Poi col Papa e ogni sacramento
andranno su come zingari

verso l'Ovest e il Nord
con le bandiere rosse
di Trotzky al vento ...

The revolutionary fervor that animated many Third-Worldist European intellectuals during the years of decolonization is well captured in these powerful verses.[1] Several years later, that same sentiment was concisely articulated by Pasolini in an interview—even though Lenin had now taken Trotsky's spot on the flag: "Years ago I dreamt of the peasants coming up from Africa with a Lenin flag, taking up the Calabrians and marching West together."[2] While from today's historical distance this statement sounds naive and historically shortsighted, it helps capture the structure of feeling of Third World solidarity and the ideological configuration of Pasolini's engagement with Africa. History moved differently, as we know, and the red of Lenin's or Trotsky's flag has been replaced by orange, the color of migrants' life vests, crossing the Mediterranean at great personal peril—welcomed not by friendly Calabrian peasants but by soldiers, cops, camps, and general hostility. The contemporary postcolonial condition, as defined by Sandro Mezzadra and Federico Rahola, has placed not the land, the worker, or the peasant (as envisioned by Marxist thought) but the sea, the border, the migrant body, and the crossing at the center of twenty-first-century struggles.[3] These are the new "permanently temporary zones" of mass migration, as defined by Federico Rahola in his eponymous volume, where the refugee camp has become a structuring model for control along Europe's borders.[4] These new areas of international law(lessness) can be read as iconic mirror images of the failure of the political vision of Pasolini, who along with so many others believed in a nonbipolar world order and the revolutionary potential of liberation struggles.

If Pasolini's dream has now been turned into a nightmare, reconstructing his geopolitical stance can help us capture that multifaceted constellation clustered around international Third-Worldist solidarity, or, using the apt definition coined by Sohail Daulatzai, that "Bandung humanism" that animated many intellectuals and activists at that time in history.[5] Taking the Afro-Asian Conference of 1955 as the pivotal moment in Third-Worldist thinking helps us come to terms with both its lost potentialities and its overdetermined historical limitations as a Global South initiative that many, Pasolini among them, wanted to read as a possible blueprint for a diffuse revolutionary method. Can the Third World lead the way in tactics, methods, and strategies of uprising? Can Europe learn the revolution from the decolonizing Third World?

Pasolini's Southern Strategy

It has become a sort of ideological pastime in leftist groups to imagine in a past conditional mode what Pasolini would have said about some current event or other and to enlist him as a comrade in contemporary quarrels. From time to time, Pasolini has been dressed as a nonglobal protester, an environmental activist, a gay rights icon, and, alas, a defender of police brutality.[6] These "ventriloquist" gestures testify to the great impact that his work and thought still has on Italian, and more generally, left-wing global culture. And yet, once we look at Pasolini's theory and practice vis-à-vis politics and society, what emerges is a very hard-to-predict and nonconformist approach. This is particularly true with regard to Pasolini's own version of *terzomondismo*, which I have defined as "heretical orientalism" in order to capture the ideological and political contradictions at the core of Pasolini's engagement with the Global South.[7] The internationalist message of "Profezia," quoted earlier, smells of pinky kumbaya to a contemporary reader, while in 1964, it was seen as a true ideological commitment and a departure from the very ambivalent position of the Italian Communist Party (PCI) on issues that were disruptive to the bipolar world order of the Cold War.

The PCI in the fifties, at the time of the Bandung conference, was largely in line with the USSR geopolitical directives, especially on issues of decolonization, postcolonial self-determination, and the Non-Aligned Movement, which the party looked down on with suspicion.[8] However, despite their lukewarm reception by the hegemony of the left-wing establishment, the liberation struggles and the war in Algeria specifically had a massive impact on the Italian intelligentsia, within both the PCI and the Partito Socialista Italiano (PSI) and all the other small political groups that will emerge before and after the *biennio rosso* (the Two Red Years, 1967–69).[9] Third-worldist thinkers were being translated and disseminated in the Italian context, and their messages adapted into a form of transnational revolutionary solidarity, which was then rather audaciously redirected toward the idea that it is the anticolonial struggle that should constitute the model of political action for the Italian intellectuals. This ideology of transnational revolution was also used by groups that were breaking away from the PCI. As Neelam Srivastava underscores, the best-known Third-Worldist revolutionary, the Martinique-born ideologue of the Algerian revolution Frantz Fanon, was speedily introduced into the Italian cultural scene. The first translation appeared as early as 1959, and all the subsequent volumes were soon thereafter published by Einaudi, thanks to the curatorial work of Giovanni Pirelli.[10]

I would suggest that considering Pasolini as an integral part of the *literature of decolonization*, alongside Jean Genet, Jean-Paul Sartre, and all the other European Marxist allies involved throughout the 1950s and 1960s in articulating a form of transnational revolutionary ethos, helps us shine a new light not just on Pasolini's own southern attitude, a pan-meridionalism well explored by Giovanna Trento, but on a large portion of the creative network of artists and intellectuals active in those years in Italy. Creating a link between the anticolonial struggle and the European leftists' intellectual movements allows us to read Pasolini less provincially and to map out a series of Euro-Atlantic networks involved in acts of solidarity.[11] It does not come as a surprise, then, that in 1968, in the "Apologia" (Apology) of his poem "Il PCI ai giovani" (Poem to young communist students), Pasolini provocatively defined himself as a Fanonian Marcusian intellectual ("intelletualli marcusiani e fanoniani, me compreso").[12] To call oneself *fanoniano* was a political and rhetorical gesture of rebellion and amounted to joining the ranks of many other Young Turks of the *sinistra extraparlamentare* (extraparliamentary Left): the radical leftist groups fighting for hegemony over the ideological leadership of the working class who coalesced around the 1968 student movement.

Pasolini's commitment to Fanon, however, needs to be explored not entirely on its own terms but in relation to his engagement with the ideas of Antonio Gramsci and Ernesto de Martino. I want to argue here that it was Gramsci and de Martino who acted as mediators in Pasolini's appropriation of Fanon's theoretical corpus. Pasolini's relationship to Gramsci's life and work has been amply investigated, and Pasolini's own debt to him was made public in his poetry collection *Gramsci's Ashes* (1957).[13] It is from Gramsci that Pasolini understood the revolutionary value of the subproletarians and the role of counterhegemonic cultural interventions, both of which form the backbone of his political activism. Moreover, it is Gramsci's meditation on the organic intellectual that informed Pasolini's own role as an engagé artist. But Pasolini's engagement with Ernesto de Martino's anthropological work is probably less known. De Martino had been working since the 1930s on different ethnographies of Italian southern peasants. With a keen interest in ancient religious practices, de Martino was among the first to make active use of "new media" (photography, phonography, film) to document his field-work. The recent translation into English of his canonical *Sud e magia* (1959) as *Magic: A Theory from the South*, which focuses on the southern region of Basilicata, allows us to fully understand the very modern conceptualizations offered by de Martino in his work, as he was moving away from the vulgar evolutionist framework in vogue at the time, which offered a racially based reading of marginal cultures.[14] While there is only one recorded instance of the two men meeting (in Crotone in 1959), Pasolini's encounter with de Martino's very peculiar and innovative form of anthropology took place during his early work as a gun-for-hire in the Roman film industry, where he contributed to anthropological films by Cecilia Mangini, a fearless documentary ethnographer strongly influenced by de Martino's writings.[15] Pasolini worked on three of her first films (*Ignoti alla città*, 1958; *Stendalì*, 1960; and *La canta delle marane*, 1952). *Stendalì* stands out because Pasolini helped solve a problem typical of ethnographic cinema: sound. Mangini did not film with a proper sound camera (unthinkable in our digital age), which left her with beautiful but silent images of funerary rites from Puglia (as this film was directly inspired by de Martino's *Morte e pianto rituale nel mondo antico*).[16] Pasolini composed a litany, sampling lines based on Greek tragedies, which was then performed on the soundtrack. This sonic approach was a particularly apt encapsulation of Mangini's own artistic method. They were highly mediated reconstructions of actual events, more docudramas or docu-fictions rather than following the pseudo-objective models of early ethnographic visual accounts. As Donatella Maraschin details, this schooling in anthropological work has been systematically neglected in studies on Pasolini in an attempt to make his work resonate directly with the European New Wave modernism rather than the ethnodocumentary strand of European visual ethnography.[17] Rather than a sign of his adherence to the aesthetic experimentations of the New Waves, it was probably the Roman anthropological circle that inspired Pasolini to mix genres and modes of filmmaking.[18] As Cesare Casarino comments, "for Pasolini, it is precisely as an anachronistic narrative straight out of the archaic substrata of folklore and myth that the history of modernization becomes conceptualizable and representable."[19] It is also through ethnographic images that this "archaic substrata" renders itself visible and (re)acquires its revolutionary potential. The same principle is at play for Pasolini here, whether the object of the ethnographic gaze is positioned in geographic proximity or at a great remove. Pasolini's work with Italian visual ethnographers had an impact on his experience of filming in Global South countries. The mixing of narrative and stylistic techniques borrowing from both fiction and documentary aesthetics that we saw in Cecilia Mangini's film, and the investigation of modernity and the decolonial era, are all conducted precisely through these hybrid techniques learned during his work with the filmmakers involved in de Martino's circle.

Nicholas Mirzoeff well captures the localization of revolutionary potential in the South for both Gramsci in the Italian Mezzogiorno and W. E. B. Du Bois in the Jim Crow–era United States:

> Writing in the 1930s with a full awareness of fascism's dominance, both W. E. B. Du Bois and Antonio Gramsci came to see the need for a new point of view that both in different ways called the "South." For Du Bois, the South was the Southern part of the United States that practiced segregation under so-called Jim Crow laws, whereas for Gramsci it was the Italian *mezzogiorno*, a mix of feudal rural areas and unregulated modern cities like Naples. The South was, of course, intensely contested, rather than some imagined point of liberation, but for both thinkers no strategy could be successful that did not imagine itself *from the South*.[20]

This Southern strategy, or precondition, is very visible in Pasolini's own thinking. What we see, as we move chronologically through his oeuvre, is a clear continuity between his early ethnographic work on the revolutionary potential of the *lumpenproletariat* of the *borgate romane*, the exploited Italian southern peasants and the decolonizing subjects of the African liberation movements. This expansion, that encompasses several parts of the Mediterranean, South America, and the black inner cities of the US urban north, infused with revolutionary Fanonian ideology, gives both continuity with earlier works and renewed political vigor to Pasolini's non-Western productions. It was at this point, under the influence of both Fanon and ethnographic theories, that he found an artistic method best suited to his political goals, in the form of the essay film.

Semiotic Counter-Strategies

Pasolini believed film to be a unique and indispensable instrument in the deployment of "semiotic counter-strategies" against capitalism, as many militant filmmakers and theorists of the long '68 did.[21] This *dispositif* acquired a

74　　　　　　　　　　　TRAVELING AUTEURS

new bent and became a precious ally when brought into the postcolony, as this passage from the section "Gennariello" in *Lettere luterane* (*Lutheran Letters*), written around 1970 on the ontological difference between the written and the visual in the postcolonial context, suggests:

> Nothing compels one to look at things like making a film. The gaze of a writer upon a landscape, rural or urban, can exclude an infinity of things, cutting out from the whole only those that give rise to emotions or serve some purpose. The gaze of a director on this same landscape, meanwhile, cannot fail to take note of—almost listing them—all the things that are found there. Indeed, while for a writer things are destined to become words, that is, symbols, in the expression of a director things remain things: the signs of the verbal system are thus symbolic and conventional, while the signs of the cinematographic system are precisely the things themselves, in their materiality and their reality. These become, it is true, "signs," but they are the livings "signs," so to speak, of themselves. . . . So if I had gone to Yemen as a writer, I would have returned with a completely different idea of Yemen than that which I have having gone there as a director. I don't know which of the two is truer. As a writer I would have returned with the idea—exciting and static—of a country crystallized in a medieval historical situation, with tall and narrow red houses, decorated with white friezes as though made by a crude goldsmith, heaped up in the middle of a burning desert and bright enough to scratch the cornea, and here and there valleys with villages that repeat exactly the architectural form of the city among sparse terraced gardens of wheat, of barley, of small vines. As a director I saw instead, in the middle of all this, the "expressive," horrible presence of modernity: a leprosy of chaotically planted light posts, houses of concrete and sheet metal built without sense there where the walls of the city once were, public buildings in a dreadful twentieth-century Arab style, et cetera. And naturally my eyes had to rest themselves on other things as well, smaller or even miniscule: plastic objects, cans, shoes and textiles of cotton, miserable canned pears (from China), little radios. I saw, in short, the coexistence of two semantically different worlds, united in a single chaotic expressive system.[22]

What makes this excerpt more than just a musing on the semiotic distinction between the representational capabilities of the written language versus the mechanical eye of the camera and its celluloid development is the foreign location, which these thoughts both address and are generated by.[23] In line with what Nicholas Mirzoeff claims in his *The Right to Look*, modernity's complexes of visuality (the plantation, the imperialist, and the military-industrial complexes) is revealed once it is looked at from a deco-lonial perspective. Rather than just being a "reverse shot," writes Mirzoeff, "this perspective is equally constitutive by means of its own reality effect of the classified, spatialized, aestheticized, and militarized transnational culture that in its present-day form has come to be called 'globalization.'"[24] Pasolini's own postcolonial semiotics of the image belong to this tradition of visual resistance to any authoritarian act of control over the right to visuality—that is, not just who has the right to look and to speak but the regimens that allow these to happen.

When Pasolini moved to Rome in 1950 from the northeastern region of Friuli, he claimed that it was *la scoperta dell'altrove* (the discovery of the Elsewhere)[25] that drove him toward writing his early realist novels, *Ragazzi di vita* (*The Ragazzi*, 1955) and *Una vita violenta* (*A Violent Life*, 1959), about marginal figures and dropouts of the economic boom in the shantytowns far removed from Rome's city center.[26] He then moved beyond Europe, and like few other Italian intellectuals of his time, Pasolini understood that the need for a radical alternative to the neocapitalist Western model required an acceptance of a true alterity, of which he felt himself to be, in many ways, the actualization, as a communist expelled from the party, a homosexual unaffili-ated with the gay movement, and a polemicist against both the mainstream and the avant-garde of Italian culture.[27] The choice to shoot in non-Western locations in most of his later cinema has been often read as just a bizarre taste for orientalist locations and exotic brown and black bodies, which Pasolini liked to shoot and to fuck.[28] But this exoticizing mode, undeniable in all Pasolini's cinema and in many, if not all, white Western travelers this book addresses, is just the first layer of a complex approach toward a place that for Pasolini is both Orient, a place of ancestral and mythical beings, and the Third World, a political, revolutionary formation.[29] This double articulation generates an engagement with the Global South that inspired two feature films, *Edipo re* (*Oedipus Rex*, 1967) and *Il fiore delle mille e una notte* (*Arabian Nights*, 1974). It also inspired the documentaries and medium and short length films *La rabbia* (*Anger*, 1963, a found-footage film); *Sopralluoghi in Palestina per il Vangelo secondo Matteo* (*Location Scouting in Palestine*, 1964); *Appunti per un film sull'India* (*Notes for a Film on India*, 1968); *Appunti per un'Orestiade Africana* (*Notes Towards an African Oresteia*, 1969); and *Le mura di Sana'a* (*The Walls of Sana'a*, 1971) as well as a screenplay for an unrealized film, *Il padre selvaggio* (*The Savage Father*, released posthumously in 1975).[30]

In addition to these completed works, there was the large and ambitious unrealized project entitled *Appunti per un poema sul Terzo Mondo* (*Notes for a Poem on the Third World*, 1968), of which the Palestine, India, and Africa films were to be parts. To this, we have to add numerous poems, essays, and articles that address non-Western issues at large.

What Pasolini wrote about/in Yemen is essential in delineating his engagement with travel outside of the West, and with the form of the essay film, which mostly shaped his nonfiction work. In this postcolonial setting, the ontology of the written and its descriptive and denotative capacity versus the filmed, with its visual referents that escape the system of signs (at least according to Pasolini's semiotics), since they are signs of themselves—that is they represent themselves with themselves, they acquire a political connotation. According to Pasolini, while the word *crystallizes* and halts representation "in a medieval historical situation," incapable of showing the dynamic of the development of a place, the camera (seen by Pasolini not as a filtering device but as a machine that represents things for what they are, "listing them") penetrates the terrible paraphernalia of modern alienation. This is how the "leprosy," the chaos, the nonsense of the displacements of modernity opens up before the film director and the spectator. While the writer cannot see certain elements because of the ineffectual nature of his language, infected with all of the unconscious traditions it brings, to fully signify—that is, it operates on a symbolic level that is removed from the things themselves by the very instrument it employs—the lens follows the eyes of the director as they "rest themselves" on this or that small or large item in the scene. It is the difference between hearsay evidence and the eyewitness, and—to continue the judicial metaphor—it makes it impossible not to indict the wasteland of the colonized Third World, a wasteland that has been made, constructed, and intended and, as such must have a perpetrator or perpetrators. This very "heretic" take on Pasolini's semiotics did sound off to semioticians at the time and now (see, for example, the rebuttals of his approach by "professional" semioticians such as Roland Barthes, Umberto Eco, Stephen Heath, Christian Metz, and Gianfranco Bettetini, among others), but it works well to explain Pasolini's own films, and his own political motivation to privilege the camera over the pen particularly when engaging with the non-Western world as precisely a third space.[31]

A Third Space

Why did Pasolini write this piece, and why about Yemen? Sunday morning of October 10, 1970, Pasolini and his director of photography Tonino Delli Colli, have just finished shooting the "Alibech" episode of the adaptation of *The Decameron* (*Il Decameron*, 1971), in North Yemen. After Campania, Lazio, and Trentino, Pasolini had succeeded in convincing producer Franco Rossellini to take the crew to Yemen for a single episode. This October Sunday Pasolini did not yet know that in the editing room, the images shot in Sana'a would not find a place in the final version of the film. He had understood, however, that he was in love with the place—and this wasn't the first time. While scouting for locations, Pasolini was often struck by the beauty of certain places, at times arid and thankless, as in Africa or southern Italy, at other times lush and rich, like certain images that remain with us of the Indian subcontinent or the Roman countryside and Tuscany. Pasolini's first visit to Yemen with the Arriflex camera (he would return in 1973 to shoot parts of *Arabian Nights*) would be remembered, however, not for the missing piece of *The Decameron* but for a fourteen-minute short film entitled *Le mura di Sana'a* (*The Walls of Sana'a*), a "documentary in the form of an appeal to UNESCO," as the subtitle states. Sana'a is crumbling, and like "Prague, Amsterdam, Urbino" (as Pasolini reports in voice-over), must be saved from itself. The inhabitants of the city have perpetrated the crime in a desperate desire for modernization.

This short film begins with a series of establishing shots of the main governmental institutions of the country. The handheld camera, with Pasolini's voice-over, lingers on the buildings of the Ministry of Public Education, the presidential palace, and the Central Bank. It is unclear whether these dilapidated edifices are halfway-built or already crumbling. Much like at the beginning of the medium-length TV film of the previous year, *Appunti per un film sull'India* (*Notes for a Film on India*, 1969) this inquisitive gaze on state apparatuses foregrounds the key issues of contact with the alterity of the decolonized Third World: the effects of modernity and technological progress on the ancient, archaic world.[32] The main objective of *Le mura di Sana'a* is to force young non-Western nations to acknowledge the absolute, universal value of their artistic patrimony; in short, it was intended to help them develop a historical consciousness. The ideological contradictions of this message—the neocapitalist West and Soviet East should halt the process of industrial modernization and thus help the Third World become conscious of its own uniqueness and alterity—brings us to the core of the privileged status of the white Western traveler, which we have already seen in Rossellini in this book. While this can be read as speaking for the Other, it is also an attempt at universalizing non-Western knowledge, and in this case, architecture. The fact that this film is an "appeal to UNESCO," the United Nations Educational, Scientific and Cultural Organization, grounds it in the Western notion of historic preservation, that is "the endeavor that seeks to preserve, conserve and protect buildings, objects, landscapes or other artifacts of historical significance," as we can read in UNESCO's mission statement. It is a philosophical concept that became popular in the twentieth century, which maintains that cities, as products of centuries of development, should be obligated to protect their patrimonial legacy. The term refers specifically to the preservation of the built environment, and not to the preservation of, for example, primeval forests or wilderness.[33] It's clear that Pasolini was responding to the cultural atmosphere of the time, since in UNESCO's 1972 World Heritage Convention, landscapes and sites of outstanding universal value could be designated as World Heritage Sites, thereby superseding national state jurisdiction as a "duty of the entire international community," as stated in article six of the Convention Concerning the Protection of the World Cultural and Natural Heritage. Who is Pasolini speaking for in this film? Himself, humanity, a sense of history? Dipesh Chakrabarty's admonition in *Provincializing Europe* seems to speak well to the universalist idea of historical preservation, where "these concepts entail an unavoidable—and in a sense indispensable—universal and secular vision of the human. The European colonizer of the nineteenth century both preached this Enlightenment humanism at the colonized and at the same time denied it in practice."[34] This concept is even better explained by Ariella Azoulay, when she writes that these "politics of preservation" are very much part of the imperial mode of engagement with colonial artifacts, and "the degree of our implication in institutionalized imperial violence through different facets of 'good' liberal citizenship [is] designed to protect the differential principle on which citizenship is predicated."[35]

But it is in the Yemen Arab Republic (YAR) created by Nasserite officials with the 1962 revolution that defeated the imamate, that is to say, in this new, socialist, pan-Arabist Yemen that Pasolini is speaking to and not just for.[36]

PASOLINI IN AFRICA AND THE MIDDLE EAST

Let's be clear, I am not denying that Pasolini, along with many Western intellectuals and artists of the long '68, was often involved in a double articulation of solidarity and orientalism, which a symptomatic reading of their work makes emblematically and embarrassingly clear, as is forcefully argued by Alan O'Leary in his analysis in *The Battle of Algiers*.[37] I think, in fact, that it is essential to highlight the asymmetrical status of these situations, as Gaia Giuliani does in a recent razor-sharp analysis of racial issues in Italian media. She cuts to the heart of the matter when, in her discussion of Italian filmmakers abroad, she immediately notices the position of privilege, actual and rhetorical, that they embody, and how their narrative is ultimately one of domination and mastery.[38] While I am fully aware of Giuliani and O'Leary's justified suspicions, I am interested here in identifying a "trans-affective solidarity" (to use the term coined by Anne Garland Mahler) that runs through the political globe of the long '68, as a network of artists and intellectuals who shared an interest in decolonial and anti-imperialist struggles, of which Pasolini was ultimately, even though heretically, part of.[39]

It should also be noted that postwar Italian society, as it underwent accelerated modernization, faced many challenges that were not so dissimilar from the postcolonial world. With its underdeveloped agrarian regions, its relative tardiness in becoming a unified state, its endemic political clientelism, and the media-led supplanting of its rural ethos by an urban, capitalist one, the dynamics of Italian modernization provided lines of shared vision between the Italian intellectuals and those of the Third World.[40]

During an interview about Sana'a, Pasolini states: "Perhaps it has to do with a professional bias, but I felt the problems of Sana'a as my own problems. The disfiguration that is invading there like a leprosy wounded me like a sorrow, a rage, a sense of impotence and at the same time a feverish desire to do something, which peremptorily compelled me to film."[41] We understand this "rage" a few minutes into the film, when Pasolini's own off-screen voice-over briefly narrates the recent years of Yemeni history (the socialist republican revolution, the arrival of the Chinese, the first consumer goods) and closes with the observation that the old city of Sana'a, "having never undergone any contamination from any other world, much less by the radically different modern world," has maintained an original pureness: "its beauty has a form of unreal perfection, almost excessive and elating." We are introduced to that "comparative ethnography" that is the main mode of Pasolini's approach to narrating non-Western locales to European audiences.[42] This comparative approach, in an attempt at solidarity with a socialist nation, materializes once we suddenly switch to images of Orte, a small hill town in the Tiber valley. These are images shot during the filming of *Pasolini e . . . "La forma della città"*, a short fifteen-minute reportage produced by RAI, directed by Paolo Brunatto in the fall of 1973, and broadcast in February 1974.[43] Orte appears in its medieval perfection, until the camera zooms out and pans left to show a new building on the slopes of the hills. Pasolini quips: "At this moment the destruction of the ancient world, that is, the real world, is taking place everywhere. Unreality spreads by way of the housing speculation of neocapitalism; in place of the beautiful and human Italy, even if poor, there is now something indefinable that to call ugly is saying little."[44] The town of Orte, like many small Italian towns during the massive campaign of housing speculation of the economic boom, had indeed radically changed. Pasolini's defense, though, is not that of late romantic upset over the ugliness of the new buildings, but that of the historical materialist terrorized by this real "leprosy" that shatters the historical, architectural, and social memory of Italy and the world at large. The modernity that for Pasolini is nothing other than a new prehistory of barbarism disfigures and disintegrates human beings just as it does the landscape. Italy and Yemen find themselves in the eyes of Pasolini united in the same destiny of forced modernization, of senseless and unplanned development. As Pasolini aptly put it: "Italy is . . . a laboratory country, because in it the modern industrial world and the Third World coexist. There is no difference between a Calabrian village and an Indian or Moroccan village; it is a question of two variations of a single fact that at the bottom is the same."[45] In the battle, shouldering the faithful Arriflex camera, Pasolini was fighting neither the quixotic windmills of the new norm for a decorum offended by the "plastic objects" nor "the little radios" he saw the world littered with but rather a political and ideological nexus that he termed *irrealtà*: "unreality." Not dissimilarly from what Guy Debord and the Situationist International in those same years called *la société du spectacle*, *irrealtà* is the neocapitalist world of audiovisual media that has replaced as second nature the daily life of Western citizens and that has led the West toward an irreversible "anthropological mutation" filled with consumerism.[46] This *"civiltà dei consumi"* (consumption culture) and its residual byproducts that Pasolini lists in his description of Yemen, this trash that should be read as signs of a "development" toward modernity of the "underdeveloped countries," are for Pasolini stepping stones on a path toward alienation, a society

PASOLINI IN AFRICA AND THE MIDDLE EAST 81

of mass consumption that eats the souls and the bodies of human beings. In an article published in the Roman paper *Il tempo* on August 6, 1968, Pasolini talks about "a very contagious disease":

> When I talk about the bourgeoisie I am not really talking about a social class, but rather a real and concrete disease. A very contagious disease: so much so that it has contaminated almost all those who fight against it: northern Italian factory workers, southern immigrant workers, members of the bourgeoisie opposing the current government, and the "lone wolves" (like myself). The bourgeois—let's say this with a bit of irony—is a vampire who is not at peace till it bites the neck of its victim for the pure, simple and natural pleasure of watching them become as pale, sad, ugly, lifeless, twisted, corrupted, uneasy, full of guilt, calculating, aggressive and terroristic as itself.[47]

The Chinese "canned pears" and "the small transistor radios" (*le radioline*) are not just objects but the first enemy encroachment that needs to be fought. Pasolini's call in *Heretical Empiricism*—"we must de-ontologize, we must ideologize"—is an appeal to battle this unreality.[48] He took aim at the ideological disengagement from reality triggered by media, urbanization, and loss of traditions; in short, the Third World is where he proposed making the last stand for a possible political alterity that cinema can help depict and narrate. As he writes in the essay "Sviluppo e progresso" ("Development and Progress"): "Progress is thus a socially and politically ideal notion, whereas 'development' is a practical and economic fact."[49] This is why the nations of the Third World would never become "developing countries" in the Pasolinian vocabulary, but stubbornly remain countries of the Third World: an external space, truly that "third space" theorized by Homi Bhabha as "that postcolonial space of liminality and hybridity that permits the possibility of new negotiations of signification and representation."[50] It is in this postcolonial space that Pasolini's representation of Yemen becomes more than a semiotic analysis; rather, it acquires generative power—this is the space for the creation of new significations in artistic terms, but also the generation of a new political subject: the European Third-Worldist.

Pasolini Travels, or the Essay Form

Pasolini's travels outside of Europe began in January 1961 with a trip to India for a conference on the poet Tagore in the company of Alberto Moravia and Elsa Morante, who will become staple fellow travelers.[51] Like many other politically engaged artists of late modernity, Pasolini was witness to a radical change, where the Other was no longer just the proletariat and the working class, but the cultural Other, whether it be a racialized non-Westerner or someone marginalized within Western society due to their race, sexuality, or difference of any sort. As Hal Foster remarked in *Return to the Real*—an examination of the relationship between modernism, alterity, and art practices—this change, from a subject defined in terms of economic relations to one defined in terms of cultural identity, is significant in as much as it forces the committed artist to move beyond national borders, to explore new expressive forms, and, above all, to turn to other disciplines, such as anthropology, sociology, and ethnography in order to conduct their creative work.[52] Pasolini's first experiment with what would become a new way of making films—a combination of voice-over narration, nonfictional documentation, choreographed reenactments, impromptu musical adaptation, and everything else that went under the hodgepodge heading of *Appunti (Notes)*—was carried out first during his trip to Palestine in 1964. Pasolini went to Palestine from June 27 to July 11, 1963, with a small crew and a few fellow travelers ostensibly in search of locations for *The Gospel According to Matthew*. Besides the technical staff, Pasolini was joined by two priests from the Pro Civitate Christiana, a post–Vatican II religious association centered in Assisi, with whom he had been in dialogue for several years.[53] The trip was apparently undertaken as an excuse to travel through the Middle East rather than to actually find locations, since at this point Pasolini had already decided to shoot his film in Matera in southern Italy. After returning to Rome, Pasolini edited the rushes, adding his own off-screen voice commentary and creating a kind of travel diary that included conversations recorded during the trip, with the title *Sopralluoghi in Palestina per il Vangelo secondo Matteo (Location Scouting in Palestine, 1964)*.

In the Middle East, Pasolini found neither the Gospel-like conditions he was searching for nor the religious conversion he was toying with. What he did find was a new filmmaking practice, which he would put into action in the years to come. As Pasolini explains in discussing the never completed mammoth project *Notes for a Poem on the Third World*:

> The feeling of the film will be violently and even foolhardily revolutionary:
> as though to make of the film itself a revolutionary action (not related to
> any political party, of course, and absolutely independent). . . . The immense
> quantity of practical, ideological, sociological, and political material that

PASOLINI IN AFRICA AND THE MIDDLE EAST 83

goes into constructing such a film objectively prevents the manufacture of a normal film. This film will thus follow the formula: "A film on a film to be made." . . . Each episode will be composed of a story, narrated with a summary and through the most salient and dramatic scenes, and by preparatory sequences for the story itself (interviews, investigations, documentaries, etc.). . . . Stylistically, the film will be composite, complex and spurious, but the stark clarity of the problems treated and its function as a direct revolutionary intervention will simplify it.[54]

The theory and praxis of this activist Third-Worldist film had its roots in different cultural trends very active in Italy toward the end of the sixties. The choice of the title "Notes," for example, resonated with experimental linguistic forms that were dubbed "open works" by Umberto Eco in his 1962 volume *Opera aperta*, which Pasolini repurposes by calling it *struttura da farsi*—structures-to-do or to be completed. *Open works*, in Eco's words, are those "that must be brought to conclusion by the interpreter at the very moment at which he benefits from them aesthetically."[55] The *da farsi* represents for Pasolini more than a simple case of "unfinished" labor: it is related to the necessity of creating a work with a fluid structure that reflects the Marxist sociopolitical vision of the *da farsi* society and a potential response to Lenin's powerful title of the 1902 pamphlet "Che fare?" ("What Is to Be Done?").[56]

This notion of Marxist-Leninist revolutionary praxis and its importance emerged at the very moment that so many African countries in the 1960s were transitioning to forms of democratic and socialist governance. Also, it resonates with what Eco—referring to Brecht's theater—calls "revolutionary pedagogy."[57] Eco clarifies the "revolutionary pedagogy" of the open work as follows: "it is the same concrete ambiguity of social existence as a clash of unresolved problems to which it is necessary to find a solution. The work here is 'open' as a debate is 'open': the solution is awaited and hoped for, but it must come from the conscious participation of the public."[58] The formal structure of the open work clearly reflects the pedagogical aspect of Pasolini's political engagement, which is never didactic, but serves as the demonstration of an open-ended process, of a *da farsi*. The self-reflexivity of the "Notes" genre, with its embrace of the unfinished, is exemplary of an aesthetic in which the artist's tyrannical authority is renounced, to use Rancière's terminology, to open spaces for new configurations.[59] Only thus could we make sense of the "direct revolutionary intervention" that Pasolini places at the base of his *Notes for a Poem on the Third World* project, transforming them from

84 TRAVELING AUTEURS

colonizing narratives into an open linguistic experience, both cinematically and philosophically.

The essay film provides a form of mediated engagement with the materiality of cinema, which lends Pasolini the ideal medium to tackle the postcolony. Pasolini's understanding of the essay film resonates with Adorno's notion of the essay as a form that actualizes the negative dialectic, which can give voice to the defeated. What Pasolini called a suspended dialectic, a form of permanent contradiction, is a fixed and yet productive dialectic where the two parts live side by side, without sublimation into a synthesis. As Antonio Vazquez-Arroyo clearly explains, Adorno in his "Essay as Form" seeks to grasp historical experience by breaking the silences pervading hegemonic historical narratives and lending voice to the suffering of the defeated, in many cases the nameless others sacrificed by the principle of identity inscribed in the idea of progress.[60] In short, blind spots outside of dialectics become a third space where the permanent contradiction allows for the emergence of unaccounted voices.[61] The essay film became, for Pasolini, a form of suspended dialectic with the potential to show our historical condition against the placating vision of progress imposed by the rest of the audiovisual media. It is not surprising, then, that Pasolini's engagement with the essay form included quite an extensive list of films, shot throughout his long career. Some are direct responses to the Italian political context, such as the found-footage medium-length *La rabbia* (*Anger*, 1963) and *12 dicembre* (*December 12*, 1972); or the cinema vérité–inflected *Comizi d'amore* (*Love Meetings*, 1964), a sociological travelogue on love, gender, and sexuality; and the architectural *Pasolini e ... "La forma della città"* (*Pasolini and ... the Form of the City*, 1975). But it is in Pasolini's Third World essay films that his political commitment to the South comes to the fore.

Although the project *Notes for a Poem on the Third World* was never completed, we fully understand what Pasolini's postcolonial essay filmmaking is. Rather than relying on the inherent postmodern nature of the essay film as a product of the diminishing authority found in and promoted by postmodern discourse as well as the "waning of objectivity as a compelling social narrative" that postmodernity generated (as for the kind of "personal cinema" of Agnès Varda, Jonas Mekas, etc.), the political brand of Pasolini's experimentation was forged in the ideological battles of the literary circles of postwar Italian Marxist culture.[62] Pasolini's approach was molded in the dialectical relationship between the powerful influence of the Lukacsian imperatives that provided the PCI with its aesthetic blueprint and the alternative, the Brechtian framework that was drawn on by the artistic and literary avant-garde of the late fifties (including both Gruppo '63 literary experimentalism and arte povera political modernism).[63] I agree with Rascaroli when she writes that "subjectivity in contemporary nonfiction films can consequently be seen as an inheritance of the decidedly auteurist and anti-mainstream, anti-establishment cinema of the new waves, and of European and North-American avant-gardes."[64] However, Pasolini's presence in these films should not be seen in traditional terms of self-expression, but rather as the unraveling of a political process of subjectivization of the Western Marxist in an encounter with the anticolonial, postcolonial, and neocolonial movements of Africa and India. If we are looking to place Pasolini's *Notes* films in a specific category or genre, we would do well to keep them apart from those of, say, Chris Marker, whose work is the product of Debordian media analysis and archival obsession, or Derek Jarman's personal meditations on sexuality. As much as these two figures may seem thematically associated with Pasolini, it is rather within the works of contemporary *vérité* and ethnographic investigation that we find connections to Pasolini, as well as within the self-reflexive examination of the author function, inherited from the European modernist tradition. Indeed, these works were implicitly in dialogue with foundational texts of European counterparts such as *Loin du Vietnam* (*Far from Vietnam*, Jean-Luc Godard, Chris Marker, Alain Resnais, Agnès Varda, William Klein, Joris Ivens, Claude Lelouch, 1967); René Vautier's explosive documentaries on Algeria, *Peuple en marche* (1963) and *Avoir 20 ans dans les Aurès* (*To Be Twenty in the Aures*, 1972); Jacques Panijel's *Octobre à Paris* (*October in Paris*, 1962) on the massacre of Algerian protesters in the streets of Paris by the police a year before; and Agnès Varda's *Salut le cubains* (1963) and *Black Panthers* (1968), along with the works of other left-bank filmmakers, as well as William Klein's films on the Black Panther expat community in Algeria, *Eldridge Cleaver, Black Panther* (1970) and *Festival panafricain d'Alger* (1969).[65]

What makes Pasolini's "Notes" films stand out might be clarified through "free indirect discourse" (*discorso libero indiretto*), a key concept for Pasolini's own self-assessment as an artist—and a term very familiar to Pasolini scholars, who generally associate it with his modernist films (think *Teorema*, 1968). This term seems to work well as a looser framework to describe his political postcolonial nonfiction films. In comments on free indirect discourse and "cinema of poetry," Pasolini took up the function and limits of the authorial intervention in cinema. As he puts it in the chapter "The Cinema of Poetry" from *Heretical Empiricism*: "The 'Free Indirect Discourse' in cinema is endowed with a very flexible stylistic possibility; that it also liberates the expressive possibilities stifled by traditional narrative conventions, by a sort of return to their origins, which extends even to rediscovering in the technical means of cinema their original oneiric, barbaric, irregular, aggressive, visionary qualities. In short, it is the 'free indirect point-of-view shot' which establishes a possible tradition of the 'technical language of poetry' in cinema."[66] Thus, what we see in cinema has a double articulation: on the one hand, it responds to the organizing will of the author, and on the other hand, it functions within the overall text of which it forms a part. Gilles Deleuze is surprisingly clear and succinct in his understanding of what free indirect discourse is: "In the cinema of poetry, the distinction between what the character saw subjectively and what the camera saw objectively vanished, not in favor of one or the other, but because the camera assumed a subjective presence, acquired an internal vision, which entered into a relation of simulation ('mimesis') with the character's way of seeing."[67] It is here that Pasolini discovered how to go beyond the two elements of the traditional story, the objective, indirect story from the camera's point of view and the subjective, direct story from the character's point of view, to achieve the very special form of a free indirect discourse.[68] The characters we encounter in Pasolini's African films speak the double language of the cinema of poetry: the *parole* of the auteur becoming subject, and the *langue* of Third-Worldist ideology. In *Notes for an African Orestes*, we see this played out; the extras in the film, citizens of newly independent Tanzania, are asked to act out scenes of the birth of the democracy from Aeschylus's trilogy. This daringly juxtaposes the supposed foundation of Western political thinking with the birth throes of the liberated African state: it "Third-Worldizes" the Athenians at the birth of modern democracy, while it "Westernizes" the Tanzanians. The scene acquires narrative and ideological validity precisely via this speaking "through," which is the key feature, stylistically, of free indirect discourse. The "Notes" films could be questioned in terms of the way in which the problematic they explore is never fully resolved by the participation of the people whose subjectivity is, quite literally, at stake. While a desire to reach out and understand the social issues at play is evident in these films, the free indirect—or poetic—style of this nonfiction film does not allow for a complete encounter with its subjects. Thus, it is not a surprise if many perceive

PASOLINI IN AFRICA AND THE MIDDLE EAST

this speaking through as a "speaking for," to evoke Gayatri Spivak's political essay "Can the Subaltern Speak?"[69]

An African Oresteia

While working on *Medea* (1969), Pasolini took a trip to Uganda and Tanzania in search of sets for a new project, a full-length film based on Aeschylus's *Oresteia* trilogy to be shot in Africa.[70] Pasolini explains the motivations behind this new experiment: "The essential and deep reason is . . . that I seem to recognize analogies between the situation of the Oresteia and that of today's Africa, above all from the point of view of the transformation of the Erinyes into the Eumenides. That is to say it seems to me that tribal African society resembles ancient Greek civilization. And Orestes's discovery of democracy, bringing it to his country (Argos in the tragedy and Africa in my film), is the discovery of democracy that Africa has made in recent years."[71] Produced by RAI and filmed between 1968 and 1969, but officially screened only in September 1973 at the Venice Film Festival, *African Orestes* is organized around material shot in three different moments. In the first, we see Pasolini and his small crew searching for characters and locations for the film; in the second, the director meets a group of African students at the University of Rome and screens for them images that he has filmed in Africa and invites them to comment on the project; in the third part, Pasolini experiments with the staging of the Greek tragedy in Rome using African American jazz singers. This tripartite division is hardly rigid: not only do the three different phases alternate in nonlinear succession but Pasolini also adds in the editing room other archival footage of the Nigerian-Biafran conflict that had recently ended. It does show a commitment to the African continent, which we see, for example, in these verses:

> E ora . . . ah, il deserto assordato
> dal vento, lo stupendo e immondo
> sole dell'Africa che illumina il mondo.
> Africa! Unica mia
> Alternativa . . .[72]

The "composite and mixed" style of the documentary (as Pasolini defines it), is programmatically evident in the first few frames. The film opens with, on the right, the cover of an Italian translation of the Greek text of Aeschylus's *Oresteia* and, on the left, a map of Africa. While the opening credits roll, the viewer is given several seconds to assess the feasibility of this project: is it possible to conceive of two texts that are so culturally and ideologically far from each other? This in-camera split-screen represents on one side the map, which stands in metonymically for the colonial dream of the imperial cartographer, while on the other side, we see the Italian version of the Greek text, the tragedy studied in school and then translated, renegotiated, and reconceived in what now aims to be a wider project of comprehending the past and alterity.[73] This was not just an effort to "translate" by putting into images the Oresteia projected onto Africa, but the programmatic manifesto of a vital artistic and political dilemma: that is, making "cinema of poetry" by bringing together antiquity, anthropology, art cinema, and political commitment. There are good reasons why the *African Orestes* has been the most successful and most widely screened and distributed of Pasolini's "Notes" films. It is an ambitious project that addresses many obviously relevant questions, and it also works as an instruction manual, offering insight into Pasolini's own world of travel films.

The opening on the in-camera split-screen gives way to a grainy image of Pasolini himself. On closer look, we realize that this is a reflection of a shop window, with the director shouldering a handheld camera, his voice-over narration announcing with his high-pitched, friendly Friulian accent: "I am mirroring myself with the film camera in the window of a store in an African city."[74] The spectator is placed in front of another double image, no longer side by side, as in the case of the book and the map, positioned opposite one another, but in a mise en abyme, with one image inside the other. Pasolini's self-reflexive gesture embodies the good and bad of this African experiment, that double articulation of solidarity and orientalism that we are now accustomed to. By inserting himself physically in the diegesis, Pasolini demonstrated his awareness of the debates surrounding issues of exploitation in visual ethnography. Many others, including Jean Rouch, engaged in participatory ethnography, as gestures that point toward both the veracity of the images shown and the sincerity, the "good intentions" of the white traveler that should guarantee a gaze freed from colonialist intent, a gesture of humility, if you will, to which Pasolini's unthreatening and dubitative voice-over contributes.

The self-reflexive choices in this powerful opening are an attack on the notion of visual proof as a direct vehicle for scientific information. Pasolini reinforces that dubitative outlook with his voice-over: "I have come,

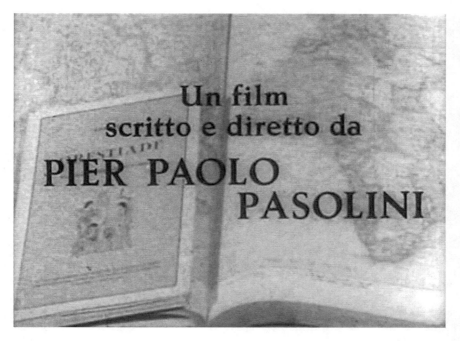

Figure 3.1. The map and the book (*Notes for an African Orestes*).

obviously, to film, but to film what?" Also, the mirror image refers back to another fundamental problematic of film that our long quote from Yemen has already highlighted, that of mimesis. If the theorem to be proved in this film is the possibility of translating Aeschylus onto Africa in the attempt to create an analogy between the two (hi)stories, the problem that arises immediately is that of the relationship between reality and representation: the problem, that is, of truth through images. A possible clue to addressing this issue might come from a deeper analysis of the first sequence of *African Orestes*. Along the reflected image of the director, we note the cheap objects in the shop window, the merchandise for sale (clothes, books, photos of Mao), and at the same time, an enormous leafy tree located in the street exactly behind the film crew. Reality emerges from this single frame: politics and nature, economics and history, compressed into a few meters of film. The voice-over continues: "I chose for the *Oresteia* an African nation that seems typical to me, a nation with socialist tendencies, as we see, pro-Chinese; but this choice of socialism is not yet clearly definitive, because alongside the Chinese attraction there

Figure 3.2. Mirroring (*Notes for an African Orestes*)

Figure 3.3. Mirroring (*Notes for an African Orestes*).

PASOLINI IN AFRICA AND THE MIDDLE EAST   91

is another, no less alluring: the American, or better, the neocapitalist." The oxymoronic image, underlined by the narration, condenses the problems of the recently decolonized African states and the political dialectic in progress. The new and the old, the archaic and the modern, prehistory and the new history of capital are collapsed at the very moment in which the semiotic and epistemological problem of the film bursts forth, to which the reflected image, mirrored *en abîme*, gives an ambiguous response. The question remains dialectically unresolved; it is a contradiction that the spectator must be able to sustain throughout the course of the film. If the unresolved, suspended dialectic is the key stylistic mode of Pasolinian art, then we see how in the first sequence this oxymoronic quality is employed by Pasolini to carry out a double action: on one hand, to unmask the filmic apparatus and therefore dislocate the spectator (a Brechtian Verfremdung to which the director has already accustomed the viewers in the past) and, on the other, to visually present the cultural and political problems of the new Africa of the 1960s.[75] Pasolinian fascination, particularly in this period, with notions of openness and suspended meaning is visible in what we might call his pedagogical style, which is never didacticism, but the demonstration of a process, of a *da farsi*. The self-reflexivity of the "Notes" genre, with its sense of unfinishedness, is exemplary of this attempt to avoid giving responses, but instead to problematize the questions. We do not have, then, a documentary *on* (Africa, India, Palestine, Sana'a), but a film *for* (Africa, etc.), where the film inserts itself into a larger debate, and promotes as immediate action the opening of potential channels of solidarity to the countries and peoples that are his film's subjects. Only thus does the "direct revolutionary intervention" that Pasolini places at the base of his *Notes for a Poem on the Third World* project transform itself from colonial narration into an open linguistic and political experience.

The anthropological dimension of this project emerges in the search for characters. Some of these chance meetings have now become part of a Pasolinian mythology: that meeting between the young Friulian poet who just arrived on the periphery of Rome in the early 1950s and the fierce Sergio Citti, as well as the fortuitous meeting with the young Spanish student who would lend his face to the Christ of the Gospel.[76] The faces and the bodies that strike Pasolini's fancy and his homoerotic desire from the *borgate* to the African villages satisfied a demand of an anthropological variety and a taste for certain human traits, but while this might work smoothly in Italy, beyond the Western context the selection process must consider the orientalist expectations of the gaze.[77] In the Third World, Pasolini is not looking for real faces and bodies, but the projections of those that his Western orientalist upbringing had already impressed on him. This is a case of "citational reality" as Rohdie defines it, in which Pasolini—contradictorily—substitutes a personal vision for the "true" reality.[78] A clear example of this can be seen in the 1969 *Appunti per un film sull'India*. Pasolini is shown in the early scenes of the film with a book of Indian prints in his arms; in short, the faces that he is looking for are these. For example, when he meets a real maharajah, he thinks him boring, bourgeois, and Westernized—he will be so disappointed that he will decide to choose a common man he meets in a market for the role. Pasolinian realism, in the face of alterity, is not ashamed to reappropriate traditional and stereotypical images.

The second of the three parts composing the *African Oresteia* directly puts into crisis the very structure of the film. In a classroom at the University of Rome, Pasolini discusses his project with a group of African students. Pasolini sits in front of the camera, and after having shown some images (we don't really know which, but we assume some rushes not dissimilar from those that the spectators of the film have seen up to that moment), he poses questions to the group: if the film would make more sense if it were set in the 1960s, at the beginning of the process of African democratization, and above all, in which parts of Africa should he shoot his film? The group of young intellectuals reacts coolly, even sardonically, to Pasolini's project: Africa is not a cultural and political unity, and democratization has not necessarily brought an improvement in living conditions. In the end, the meeting with the students is a resounding failure. Why then did Pasolini want to leave this interview as part of the film? Why did he decide to incorporate a sign of the ideological and political failure of his hard-thought theorem? A possible answer comes from Pasolini himself when, in response to a pressing critique of one of the students about the fact that Europeans seem obsessed with images of a still-tribal Africa, he responds, "There is no need to be afraid of reality."[79] As Shelleen Greene points out, when Pasolini argues for reality, he wishes to argue that prior to European colonialism, there existed within the continent a diversity of peoples with their own languages, cultures, customs, and so on, that was somehow subsumed or lost by the artificial division of the continent. However, in his reply, the student argues that this precolonial reality, what Pasolini calls "tribalism," was as much imposed on Africa as was colonial separation. The student's response challenges Pasolini's conception

PASOLINI IN AFRICA AND THE MIDDLE EAST

of a reality that seeks to uncover heterogeneous cultures prior to Western intervention.[80] In short, Pasolini is annoyed by the bourgeois students, dressed in nice ties and turtlenecks, sons of rich families sent to Rome to study, and this harsh reply intends to point to their desire to look good, the *bella figura* at the heart of Italian petit bourgeois decorum. These students, who we understand are mostly from Italian ex-colonies, are neither the free-spirited youth that Pasolini shot in Africa, the underprivileged African masses that triggered his political and libidinal interests, nor the politically conscious Third-Worldists he had wanted his film to depict—they obviously belong to the elite of their country, and they are the properly colonized intellectuals that Fanon dubbed *hommes de culture colonisé* and "mimic men" (*béni-oui-oui*, in Fanon's original French, a term that we can translate as "the yes men," and that was used to derogatorily define all the Muslim collaborators of the French occupation of Algeria).[81] These future scientists, engineers, and bankers are perceived by Pasolini as part of the problem since they are neither able to be rendered exotic (and erotic) nor are they part of a solidarity movement. As Pasolini had written in the introduction to the collection of poetry *Letteratura negra* (Black literature) published in 1961 and titled *La resistenza negra* (The Black resistance):

> The concept "Africa" is an extremely complex subproletarian condition that is not yet utilized as a real revolutionary force. Perhaps I am best able to define this concept if we identify Africa with the entire world of Bandung, Afro-Asia, which saying clearly, begins at the peripheries of Rome, encompasses our South, parts of Spain, Greece, the Mediterranean states, the Middle East. Don't forget that in Turin, there are writings on the walls that say "Via i Terroni = Arabs." In such a sense, the concept "Africa" encompasses the world of the subproletariat "consumer" with respect to capitalist production, the world of the under-governed, of the subculture, of the pre-industrialized civilization exploited by the industrial civilization. . . . The Black Resistance is not finished; and it seems it will not finish as it is finished here by us, with the clergy and De Gaulle in power; while if for us "Resistance" is still equivalent to "hope," the historical resistance that has concluded culturally, a decade or so ago, is already without hope. In Africa, it's clear the split between resistance and Resistance has not come. The struggle is everywhere.[82]

These actual physical people in a classroom in Rome do not fit Pasolini's paradigm of resistance, but they are still useful to the film as they point to that contamination or, to use the apt definition of Shelleen Greene, "a miscegenous cinema," where miscegenation and contamination take place in the merging of the white, male, leftist intellectual with the Black, postcolonial subject to "undermine binary constructions of the relationship between Italy and Africa, and further between the West and non-West," constructions that Pasolini is eager to investigate.[83]

The second part of the film ends with a memorable shot of the Furies as trees swaying dramatically in the wind, "the goddesses of man's animal moment." The voice-off narration continues, "The Furies of the *Oresteia* are destined to be vanquished, to disappear. With them disappears the world of the forefathers, the ancestral world, the ancient world; and in my film, with them, a part of ancient Africa is destined to disappear." This poetic moment is followed by stock footage of the war in Biafra, which Pasolini uses to depict the return of the soldiers from the Trojan War, to underline once again the connection between the ancient and the modern that runs throughout the film. It is at this point that the third part of the film bursts onto the screen, with Pasolini remarking, "But a sudden idea forces me to interrupt this kind of story, rending that style without style that is the style of documentaries and notes. The idea is this: to have the *Oresteia* sung instead of read. To have it sung, to be precise, in the style of jazz and, in other words, to choose as singer-actors some black Americans."[84] The choice of jazz music is directly influenced by the emergence of Black Americans within the civil rights movement in the United States, and free jazz had become a signifier of radical politics thanks, at least in Europe, to the dissemination of American Black writers such as James Baldwin, as well as volumes such as *Free Jazz / Black Power* by Philippe Carles and Jean-Louis Comolli (the film critic and theorist) published in 1971 and translated into Italian by Einaudi two years later.[85] As Karen T. Raizen has aptly noted, while often in Pasolini's films sync sound, or lack thereof, is often used as a Brechtian strategy of alienation, to point to the artificiality of the medium, "these mouths are not disjointed from their voices: they produce their own speech, their own song."[86] In a twelve-minute diegetic performance, Yvonne Murray and Archie Savage sing the roles of Cassandra and Agamemnon, in English, to jazz music. The piece is obviously derivative of John Coltrane's *A Love Supreme* (1965), composed by Argentinian saxophonist Gato Barbieri (a staple of Italian art cinema at the time, providing quick sax riffs for Bernardo Bertolucci's *Ultimo tango a Parigi* [*Last Tango in Paris*, 1972] and Gianni Amico's *Tropici* [*Tropics*, 1968], to name but a few), and a star-studded band with Marcello Melio on acoustic double bass and Don Moye (from the Chicago Art Ensemble) on drums. Pasolini and Gian Vittorio Baldi, producer of *African Orestes*, for this surprise finale take advantage of the musicians regularly performing at the time at the Folkstudio jazz club in the Trastevere neighborhood in the heart of Rome. Founded by Chicago artist and musician Harold Bradley in 1960, Folkstudio became a very popular stop for jazz and folk artist expats or those just traveling through Europe. This last act of the three-part film is directly inspired by the diffusion and dissemination of jazz in Italy that Folkstudio helped kick-start and an interest by Italian high-brow audiences for this genre. A few years before, Gianni Amico's *Appunti per un film sul jazz* (*Notes for a Film on Jazz*, 1965—notice the consonance of the title), a documentary shot in sync-sound at the Bologna Jazz Festival of 1965, featured precisely Gato Barbieri as one of the performing stars. It is clear that Pasolini, or more probably the producer Gian Vittorio Baldi, was aware of this film, and there they gathered the concept, the title, and the musicians. In his off-screen narration Pasolini clarifies: "It is now very clear to everyone that twenty million American black subproletarians are the leaders of a revolutionary movement of the Third World."

The conclusion of the film is suspended: the *sineciosi* (to use the term devised for Pasolini's poetics by Franco Fortini), the oxymoron, the unresolved dialectic so dear to Pasolini's own aesthetics concludes the film and the director's African experiment.[87] A group of African peasants are bent over their harvest while a revolutionary Soviet song, "Varshavianka" (a tune that is known in English as "Whirlwinds of Danger"), accompanies their work. If the questions have not found adequate responses, it is only because the new questions that this film has generated and continues to generate are more important to Pasolini than a final answer.

The Color Line

With his essay films in the Global South, Pasolini seemed to foresee a theoretical stand pioneered a few years later by Clifford Geertz, James Clifford, and the reflexive turn of American meta-anthropologists such as Paul Rabinow and Renato Rosaldo. James Clifford in *The Predicament of Culture* attacks both the superficiality of liberal thought—fighting globalization by preserving Indigenous cultures in a (failed) attempt to re-create "artificial aesthetic purifications"—and the orthodox Marxist position, which sees local realities as obstacles on the road to progress (such, for example, is Moravia's stance on the socioeconomic immobility of India, which informs his *Un'idea dell'India* [An Idea of India] published in 1962).[88] For Clifford, the world is not populated by "endangered authenticities"; he is instead concerned with "mak[ing] space for specific paths through modernity," a new "inventive poetics of reality" where "the time is past when privileged authorities could routinely 'give voice' (or history) to others without fear of contradiction."[89] If we can free ourselves from the nineteenth-century notion of culture as occidental progress, Clifford argues that we can rethink the concept of ethnography as "writing about culture from the standpoint of participant observation."[90] Clifford's positions seem at first sight an act of accusation against Pasolinian incursions into foreign territories, such as his attempts to impose ancient Greece on the nascent African democracies in the *Oresteia*, the anything but apologetic use of Western visual models in the search for characters in *Notes on a Film about India*, or the use of exotic nudes in *Arabian Nights*. Hopefully, however, the analysis conducted throughout this chapter of Pasolini's African *Notes* as essay films reveals not only that Pasolini was profoundly conscious of his own Western ideological burden but also that his Third-Worldist experiments were carried out with the aim of going beyond the desire to represent and translate other cultures for the orientalist scopophilia of the European spectator. Instead, they can be thought alongside a line of shared global solidarity. The Pasolinian postcolonial attitude develops into a combination of visual experimentalism and comparative anthropology that I called "heretical orientalism," that is, the desire to translate for the Western spectator by didactically establishing continuous connections with Italy, in such a way so as to give points of reference to the reader or spectator, while simultaneously experimenting with new visual and narrative techniques that would methodologically break with the imperialist aura of the methods honed in the nineteenth century.[91] It certainly anticipates much of the 1970s and '80s postcolonial filmmaking, from William Klein's documentaries in Algeria to the feminist self-reflexivity of Trinh T. Minh-ha's early works, and it prefigures some of the challenges to political nonfiction films in the era of globalization, such as the implicit dialogue between Pasolini and Harun Farocki on the ontology of the medium, and with Isaac Julien on gender and postcoloniality.[92]

To conclude this chapter with the same suspended dialectic that animates so much of Pasolini's own work, and with the same global geography of the decolonizing 1960s, I would like to point to *La rabbia* (*Anger*, 1963), a montage

PASOLINI IN AFRICA AND THE MIDDLE EAST

film about nuclear war and Marylin Monroe. This film, which was originally screened as one half of a monstrous diptych conceived by producer Gastone Ferranti as a boxing film-match between Pasolini and Giovannino Guareschi's folksy right-wing ideology as a response, was at the time of its release quickly forgotten. But thanks to a brilliant work of restoration by Giuseppe Bertolucci and the Cineteca di Bologna, it has been brought back to its original intent.[93] Upon removing the horrifying responses by Guareschi, we can enjoy Pasolini freewheeling on images and politics, a cinema of poetry for free jazz on found-footage material. It gives a taste of Pasolini as a film editor, picking and choosing images from the large collection of the *Mondo Libero* news reports, a populist and popular newsreel that provided him with the whole world within reach of his editing table. In this film, Pasolini deals with the 1956 invasion of Hungary and Castro and the Cuban Revolution as well as takes Marilyn Monroe's death as a starting point to speak about the death of beauty, to complain about the disappearance of the rural world, and to heavily criticize industrialization, conservativism, anticommunism, and (his archenemy) the Italian bourgeoisie.

Pasolini's geography in *La rabbia* represents a particular image of the globe: where, in the summary of Silvestra Mariniello, "Bandung is the capital of three quarters of the world . . . even of half of Italy"; where the Appian Way leads to Cochin; where Guinea is continuous with the Po plain or the Apulian countryside; and where Lucania, resembling Morocco, is near Vietnam.[94] This Third-Worldist geography has in the color of its people the unifying message that Pasolini sings in his poetry: "They are the days of joy, / the days of victory. / People of color, / Tunisia lives its liberation." And once again, "Joy after joy, / victory after victory! / People of color, Tanganyika is free." Addressing the Congo, the voice-over in the film returns with the same formula: "Joy after joy, / victory after victory! / People of color, another nation / of Africa is independent!" and a little later, referring to Central America, "Joy after joy, / victory after victory! / People of color, Cuba is free."[95]

In one of the most emotional moments, as images of violence against black bodies roll across the screen, Pasolini's own voice recites:

A new problem breaks out in the world.
It's called color.
The new extension of the world
is called color.

One has to admit the idea
of thousands of black and brown children,
black-eyed
infants with curly hair.
One has to accept endless multitudes
of real lives that,
with innocent ferocity,
want to enter our reality.
Other voices.
Other glances.
Other dances.
Everything will become familiar
and expand the earth![96]

It is probably this interpretation of blackness and the new color line as a key concept in the postcolonial condition that makes it easy to understand why Pasolini has been appropriated in contemporary artistic productions, especially those originating beyond Europe. Malini Guha, in her analysis of the shift from the vision of the empire to the vision of the world in British and French cinema, points to a key text by Homi Bhabha, "Notes on Globalization and Ambivalence," where he identifies the time of globalization as the "anxious and impossible temporality, the past-present."[97] The "past-present" is the time of the colony, which reappears in every attempt of erasure. It is also the time of the "great cultural archive" as identified by Edward Said in *Culture and Imperialism*, where the "rich cultural documents" of the encounter between East and West, periphery and metropole, colonized and colonizer are continuously played out. The reworking of Pasolini's documentaries in Africa and Asia similarly presents an ambitious attempt to negotiate the aesthetic ideologies of the postwar European art cinema with the more radical currents of a postcolonial ethos. As such, these "remakes" highlight with particular force the complexities and limitations of Pasolini's original engagement with the Third World, and the legacy of that historic moment within today's culture.

Two powerful contemporary responses to Pasolini's Third-Worldist works, *Waiting for Pasolini* (2007), directed by Daoud Aoulad-Syad and produced by Abderrahmane Sissako, and a short experimental film by Ayreen Anastas, *Pasolini Pa* Palestine* (2005), each directly address the issue at the core of the "past-present" and are generated in that Global South that Pasolini's essay films tried to imagine. *Pasolini Pa* Palestine* rethinks Pasolini's documentary *Sopralluoghi in Palestina*, translating its script into Arabic and taking his film survey and location scouting as a map for exploring contemporary Palestine.[98] Both of these contemporary films are important to address in so far as they allow us to focus on the modalities of production, reception, and dissemination of Western cultural products of *tiermondiste* narratives and to assess their role on a more global and contemporary scale. *Pasolini Pa* Palestine* engages with Pasolini's Third World essay films—in particular *Sopralluoghi*—on the level of both form and content. Sponsored by the Al-Ma'mal Foundation for Contemporary Art in Jerusalem, this medium-length film starts with a female voice-over (Ayreen Anastas) asking, "Should we start?" The images of Pasolini's film, with French subtitles, are projected over a map of Israel/Palestine, prepared by the artist in her attempt to follow (quite literally) in Pasolini's footsteps—retracing the same route that he took during the making of the film in 1962, as a way of "visiting [its] places and the ideas" (as the voice-over clearly states). The initial superimposition, the celluloid projection of Pasolini's film and the map with the highlighted path, creates the first past-present temporal disjunction of the film. Built as a dialogue with four voices (Ayreen Anastas is "the director"and Karam Tannous "the voice," while Suhail Shadoud is Pasolini and Haissam Zaina plays Don Andrea) the first scene sets the tone for the film, which starts with Pasolini and Don Carraro looking at a peasant separating wheat from the chaff. The scene is repeated until the voice of the artist interrupts the joyful reconstruction of events, and a split-screen appears. The female voice-over of "the director" demands for temporal continuity to be respected and asks to go to the actual location in Bethlehem where the movie starts, even though logically it would appear at the end of the trip. These sudden breaks of the narrative punctuate the film to point out mistakes, inaccuracy, and, more generally, to make snarky comments on the teleology of the foreigner who came to superimpose a fundamentally Western narrative over Palestine. It will be this female voice that calls for "music!" as they ascend Mount Tabor by car and visit the Basilica, as Bach's Passion (a Pasolini staple!) blasts. This feminist and Global South rewriting of Pasolini, blending issues of gender and geopolitics not addressed in the original film, makes this work speak dialectically to the original, confronting and updating Pasolini's own vision. The superimposition and the split-screen used by Anastas are in fact visual citations borrowed from Pasolini's own nonfiction *appunti* playbook, which we saw in the profilmic split-screen of Euripides on one side and a map of Africa on the other at the very opening of *Appunti per un' Orestiade Africana*. This repurposing of Pasolini's art film toolbox highlights the complex entanglement of politics, orientalism, and European art cinema. In *Pasolini Pa* Palestine* the filmmaker is fully aware of the powerful self-inscribing incipit of the *Orestes*, as she reenacts the opening sequence of the film in front of the shopping window. But in *Pasolini Pa* Palestine*, the male voice-over mocks Pasolini's, appropriating his lines. One of the male voice-over narrators (Suhail Shadoud as Pasolini) claims: "After forty years, I am making the same mistakes," as the image of Anastas appears on screen, this time in color, asking herself the same question Pasolini asked himself then: "To film what?"

While *Pasolini Pa* Palestine* makes an explicit reference to Pasolini as a father figure for the engaged filmmaker of the Elsewhere (the *Pa**, with an asterisk in the title), *Waiting for Pasolini* is a fictional account that offers a well-informed glimpse into real issues of labor and the impact of Western filmmakers on non-Western countries, as it is infused with a nostalgia both for a better political life that never was and for European art cinema. It tells the story of a remote village in Morocco, where satellite dish salesman Thami announces to his fellow villagers the imminent arrival of a troupe of Italian filmmakers who will shoot a film. The film is a bittersweet comedy, offering many hilarious moments that explore a cross section of a Moroccan village, whose only regular contact with the outside world is through satellite TV, but that suddenly becomes involved in the movie-making world. After the announcement by the satellite dish vendor, mayhem erupts in the village, with children running in the streets shouting "the cinema is coming" while all the residents get ready to appear as extras in the film, from the women, who rush to put on their makeup, to Fakih, the preacher of the local mosque who invites all to prayer. Such is the level of excitement that it seems the arrival of the cinema troupe will solve all the problems in the small village. "Pasolini will pay amounts which will be sufficient for you, for the lives of your children and grandchildren," Thami tells the citizens of the village, boasting to have been a personal friend of Pasolini when he was in town—we are near the city of Ouzazarat, in southern Morocco, where *Oedipus Rex* (*Edipo Re*) was filmed in 1967. But Thami suddenly finds out that Pasolini had died thirty years before and that he will not be coming back to this village. He falls on his knees in front of the poster of the Italian artist hanging in his house and asks: "Why did you die? Why didn't you wait for me?" The Italian troupe

Figure 3.4. "To film what?" (*Pasolini Pa* Palestine*).

that takes hold of the village is shooting some sort of *cinepanettone*, a farcical comedy about Italians in Africa.[99] But even this new source of income for the local villagers quickly dries up. With a phone call the producers cut the funding for the film, the crew dismantles everything, and they leave the village after just two days of shooting. In the end, there is nothing else left for Thami than to go back to climbing on roofs and installing satellite dishes, with the awareness that Pasolini will never come again, and that cinema is now tailored exclusively for the TV, as the not-so-subtle finale informs us. This new death of Pasolini, both as an auteur and as a political figure, is to be read as a tribute from this African director to European cinema and as a critique of new neoliberal mass-produced entertainment. While the impact of Pasolini on the Moroccan film industry has just begun to be explored, we are aware that European art cinema represented an important alternative venue of political and aesthetic solidarity among intellectuals involved in different democratizing processes.[100] The new globalized productions are, then, symptomatic not just of a new world order, very remote from any Third-Worldist aspirations, but of a new World Cinema of flattened and ready-for-streaming standardized products.

The subaltern rewritings conducted by Aoulad-Syad and Anastas, as well as Pasolini's reinscription into the transnational networks of artists and filmmakers who form part of a shared history of geopolitically engaged cinema (that same geography that he first engaged with), have at least two clear outcomes. On the one hand, this reassessment can be thought of as reconnecting the decolonizing efforts with the current antineocapitalist struggle via the Western solidarity movement of the European Left and, in so doing, redeploying all the political weight of countercultural Italian political cinema. On the other, both films I engaged with here highlight the problematic power relations at play, such as exploitation of labor and exclusion from distribution networks. As our understanding of World Cinema shifts on its axis under the stress test of postcolonial theories and practices, Pasolini's work could be, one more time, heretically useful.[101]

Notes

1. Blue-eyed Alì, / one of many sons of sons, / shall descend from Algiers / on sailboats and rowboats. With him / shall be thousands of men / with tiny bodies and the eyes / of wretched dogs of the fathers / on boats launched in the Realm of Hunger. With them they shall bring little children, / and bread and cheese wrapped in yellow paper of Easter Monday. / They shall bring their grandmothers and donkeys, on triremes stolen from colonial ports. / They shall land at Crotone or Palmi / by the millions, dressed in Asian / rags, and American shirts. / The Calabrians shall say at once, / as ruffians to ruffians: / "Here are our long-lost brothers, / with their children and bread and cheese!" / From Crotone or Palmi they'll go up / to Naples, and from there to Barcelona, / Salonika and Marseille, / to the Cities of Crime. . . . Then with the Pope and all the sacraments / they shall go like gypsies / up, to the West and North / with the red banners / of Trotsky in the wind.

2. Pasolini, *Saggi sulla politica*, 1638. In that same interview, Pasolini speaks of the "idealization of the Third World" and admits that it did make sense five or ten years prior, while "today, that seems to me an idea that needs to take into account history, reality, truth. . . . Today, that idea reveals its force as purely psychagogic and mythic." My translation.

3. Mezzadra and Rahola, "Postcolonial Condition." For a critical reading, see Walker, "Postcoloniality in Translation," and Walker, "Postcolonial."

4. Rahola, *Zone*.

5. Daulatzai, *Fifty Years*.

6. On March 1, 1968, students of the Movimento Studentesco (MS) and police forces were involved in a melee in Valle Giulia's Faculty of Architecture campus.

PASOLINI IN AFRICA AND THE MIDDLE EAST 103

Pasolini, in an often misunderstood poem titled "Il PCI ai giovani" (poem to young communist students), states his surprise for the violence shown and takes the policemen's side (not the police's) as the true proletarians versus their counterpart of bourgeois students.

7. Caminati, *Orientalismo*.

8. For example, issue 11–12 of *Rinascita* (published in December 1958), with the Diego Rivera mural *La conquista de Mexico* on the cover, titled *Crepuscolo del colonialismo* (*The Twilight of Colonialism*), was, according to Marco Galeazzi, a clear attempt at containing the dissemination of these ideas in the party. In its opening statement, titled "Guardando il futuro" (Looking at the future)—submerged in the fuzzy talk of brotherhood, such as in the claim that "the people that fight or have fought to break the colonial yoke are natural allies . . . we already perceive the rise of a vast brotherhood of nations . . . advancing towards socialism"—we can detect Togliatti's PCI vision of the revolution. This was a manifesto of *gradualismo* (gradualism), a policy of small steps toward the revolution under the watchful eye of the party and the loving embrace of the Soviet Union that was at the core of the post–World War II political etiquette among workers' parties on this side of the Iron Curtain. Thus, Togliatti wanted to control those radicals who were eager to contribute to the Third World struggle as well as the more cosmopolitan intellectuals. I discuss this more at length in Caminati, "Southward."

9. Le Sueur, *Uncivil War*; Shepard, *Invention*.

10. Srivastava, "Frantz Fanon," and Love, "Anti-Fascism." As Trento notes, Pasolini's understanding of a global Africa was also shaped in part by the work of Senegalese poet and politician Léopold Sédar Senghor, whose influence can be found, for example, in Pasolini's poem "La Guinea," as well as throughout his *Appunti per un'Orestiade africana*. See Trento, *Pasolini*, 33; see also Trento, "Eritrea."

11. Trento, *Pasolini*.

12. Pasolini, *Saggi sulla letteratura*, 1450.

13. Barański, "Pasolini"; Sillanpoa, "Gramsci," 120–21; Greene, *Heresy*.

14. De Martino, *Magic*.

15. Cecilia Mangini very generously allowed me to interview her in Rome in April 2010 at the American Academy about her relationship with de Martino and Pasolini.

16. de Martino, *Morte*.

17. Maraschin, "Ricerche."

18. Houcke, "Ignoti." Recent in-depth studies by Anne-Violaine Houcke have also pointed out the impact of Mangini's first short, *Ignoti alla città* (1958), which documents the life of *borgatari* displaced by the gentrification of the Roman city center. Quite interestingly, Mangini's style in *Ignoti* is closer to Soviet-style filmmaking, favoring dramatic close-ups and camera movements, which are fully rejected by the iconoclastic film style of early Pasolini, devoted as it was to

dedramatizing long shots and close-ups to obtain a "hieratic," fresco-like effect (Houcke, "Affinités").

19. Casarino, "Southern Answer," 676.

20. Mirzoeff, *Right to Look*, 27, my italics.

21. Wollen, *Reading*.

22. Pasolini, *Lutheran Letters*, 31.

23. See de Lauretis, "Language"; Bruno, "Body."

24. Mirzoeff, *Right to Look*, 9.

25. Anzoino, *Pasolini*, 2.

26. For an analysis of the role of Roman locations in Pasolini's films, see Rhodes, *Miserable City*.

27. Casarino, "Southern Answer," 680. On Pasolini's complex relationship with the Italian art and literature avant-garde, see Caminati, *Cinema as Happening*, and Merjian, *Avant-Garde*.

28. On the very few that wrote on Pasolini's sexuality and his artistic practice and theory, I suggest the provocative piece by Wark, "Sexting." On Pasolini's own orientalist erotics, Joseph Allen Boone's work has opened up an interesting path beyond resentment and condemnation in his discussion of *Arabian Nights* where he quotes Pasolini as saying, "May I say, a bit tautologically, that for me eroticism is the beauty of the boys of the Third World?" (Boone, *Homoerotics*, 223). This quote was originally from "Eros e Cultura: Interview with Massimo Fino" in *Europeo*, October 1974. More recently in Humphrey, *Archaic Modernism*, the author makes an argument for the "queer aesthetic" of Pasolini's films, with particular emphasis on Pasolini as a queer orientalist, where the body of the black Other is reinvested with homoerotic desire, therefore rewriting his work through a queer lens.

29. In a letter to *Paese Sera*, published on March 23, 1966, and titled "I diseredati sono il nostro Terzo Mondo" (The outcasts are our own Third World), Pasolini already delineated the connection between Italian and global subproletarians. Now collected in Pasolini, *Politica*, 825–29. I elaborate on Pasolini's extension of his thinking on the Global South in Caminati, "Southward."

30. For a comprehensive analysis of *Il padre selvaggio* and its rightful place in Pasolini's third worldism, see Verdicchio, "Colonialism."

31. See Bruno, "Heresies," for a thorough discussion of this debate.

32. I discuss the Indian film at length in Caminati, *Orientalismo*.

33. Caves, *Encyclopedia of the City*, 345.

34. Chakrabarty, *Provincializing Europe*, 4.

35. She continues:

> "conceiving of art and museums as signs of progress, caring for the preservation of the past by saving documents, rescuing endangered cultures, feeling compassion for and expressing solidarity with people living in poverty as though they are dwellers of other planets, supporting

reform initiatives for the victims of the regimes under which citizens are ruled, and endorsing progressive social projects aimed at 'improving lives' in other places by enabling their inhabitants to benefit from seemingly advanced and transparent institutions for managing populations, debts, and cultural traditions. Unlearning is a way to reverse the role of the normalized milestones that structure the phenomenological field out of which modern history is still conceived and narrated, such as those of progress and democratization in the place of (for example) destruction, appropriation, and deprivation, followed (as if in later phases) by the imperial 'generosity' of providing for those dispossessed by imperialist policies." (Azoulay, *Potential History*, 11)

36. Maggi, "*Walls*."

37. O'Leary, *Battle of Algiers*.

38. Giuliani, *Race*.

39. Mahler, *Tricontinental*, 10. Some recent projects have a similar aim of reconnecting the arts and politics of the Global South to solidarity movements of the metropole. See De Groof, *Lumumba*; Nash, *Red Africa*. On cinema, see Eshun and Gray, "Special Issue," in particular Hadouchi, "African Culture."

40. See Casarino, "Southern Answer."

41. "Si tratterà forse di una deformazione professionale, ma i problemi di Sana'a li sentivo come problemi miei. La deturpazione che come una lebbra la sta invadendo, mi feriva come un dolore, una rabbia, un senso d'impotenza e nel tempo stesso un febbrile desiderio di far qualcosa, da cui sono stato perentoriamente costretto a filmare" (Pier Paolo Pasolini, "Corriere della Sera," June 29, 1974, quoted in Chiesi, "Sguardo," my translation). On the two versions on this film, see Chiesi, "Sguardo."

42. Maraschin, *Pasolini*.

43. The very first version of *Le mura di Sana'a* was broadcast by Radio Televisione Italiana (RAI, the state-owned Italian national channel) on February 16, 1971, without the Orte portion of the film, shot three months after the broadcast. It's only in 1974 (a few months after the broadcasting of *La forma della città*) that Pasolini presented in Milan a second version of *Le mura di Sana'a* (which has since become the official version), which included the Orte sequence. As Chiesi notes, the images of Orte are not exactly the same as those shown in *La forma della città*, albeit they are clearly from the same shooting day.

44. "Ormai, del resto, la distruzione del mondo antico, ossia del mondo reale, è in atto dappertutto. L'irrealtà dilaga attraverso la speculazione edilizia del neocapitalismo; al posto dell'Italia bella e umana, anche se povera, c'è ormai qualcosa di indefinibile che chiamare brutto è poco" (Pasolini, *Per il cinema*, 2108).

45. "L'Italia è . . . un paese da laboratorio, perché in essa coesistono il mondo moderno industriale e il Terzo Mondo. Non c'è differenza fra un villaggio

calabrese e un villaggio indiano o marocchino, si tratta di due varianti di un fatto che al fondo è lo stesso" (quoted in Camon, "Conversazione," 116; now in Pasolini, *Politica*, 1638).

46. Debord, *Spectacle*. See Pasolini, "Studio sulla rivoluzione," or Pasolini, *Politica*, 307–12. Quite interestingly, and as far as I know unrelated to Pasolini's own definition, Nicholas Mirzoeff uses the term *unreality* to define the visuality imposed by structural exploitation: "The 'realism' of countervisuality is the means by which one tries to make sense of the *unreality* created by visuality's authority from the slave plantation to fascism and the war on terror that is nonetheless all too real, while at the same time proposing a real alternative" (*Right to Look*, 5, my italics).

47. Pasolini, *Politica*, 1097, my translation. The original reads "Io per borghesia non intendo tanto una classe sociale quanto una vera e propria malattia. Una malattia molto contagiosa: tanto è vero che essa ha contagiato quasi tutti coloro che la combattono: dagli operai settentrionali, agli operai immigrati dal Sud, ai borghesi all'opposizione, ai 'soli' (come son io). Il borghese—diciamolo spiritosamente—è un vampiro, che non sta in pace finché non morde sul collo la sua vittima per il puro, semplice e naturale gusto di vederla diventar pallida, triste, brutta, devitalizzata, contorta, corrotta, inquieta, piena di senso di colpa, calcolatrice, aggressiva, terroristica, *come lui*."

48. Pasolini, *Heretical Empiricism*, 226.

49. "Il 'progresso' è dunque una nozione ideale (sociale e politica): là dove lo 'sviluppo' è un fatto pragmatico ed economico." Originally published in *Scritti corsari*, now in Pasolini, *Politica*, 455.

50. Rutherford, "Third Space," 220. Bhabha refers to the interstices between colliding cultures, a liminal space "which gives rise to something different, something new and unrecognizable, a new area of negotiation of meaning and representation." In this "in-between" space, new cultural identities are formed, reformed, and constantly in a state of becoming. I am not thinking here of Edward Soja's notion of Third Space.

51. Naldini, *Vita*, 240.

52. Foster, *Return*, 177. The notion of the "artist-as-ethnographer" developed by Foster is at the core of my understanding of Pasolini's documentary. A similar concept is expressed by Rancière, who sees the worker and the colonial subject at the core of 1968 political opening to Otherness, see Rancière, "Democracy," 33.

53. Subini, "Carteggio inedito." See also Steimatsky, *Italian Locations*, 121.

54. Quoted in Mancini and Perrella, *Corpi*, 7, my translation.

55. Eco, *Open Work*, 33. This book was originally published in Italy in 1962.

56. An excellent bibliography on the notion of the *da farsi* is in Rumble, "Contamination," 361. Also, see Benedetti, *Pasolini contro Calvino*, particularly her analysis of *Petrolio* as a work of "eterogeneità costitutiva" (constitutive heterogeneity),

that is to say a mix, as Pasolini refers to his own *Divina Mimesis*, "di cose fatte e di cose da farsi, di pagine rifinite e di pagine in abbozzo, o solo intenzionali" (things done, and things that have to be done, pages completed and sketches, or only intentional) (Benedetti, 47).

57. Eco, *Open Work*, 45.

58. Eco, 45.

59. Rancière, *Emancipated Spectator*, 18.

60. Vázquez-Arroyo, "Universal History."

61. Adorno, "Essay as Form," 171.

62. Rascaroli, *Personal Camera*, 14; Renov, *Subject of Documentary*, xvii.

63. For the rich and complex relationship between Pasolini and the avant-garde, see Merjian, *Avant-Garde*.

64. Rascaroli, *Personal Camera*, 6.

65. See Stark, "Militant Film."

66. Pasolini, *Heretical Empiricism*, 178.

67. Pasolini, 178.

68. Deleuze, *Cinema 2*, 148.

69. Spivak, "Subaltern."

70. No record exists of an actual plan to shoot this film, which leads many scholars, myself included, to believe that these "Notes" are indeed all that Pasolini ever planned to actually shoot.

71. Naldini, *Vita*, 341.

72. Pasolini, "Frammento alla morte"; "And now . . . ah, the deafening wind / of the desert, the stunning, squalid / sun of Africa / that lights up the world. / Africa! My sole / alternative . . ." Commenting on these lines in a letter to Francesco Leonetti, dated the summer of 1961, Pasolini writes, "You misinterpreted 'Africa, my only alternative': it is a 'decadent,' defeated interjection, where Africa is not Lumumba's Africa, but rather Rimbaud's" (*Lettere*, 494). Following Mariniello, we can take Pasolini's statement on his final lines symptomatically, as exposing his torn commitment between Rimbaud and Lumumba. As in all of Pasolini's examples of "suspended dialectics," the two live unhappily side by side.

73. Pasolini's translation of the Oresteia was commissioned by Vittorio Gassman for the Greek Theatre in Syracuse in 1960. See Piva, "Traduttore."

74. "Mi sto specchiando con la telecamera in una vetrina di un negozio di una città Africana."

75. Costa, "Effetto dipinto," and Rumble, "Contamination." Pasolini discusses Brecht quite often in his writings. In relation to cinema, see Pasolini, "Teatro di parola," and the interview Pasolini, "Mamma Roma." Pasolini was also fully aware of Shklovskij's theory of *ostranenie*. On Brecht and Shklovskij's alienation theories, see Jameson, *Prison-House*, 57–59.

76. Naldini, *Vita*, 153, 272.

77. The most accessible summary of the racially marked stereotypes prevalent in modern Italian culture is in Ponzanesi, "Black Venus."

78. Rohdie, *Passion*, 71.

79. Rohdie, 1182.

80. Greene, *Equivocal Subjects*, 221.

81. Fanon, *Damnés*, 56. For the English version, see Fanon, *Wretched*, 13.

82. Quoted in Greene, *Equivocal Subjects*, 217. In this collection that he curated, Pasolini enters into contact with Léopold Senghor and Aimé Césaire, among others. See de Andrade and Sainville, *Letteratura negra*. *Terrone* is a derogatory term for Italian southerners similar to "redneck" in US English.

83. De Andrade and Sainville, 211–12.

84. Pasolini, *Per il cinema*, 1185.

85. Carles and Comolli, *Free Jazz*. The Italian edition was edited and translated by Giorgio Merighi and Patricia De Millo, and was published by Einaudi in 1973.

86. Raizen, "Voicing."

87. Fortini, *Attraverso Pasolini*, 12. For a thorough discussion of the term, see Gatto, "Sineciosi ideologica."

88. Clifford, *Predicament*, 4; Rumble, "Ideas vs. Odors."

89. Clifford, *Predicament*, 5.

90. Clifford, 9.

91. Caminati, *Orientalismo*.

92. On the rich afterlife of Pasolini in contemporary art, see Merjian, *Avant-garde*.

93. Chiesi, *Rabbia*.

94. Mariniello, "Temporality," 118. The quotes are from Pasolini, *Belle bandiere*, 145; Pasolini, "Bandung Man"; and Pasolini, "Guinea."

95. Pasolini, *Per il cinema*, 373.

96. Pasolini, 374.

97. Bhabha, "Notes," 38. See also Guha, *Empire*.

98. For an insightful reading of Anastas' film see "Between Basilicata and Bethlehem: Pasolini, Palestine and the non-European" in White, *Atonal*, 113–42.

99. On this very popular trend in Italian cinema, see O'Leary, "Phenomenology."

100. See the talk Limbrick, "Morocco." Also, on the entanglements between Moroccan and European cinema, see Limbrick, *Arab Modernism*.

101. See Caminati, *Stress Test*.

4

Antonioni in China, Mao in Milan

A Postcard

In *Videocartolina dalla Cina* (*Videopostcard from China*), a short eight-minute video made in December 1985 (on behalf of and "mailed to" the third channel [RAI 3] of the Italian national television broadcasting company RAI to celebrate ninety years of cinema), Italian director Bernardo Bertolucci is depicted in China while scouting locations for an ambitious project about the life of the last Chinese emperor Puyi. The first shot is an image we have become familiar with—Bertolucci is reflected in a mirror holding a Sony Handycam Video8 camcorder. Very much like Pasolini in his *Notes for an African Orestes* (1970), Bertolucci learned the good lesson of cinéma vérité as they insert themselves into the narrative, to prove that they are, indeed, "there." Bertolucci is also there to promote his "film to be made" to Italian audiences and to RAI corporate executives, who were one of the major financiers and producers of the final version of the film, *The Last Emperor* (1987).[1] As he states on December 7, 1985, in these opening shots we start making sense of the surroundings: the Sony logo of the camera, very fashionable in the '80s as a marker of technological innovation; the Western-style outfit of the speaker; and Bertolucci's own Emilian accent, born and raised as he was in the city of Parma. Like Pasolini, it is the voice that is the first signifier for an audience in the know to cling to so as to orient themselves in these first very grainy, pixilated images characteristic of early video camera footage.

It is a powerful opening for a "location-scouting" film, to which Pasolini had already accustomed his audiences: a comparison with the opening of the *African Orestes*, shot exactly fifteen years earlier, shows us how both worldviews and modus operandi of Italian filmmakers in the land of the Other and the Elsewhere have changed. These fifteen years had brought not just new,

109

cheap portable camera technology; they also brought along the end of the dream of a revolutionary Third World that Pasolini and Rossellini (with his Indian portrait of the Non-Aligned Movement first conceived in Bandung in 1955) were so enthusiastically willing to explore. The 1985 China that Bertolucci is traveling through has done something different: it has just opened up its borders to British pop band Wham!, whose memorable performance, according to the BBC, "left an indelible impression on the audience."[2] This new "open" Dengist China, as Deng Xiaoping has taken over from Mao after his death in 1976, will have its moment of demise with the Tiananmen Square massacre of 1989. Bertolucci's timing for this trip speaks of possibility, present as he was in this very brief window, so rare in recent Chinese history. Bertolucci muses, "la Cina che così vicina non è, ma un giorno forse lo sarà, allora la chiamaremo Cina-città" ("China is not so near after all, but one day it might be, then we'll call it China-city"—a pun on the Cinecittà Roman film studios). This can be read as quite a prophetic statement on the future of China as a global visual media producer, as well as an acknowledgment of the Fifth-Generation new wave that was happening precisely during his trip (Zhang Yimou's *Yellow Earth* was released in 1984). Bertolucci is both looking forward to the massive expansion of Chinese productions in the years to come and looking backward to the expansive history of Chinese cinema, in particular starting with 1921, the year of the Communist Revolution.[3]

This "video postcard" made by Bertolucci had a privileged temporality, as it sits right in between the end of the Cultural Revolution and the new state capitalism of the post-Tiananmen era; it also has the quality of a "double exposure," as conceived by Cahill and Holland, channeling Derrida's ghostly worlds.[4] In the technical language of photographic media, the term "double exposure" refers to an image produced when a camera's aperture allows light to pass through the lens and onto a sensitized substrate within its dark chamber more than one time. The outcome is a superimposition of several temporally discrete impressions within the same frame, which, either by accidental development or by design, simultaneously testifies to these separate instances and their mutual entanglements by virtue of being together in a single visual field. Bertolucci's video camera is a time machine of sorts that looks backward to China's past, both as the primary locus of orientalist projections and as site of political experimentations for the European Left, as well as to the digital future of the "Cina-città," the China/Cinema/City of twenty-first-century media. In this film, the double exposure of the

Westerner traveling in China (the present/past bind that all images carry with them, in their "I was there") is filtered through the trope of the dialectic of the ancient versus the modern: China as the site of both the imperial past and the hypercontemporary. Quite amusingly, as he speaks of this China-city to come, Bertolucci is located exactly in the same Peace Hotel in Shanghai (now Fairmont Peace Hotel) and even probably in the same room, where other travelers through Cultural Revolution China were, all composing that same shot right below their window of the square, on the "waterfront gathering spot with a statue" (as defined by Google Maps) and the vast Huangpu River right behind it. This same shot will reappear in Antonioni's, Joris Ivens and Marceline Loridan's, and Shirley MacLaine's films, each with that same surprise at the crowd of the young and the old all performing calisthenics right below their window.

But a few minutes in, Bertolucci's film shows a close-up of a woman hanging some laundry to dry on a boat, which prompts him to say: "for a shot like this Antonioni was punished by the Gang of Four." This sudden mention of *Chung Kuo, Cina* (hereafter referred to as *Chung Kuo*), and the memory of Antonioni's trip points to an afterlife of this film as a living memory in the history of Italian cinema in and about China. Antonioni's film has become for both Italian and Chinese scholars a sort of dark kernel that everyone seems almost compulsively forced to engage with. In fact, as I was researching for this chapter, I was very surprised by the large number of young scholars of the Cultural Revolution (mostly members of the Chinese diaspora) who engage with the Antonioni affair: the actual film, which has now become a rare document of life in China in the early '70s, and its complex aftermath and political repercussions.

A good example of the living memory of Antonioni's film is the 2010 documentary *I Wish I Knew* by celebrated sixth-generation director Jia Zhangke. The film, made up of a series of interviews on life in Shanghai, includes Zhu Qiansheng, one of the minders of the Italian crew in China, who recounts how he became progressively concerned during the shoot. The scene takes place in the Yu Garden teahouse, where Antonioni had shot a scene about Chinese sociability. As tea is served, Antonioni discusses the blending of present and past on contemporary China, while in Jia's film the scene takes advantage of the memory of the witness of these events to provide some context—how the handlers, including Zhu, were worried about Antonioni focusing too much on the country's backwardness and how unruly the crew was in their attempt at shooting what they pleased. Two years later, Zhu was arrested, after the Gang of Four supposedly watched the film, deemed it anticommunist, and used it to mount a campaign against their political adversary. He was forced to go back to all the places where the movie was shot and do self-criticism. Up to that moment, Zhu confesses, he had not even seen the film.

Bernardo Bertolucci's and Jia Zhangke's films clearly demonstrate that the incursion of Antonioni into Chinese culture acquired, in spite of the very minor ambitions of that project, a long-lasting signifying presence in world-cinema culture both in China and in the West. In this chapter, I want to provide a cultural analysis of this film and to offer a reading of it as a traveling culture object as defined by Said in his essay on "Traveling Theory," in which he invites scholars to move beyond analysis of reception and, instead "to map the territory covered by all the techniques of dissemination, communication, and interpretation."[5] In this chapter, I map and reorient Antonioni's China project through a multipronged approach—an analysis of the film itself, a comparison with Cultural Revolution visual culture, an assessment of the impact on how the Cultural Revolution was perceived in Italy, and an analysis of films of other Western travelers in the Cultural Revolution—to understand both its exceptional status and its ordinariness as a cultural product that acquired real meaning as part of a series or genre. In spite of textual reading being the main exercise of this chapter, I am interested in the metacinematic aspect of *Chung Kuo*. Specifically, what interests me most is evaluating how *Chung Kuo* is very much a variation on a simple model of the travelogue of a white Westerner in a faraway land, including the leftist-intellectual self-appointed burden to explain how that very specific moment of Chinese history was having a massive impact on Western leftist culture. In short, it was a trip "there" to explain "here," as is often the case of amateur "comparative anthropologists," a strategy that spawned a long and nightmarish wake that continued to haunt this project in the years to come.

The Scramble for China

Of the period known as the Cultural Revolution, which historians conceive roughly as the ten-year period from 1966 to 1976, what stands out for those of us who are interested in issues of audiovisual representation was the high level of control implemented by the Chinese Communist Party (CCP).

In her insightful *Utopian Ruins*, Jie Li argues, quoting Ban Wang, "the Cultural Revolution created not only its own art but also a 'way of life' that was aesthetically driven, ritualistic, and theatrical."[6] The regime forced millions into becoming actors of their own life, staging a living theater or a happening, in which every individual would perform a role with the underlying assumption that it was for the best of oneself, the party, the country, and Chairman Mao. After all, "in the violent overhaul of the old and the introduction of the new, there was no longer a 'natural way' of carrying oneself and living one's life. One had to enter a prescribed 'theatrical' realm in which the individual acted out well-demarcated roles." Prevalent in the Mao era and culminating in the Cultural Revolution was a competitive and exhibitionist performance of revolutionary fervor intended for the eyes of the authorities and the "masses."[7] While historians are still caught between reading this period as either a political scheming of different competing factions or a massive sociopolitical upheaval, in this chapter, I would like to describe the cultural and cinematic climate around the time of Antonioni's visit in 1972, connecting it to both the other "fellow travelers" filming in China at the same time and the Chinese visual culture of the time. I am to place Antonioni's trip within a larger mediatic contest that connected Beijing to Paris, New York and Milan in a fil rouge of Maoist sympathies, political realities, and sheer cathectic projections of utopian desires completely detached from actually existing Maoism. All films shot in this period show that Chinese society under Mao was also mediated by images, but instead of the "commodity fetishism" in Debord's theory, the Maoist "society of spectacle" was constituted through revolutionary performances and mutual surveillance.[8]

The political and affective closeness associated with China's Cultural Revolution in the West during the long '68 generated an uncanny desire from many leftists to be able to catch a glimpse of what was going on in the country idolized by scores of young and less young revolutionaries in Paris, Rome, and everywhere else in western Europe. China at the time was not well known or seen, since very few travelers were allowed to visit, at least until Zhou Enlai's "cosmopolitan" opening, very limited in reality, but big enough to allow all the major players of the European Left to be there. Tiananmen Square looked like the place to be seen if you wanted your revolutionary stocks to go up in the volatile market of the long '68 leftist world, where groups and parties were born and died in a matter of months, if not days. This Western Sinophilia quickly turned into sheer *maolâtrie*. Essentially, as a cultural phenomenon, Maoism turned into an ideal scenario in which everyone was able to invest whatever they wanted; each country developed and reinvented its own Maoism with specific characteristics that were often completely different from the original.[9] As we will soon see, none of these Western intellectuals spoke Chinese, and reliable information about contemporary China was nearly impossible to come by. "Cultural Revolutionary China became then a projection screen, a Rorschach test, for their [Western intellectuals'] innermost radical political hopes and fantasies," as clearly stated by Richard Wolin.[10] Mao entered quickly into popular culture as a true icon. In her thorough investigation, Julia Lovell points out all the different formats of this folly, such as a 1967 issue of *Lui* magazine (a homegrown French Playboy) that included a special China supplement with young women dressed—if at all—in Mao jackets and playfully assuming faux-militant Cultural Revolution, Red Guard–style poses.[11]

Back home, it was France and its homespun Maoism that percolated through the Italian peninsula. It was because of the early interest by French intellectuals in traveling through and writing about China, and their works' prompt translation into Italian, that a copycat effect was generated through Italian lefties. The ur-trip to China must be that of Simone de Beauvoir narrated in her monumental *La longe marche* (*The Long March*, 1957). Beauvoir decided to stop there on her way back from the Bandung conference in 1955, and even though she spent but six weeks in China, knew no word of Chinese, and had little background of local history at the time of her trip (she managed to acquire most of the information reported in her book once she was back in Paris), she wrote an engaging report of a sympathetic intellectual, blending her own impressions with detailed accounts on policies, such as the agrarian reforms or industrialization in the cities. Her book definitely had a powerful impact and many French intellectuals followed in her footsteps, both literally (as the route was designed by zealous Party members) and stylistically, since these travelogues tended to bring the personal and the political together.[12]

The history of travelers through Cultural Revolution China would be long and fundamentally tedious, as most were required to visit the same locations. Most of their Chinese sentiments were dictated by their predisposition toward this specific brand of socialist life, their editors, and their eager audience.[13] Few stand out, among them Roland Barthes: "When you go to China, you carry in your baggage a thousand urgent questions, urgent and seemingly natural ones. What are things like there with respect to sexuality, women, the family, morality? What is the situation in the humanities, in linguistics, in psychiatry? We shake the tree of knowledge hoping the answer will fall to the ground and we will be able to return home bringing back with us our chief intellectual nourishment: a secret deciphered. But nothing falls from the tree. In a way, we go back home (except for the political answer) with nothing."[14] This quote, in its obscurity and well-meaning attitude, signifies the combination of orientalism and political libido with which the People's Republic of China was invested by leftists of all stripes.[15] His "Alors, la Chine?," published in *Le Monde* on May 24, 1974, three weeks after the *Tel Quel* delegation's return from China, has all the ticks typical of his writing. In spite, or because of the famous traveler, this trip generated a lot of criticism as it was considered too filo-Maoists.[16]

Many Italian writers did the same.[17] Among the writings of those who managed to travel through China, works worth mentioning include Franco Fortini's *Asia Maggiore: Viaggio nella Cina e altri scritti* (1956), which stands out as a clear attempt at keeping one's own narcissism under control. Fortini was one of the first witnesses of the revolution; it shows all of Fortini's ability to engage in what Benvenuti calls "Brechtian alterity," that is to say an encounter with the Other that generates reciprocal estrangement, thereby accepting his own role as Other.[18] Fortini's exceptionality as a Marxist intellectual, contributor to *Quaderni piacentini*, and one of the more open to Third World issues, makes this travelogue one of the few that is bearable to our twenty-first-century eyes. Alberto Moravia in his *La rivoluzione culturale in Cina ovvero il Convitato di pietra* (1968) wrote reportages for the *Corriere della Sera*, as Dacia Maraini was taking pictures (badly, it must be said).[19] Moravia was the "traveler in chief" of Italian intellectuals. His trip to India with Pasolini generated his *Un'idea dell'India* (An Idea of India) in 1960 and spun a large series of travel reportages that made Moravia the travel writer par excellence of the Italian leftist intellectuals. Usually accompanied by Pasolini, Elsa Morante, and later Dacia Maraini, Moravia presented the Italian reader with a combination of politically savvy readings of the field as well as a nice mélange of orientalist and at times disconcerting comments about daily life outside of the West. Moravia in this sense is the ideal "Italian" traveler: properly educated, sophisticated in his writing, and yet fully unaware of his Western privilege, that "imperial eye" that ultimately lies at the core of his surveying look at the world. This China reportage is not that different from the others, as it blends very personal banal experience with political analysis, as if he was fundamentally positive of what was happening in China. Giorgio Manganelli's travelogue *Cina e altri orienti*, originally published for the Milanese daily *Il Giorno* in the autumn of 1972, is dominated by Manganelli's own unremitting neurosis. But at least its many pages devoted to the culinary ambitions of the Chinese restaurants he excitedly visited and fully enjoyed prevents us from hearing another old man pontificating on how unsexy girls are (their lack of makeup and proper outfits being often singled out as serious problems), a sentiment that dominates the narrative of many fellow Italian travelers. We can think of an Italian response to de Beauvoir in the celebrated Franco-Italian feminist intellectual and member of the Italian Communist Party (PCI) Maria Antonietta Macciocchi (1922–2007), whose 1971 book *Dalla Cina: Dopo la rivoluzione culturale* (*Daily Life in Revolutionary China*, 1972) was the first major European encounter with and celebration of the Cultural Revolution. De Beauvoir's and Macciocchi's massive works could be thought of as bookending the most troublesome parts of contemporary Chinese history, as de Beauvoir anticipated the Great Leap Forward while Macciocchi arrived at the end of the Cultural Revolution.

Filming the East

The idea that there is something implicitly cinematic about China and the Chinese, and therefore worthy of being filmed, is well put by Umberto Barbaro in his 1957 essay "Paradosso sulla fotogenia della Cina di Mao" ("Paradox on the *photogenie* of Mao's China"). Barbaro, former director of the Centro Sperimentale in Rome, a communist in the heart of Mussolini's Italy, was traveling through China with a PCI delegation when he wrote this essay.[20] He is thoroughly taken not by the beauty per se but by precisely the *photogenie* of the country and the people:

> il mio desiderio di guardare, soprattutto e soltanto guardare . . . era cosi forte, che io vi arrischiavo, con sorprendente naturalezza e contro ogni mia abitudine, la posta maggiore che possa mettere, in un simile gioco, un uomo, che sia tale: mi esponevo semplicemente al pericolo di guardare senza vedere, al pericolo di non capire . . . (my desire to look, above all and only look, was so strong that I bet with surprising nonchalance and against my habit the highest possible bid a man can gamble: I would expose myself to the danger of looking without seeing, the danger of not understanding).[21]

Barbaro's claim to let himself just look, and to be charmed by the photographic predisposition of the people and the place, has its roots in the double articulation of the exotic and the political that continues to grip many Western travelers. As Barbaro states: "la Cina di oggi, la Cina di Mao Tse-tung è un paese di grande trasparenza, un paese che si capisce tutto d'acchito. Un paese limpido, un paese fotogenico" ("China today, the China of Mao Tse-tung is a country of great transparence, a country you immediately get. A limpid country, a photogenic country"). This vision of modern China, built, as Edward Said would say, through repetition of certain strategic formations, is repurposed here by Barbaro to promote the Chinese road to socialism.[22] The clarity that Barbaro alludes to is of course that of the new socialist state, one that allows you to just be in it. But I see also an element of criticism in Barbaro, as this clarity might speak to that "theater of life" that Jie Li has discussed as the mode of life in Cultural Revolution China. Barbaro seems to understand this aspect, as the limpid and photogenic China can also be understood as an uncomplicated one, where lack of conflict means lack of dialectic, which makes the country good for looking at but nothing more.

This double bind of politics and orientalism is visible in the very first Italian filmmaker in China: the neorealist director Carlo Lizzani. His *La muraglia cinese* (*Behind the Great Wall*, 1957) is the first Italian-Chinese coproduction. Advertised as a documentary, it is more a series of vignettes mostly reenacted by local actors and shot in stunning Technicolor. The film opens in Hong Kong with the stock character of an "exotic woman" who helps the Italian crew move around the city. The atmosphere is sensual and is in line with certain erotic comedies like *Europa di notte* (*European Nights*) by Alessandro Blasetti, which was released in 1958 (and was written by Gualtiero Jacopetti, who was soon to make the first of the erotica-exotica films, *Mondo Cane*).[23] The film is an incredibly rich production, and it is clear that the Chinese government provided the Italian crew with all the means at their disposal. But ultimately it is just another orientalist/political monster where vignettes on the strangeness of the Other (fishermen using cormorant to fish, capturing a tiger with a baby goat) alternates with stilted didactic moments on how life has improved since the revolution (the story of Lian Chi, the last sold wife, the last child groom, and so on). The voice-over commentary, which the Italian Communist Party directly supervised, makes the film even more innocuous, as it smooths out every possible edge in these stories. Quite stunning is the finale of the film, which shows the massive display of people in Tiananmen

118 TRAVELING AUTEURS

Square celebrating the successes of the party. In short, *La muraglia cinese* looks like an odd combination of an exploitation flick and a socialist realist didactic piece. It certainly stands out in Lizzani's filmography as an oddity of sorts, and it was pretty quickly forgotten, along with the English version released in 1960 with its voice-over by Chet Huntley.[24]

One of the first and most interesting short travel diaries is Chris Marker's *Dimanche à Peking* (*Sunday in Peking*, 1956). The film, one of the first of the French director, was generated by a trip organized for a special issue of the French magazine *L'Esprit* entitled "La Chine, porte ouverte" ("China, Open Door").[25] The China of *Dimanche à Peking* begins as a memory: the recollections of the unseen narrator in Paris, who pans a subjective camera across a treasure trove of souvenirs within sight of the Eiffel Tower. He recalls a dream of China triggered by a picture in a childhood book where the close-up dissolves into a location shot of the same spot: the avenue bordered by carved stone animals to the tombs of the Ming emperors. As always, Marker has a dialectical approach to filmmaking that shows discordances rather than unity and, through irony, allows images and words to create a new meaning for the curious viewer. Marker acknowledges the orientalist cinematic quality of this "a day in the life"–style travelogue, reminiscent of city-symphonies in a minor key, like Cavalcanti's *Rien que l'heur* (*Nothing but the Time*, 1926), as the voice-over reminds us that there's no more Bogart or opium dens created by Hollywood for the pleasure and consumption of Western viewers.[26]

If most of the writers who wrote about their travels through China and had some resonance in Italy were French, there seems to be a more diverse group of filmmakers shooting in China right around, and mostly right before, Antonioni's trip. While Antonioni probably did not see any of the films I address here, either because they did not receive proper distribution or because they were released after his own, they nonetheless share with Antonioni's film most of the locations and a lot of their affect and pathos. Specifically, there is a handful of films that need to be looked at, either because of their innovative approach to a trite subject or because of the relative fame and impact they had. Among them, and at the top of my own personal ranking, is Canadian Don McWilliams's *Impressions of China* (1976), a short compilation of slides and Super 8 footage taken by a group of Canadian high school students; this is one of the smartest attempts at reporting and representing China. In 1972, twenty-five students from Ontario traveled around the country for three weeks, and in 1976, McWilliams assembled all the material shot during that trip to make this "memory piece" that ended up twenty-one minutes in length. Made by another Canadian, Marcel Carrière's *Images de Chine* (*Images of China*, 1974), is a brilliant sound investigation and was probably one of the sharpest films shot in China during the Cultural Revolution. Carrière, a NFB filmmaker and sound person at the core of the cinema-direct movement in Quebec, manages to break through the CCP-induced theatricality through direct sound. What emerges are glimpses of real life: bicycle bells, the rustling of leaves, children crying. Structured mostly around interviews—all repeating the same mantras about "higher political consciousness," giving "thanks to Chairman Mao," and reminiscing about life "in the old society"—the mixing of the sound levels allows the *hors-champ*, the sound coming from outside of the frame, to tell a counternarrative about life in China. I found this film to be a true achievement, particularly if you compare it with the crushing failure of many Western filmmakers on missions to find the truth, or the real China, or whatever orientalist trope animated their endeavors. Here Carrière uses sound to attract his audience aurally, therefore bypassing the firewall of the ideological. Carriere is also the director in 1974 of the purely observational *Ping Pong*, in which the NFB filmed the table tennis competitions between teams of young Canadian and Chinese athletes that took place in China in the summer of 1973.[27] Of a similar vein are the TV films by Dutch journalist Roelof Kiers. His *Toerist in China* (*Tourists in China*, 1972) accompanies a group of young Dutch men and women as they travel, collecting their thoughts and impressions.[28]

One of the most fascinating films of the Zhou Enlai period is *The Other Half of the Sky: A China Memoir* by Shirley MacLaine and Claudia Weill (1975). This is a real women's film, in the 1970s activist sense of the term, and it is staged as both observational and participative. It is conceived as a fly-on-the-wall travelogue accompanying a "women's delegation" to China, headed by activist and Hollywood star Shirley MacLaine. The film does more than that, though, providing a rhythm to the visit, a pace to the encounters, and conciseness to the official speeches of the women of the CCP. As we know by now, all the places that this group visited are exactly the same as all the other preapproved sites that every single crew traveling through the Cultural Revolution were assigned—not just the same places, but also the same hotel rooms, with the same view, the same choreographed kinesthetic exercises prepared for the Western audience. But while Antonioni and other Western filmmakers live this social predetermination (the Cultural

Revolution's "theater of life") with resentment, for better or worse masked under a veneer of politeness or contempt, here Weill manages to give us an impression of enjoyment—every minute for these women seems to be one of sheer joy and pleasure, including the most canned political speeches and highly vetted dialogues: "What do you like in a man?" asks MacLaine. "A high level of political consciousness," answers the translator/minder who is accompanying them around the country. Nobody challenges it, fully aware that not much can be challenged at this point. Even when meeting with Deng Yingchao, referred to in the film as Madam Zhou Enlai (her husband), one of the leaders of the party and an icon of women's liberation, Weill keeps this encounter fast-paced and meaningful. Another great idea for this film was the choice of the "non-fiction actors" as defined by Tom Waugh, who animate the encounters with the natives.[29] While obviously politically risky, narratively this trick works and the "regular American women" (as MacLaine defines them in the voice-over commentary) add something new to the mix. They are a white southerner, Pat Branson, an employee of Texaco with "a profound allegiance to governor George Wallace" (the racist Jim Crow–era democratic politician), and Unita Blackwell, a Black voter registration drive activist who "wants to see how communism looks like since she was accused of being one [a communist] for trying to vote." With them, and somewhat in the background, there was also a Navajo woman "out of the reservation for the first time" (Ninibah Crawford), a California psychologist (Phyllis Kornhauden), a conservative Bostonian (Margaret Whitman), a Puerto Rican sociologist (Rosa Marin), and a thirteen-year-old Californian (Karen Boutilier).[30] In spite of some naiveté, this film, along with *Images de Chine*, manages to break through the CCP staging of life through its focus on women's issues—the surprise on the characters' faces at questions about individual freedom, such as the right not to marry or give birth, the right of women artists to create, questions about family structure, and so on, seem to actually surprise the Chinese women appointed to entertain the guests, probably more trained in responding to frontal ideological attacks by Westerners rather than this American feminist approach. Beyond the most memorable moments from a historical point of view, such as the meeting with Zhou Enlai's wife and the long, prolonged birth scene, the best parts are the more candid camera moments that capture snippets of conversation. This film has been rightly read as a smart attempt from the Chinese government to create a link between the US liberation movement and the CCP policies, generating a form of "radical

ANTONIONI IN CHINA

orientalism" that "idealize[s] the East and criticize[s] the West."[31] It manages to say a lot about both China and the United States, and it does so with its smart direction.[32]

Other films, mostly made-for-TV documentaries, tend to follow a more traditional expository, voice-of-God narrative structure. Such is the case for *Chine* by Gérard Valet and Henri Roanne (1971), in which the filmmakers try to make sense of what they see in an earnest and time-enlightened fashion. The film was first broadcast in prime time in October 1971 by the French ORTF and the Belgian RTBF, then across the world through PBS in the United States and CBC in Canada. The film was such a wide success that it was awarded the documentary film prize at the Viennale. It was then screened in theaters in Paris and Brussels with the claim: "Avant Nixon, découvrez la Chine de Mao" ("Discover Mao's China before Nixon"), referring to the trip of the US president in February 1972.[33] I will go back to these films in my discussion of Antonioni's *Chung Kuo*, as they provide an excellent paragon for our discussion.

The most compelling and thorough of all Western films in China in the early 1970s is definitely the twelve-hour-and-forty-three-minute-long *How Yukong Moved the Mountains (Comment Yukong déplaça les montagnes*, hereafter referred to as *Yukong*), made by bona fide fellow travelers Joris Ivens and Marceline Loridan (shot in 1972 but released in 1976). Ivens and Loridan arrived in China before Antonioni and spent eighteen months there, between September 1972 and March 1974. The Cultural Revolution, as encountered, recorded, and transmitted by Ivens and Loridan, is narrated as a living struggle rather than as a fait accompli. According to Loridan, it was the release of the Italian documentary that pushed them to finally complete the film in 1976, in order to correct the mistakes and the superficial representation they had noticed in *Chung Kuo*.[34] But at that point Chairman Mao was dead, and their twelve-part vérité effort was quickly forgotten.

To the cognizant viewer, fully aware of the past and present of China, and even more aware of the fight over discourses that the Cultural Revolution has generated, *Yukong* is an infinitely superior film. To the distant observer, Antonioni might look in his ingenuity more authentic, even sincere in his representation of daily life.[35] But in any case, *Yukong* is a key text to understand the intricacies of the traveling auteur, and I devote more time to it as we move forward.[36] What these "travelogues" have in common is their deep ambivalence about orientalism and romanticized militancy for

Western travelers, as well as the state-prepackaged documentary experience for Western filmmakers.

Antonioni for the People:
Thirty Thousand Meters in Twenty-Two Days

In Italy, *Chung Kuo* was broadcast by RAI as a three-part TV series in January–February 1973. This project to make a major TV documentary about China had been initiated by the Chinese Embassy in Rome, in conjunction with the Italian state broadcasting corporation, RAI; behind it lay an agreement to promote bilateral relations through cultural interactions, the outcome of an Italian government delegation's visit to China in May 1971.[37] According to Chinese sources, RAI had proposed the film concept and had suggested Antonioni to helm the project. When he and his team arrived in Beijing in 1972, most of the country was still inaccessible to Western visitors, and throughout their five-week journey, the logistics were in the hands of official government minders. Nevertheless, Antonioni was able to shoot some thirty thousand meters of footage and eventually produced a 220-minute film.[38]

The film is divided into three parts, with no titles except a number at the beginning of every section. Seymour Chatman has attempted to make sense of this film by looking for an organizing principle: north to south, inland to sea, present and past, activities of life, ages of man, from Beijing to Linzhou in Henan Province to the call of the Ynagzee, Suchow, Nanking and Shanghai, but with little success.[39] Antonioni's film in fact is built geographically and temporally in accordance with the physical trip he took while filming.[40] It starts right at the center of everything in Tiananmen Square and then expands to different locations in Beijing, moving south and then back north. This trip follows the same path organized by government officials that all the other official travelers followed.

The documentary opens with a still image borrowed from the PCC iconography—a painting of children on a red background, as the Beijing Railway Workers Children Choir intones the stirring opening bars of "Wo ai Beijing Tiananmen" ("I Love Beijing Tiananmen") over the title credits.[41] This song is a very recognizable marker that provides the viewer with multiple reading keys. The music defines this product as markedly "oriental" (the high-pitched voices, the string instruments, the melody close enough to an "oriental riff" to create the connotation for a Western audience), while the scene that immediately follows, depicting blue- and green-clad Chinese citizens wandering about in the square points to the political stereotype of a country in uniform. Likewise, the close-ups of girls standing together holding hands point to Antonioni as an "author," free to use the camera creatively, unbound by norms of traditional documentary footage. In short, we have in this first sequence each of the three vectors that will animate the film—the orientalist, the political, and the authorial.

The very astute critique published in *Renmin Ribao* (*The People's Daily*) in 1974, the piece that sealed the destiny of this film in China and all over the world, well captures the tone of this scene:

> The film . . . does not show the panorama of this grand, magnificent Square and takes shots of Tien An Men Gate, which the Chinese people ardently love, in such a way as to strip it of all grandeur. On the other hand, a lot of film is used to photograph crowds in the Square; there are sometimes long-shots, sometimes close-ups, sometimes from the front and sometimes from behind, at one moment throngs of heads and at another legs and feet moving helter-skelter. These shots are intended to make Tien An Men Square look like a boisterous marketplace. Is this not aimed at defaming our great motherland?[42]

The answer to the question of these zealous reviewers lies at the core of this chapter. History has definitely clarified certain aspects of this attack on Antonioni and his film, as Mao's wife, Jiang Qing, and the Gang of Four got involved in a power struggle against Zhou Enlai, which transformed Antonioni into a target in the then ongoing "Criticize Lin (Biao), Criticize Confucius Campaign," part of this later phase of the Cultural Revolution.[43] Mao's wife, Jiang Qin, is at this point in time the very powerful architect and orchestrator of most of the cultural artifacts of the Cultural Revolution; she also promoted the adaptation of the "eight model operas" into films as exemplary products of the Cultural Revolution.[44] Mao's demands for a new revolutionary national art enabled Jiang Qing to start her crusade to dominate the art world. In 1963, she started with the revision of a number of Beijing Operas on contemporary themes, and some of these titles are inscribed in the memory of many who were directly associated with the Cultural Revolution: *The Story of the Red Lamp, Shajia Village, Taking Tiger Mountain by Strategy*, and *Raid on the White Tiger Regiment*. In the summer of 1964, these works were performed for the first time at an Opera Festival in Shanghai and by then already were called "model works" (*yangbanxi*).[45] Most of these works will go on to be adapted to cinema, either as filmed versions of the operas or as full-fledged adaptations.

Quite interestingly, the arts, and more specifically art reviews, were at the very core of the new political phase which came to be known as the Great Proletarian Cultural Revolution. Two key episodes of this phase are often highlighted by scholars. The first is the 1951 *People's Daily* editorial attack on the film *The Life of Wu Xun* (Sun Yu, 1950), which was the first major national criticism of a work of art or literature after the founding of the People's Republic, a criticism in fact written by Mao Zedong himself. The second episode occurred in 1961 when *The Shanghai Wenhui Daily*, under the direction of Jiang Qing, published a harsh review of the theater play *Hai Rui Dismissed from Office*, a staple of Chinese socialist canon, since it was now perceived as a criticism of Mao. This tradition of belligerent reviews of work considered out of line with the regime shines light on the importance of the *People's Daily*'s review of Antonioni's film.

According to Paul Clark, one of the consequences of the regime of terror initiated by Jiang and her associates brought the arts, and especially the film industry, to a standstill.[46] Several feature films were among the first products to be attacked in the mass media across the nation. This fear of images made it so that most cultural production halted in the first years of the Cultural Revolution. This suspicion of film professionals and the acknowledgment of the power of the medium help explain why feature film production effectively stopped for the first four years of the Cultural Revolution. This fear of showing and saying the wrong thing led to the focus on filming "model operas," the results of which were mocked as model films.[47] These productions were highly supervised attempts at creating a new cult of personality for Chairman Mao, and the films had at their core the notion of the "three prominences." This is a reference to the formula coined by Jiang Qing for artists to follow in their creative work: give prominence to positive characters among all the characters; give prominence to main heroes among the positive characters; and give prominence to the central character among the main heroes.[48] To put it briefly, this served as an aesthetic sanctioning of the political cult of personality that made Mao the only comrade ultimately worthy of praise. The restricting circular model of the "three prominences" will play a key role in the cinema of the Cultural Revolution, which, out of fear of retribution and puzzlement over the banality of these directives, often ended up shining a constant spotlight on the protagonist and his inner circle.[49] The same directives applied to nonfiction as well: documentary film had to follow the principles of "facts serve politics" (*shishi yao wei zhengzhi fuwu*) and "truthfulness serves politics" (*zhenshi yao wei zhengzhi fuwu*). As is documented by Yingchi Chu in her *Chinese Documentaries: From Dogma to Polyphony*, this amounted to no less than a political definition of truth. In short, documentaries depicted only what the party or a particular group of party leaders felt was worthy of public consumption. During this period, when fiction films were close to absent, news and documentary films constituted the bulk of moving image productions. The main production company was the Central Newsreel and Documentary Film Studio, which was directly connected to the Propaganda Department. Typically, they would portray "Mao in meetings with the representatives of the Red Guards, the workers, peasants, soldiers and minorities, or celebrations of his new policies, the founding of Revolutionary Committees, mass meetings denouncing counter-revolutionaries, and youths following Mao's call for the extension of national re-education to the rural areas."[50] This singular narrative did not allow for dissenting voices or contradictory perspectives to be voiced. In short, Mao's theory of revolutionary art about and for the workers, peasants, and soldiers had turned out to be fundamentally a tool for Communist Party politics.

This is the cultural milieux in which Antonioni's film entered as a foreign object. It was totally unreadable according to contemporary standards of "model works" and the "three prominences" and was far too legible as counterrevolutionary propaganda. In spite of its obvious banalities, pointed out in the film review published by Renmin Ribao, the largest newspaper in China to this day, it captures something that goes beyond political trickery. The film is obviously not an attack on China, or on the CCP, or on, well, absolutely anything. And that is probably the biggest issue with "Antonioni in China" as a project. The director claimed to arrive in China with no other idea but to "observe," as he clearly states this is his "method": "The people around us, the places we visit, the events we witness—it is the spatial and temporal relations these have with each other that have a meaning for us today, and the tension that is formed between them. This is, I think, a special way of being in contact with reality. And it is also a special reality. To lose this contact, in the sense of losing this way of being in contact, can mean sterility."[51] But he and his crew fell into the most banal of orientalist traps—that conception of "being first" that both Rossellini and Pasolini so astutely avoided in different ways, as we have seen in the preceding chapters. While both Pasolini and Rossellini had a "political project" when traveling outside of Europe, Antonioni presumes an apolitical approach that ends up normalizing both the orientalist gaze and Western liberal capitalism as a single mode of living and seeing. Serge Daney has already noted this dilemma in his "review of the review" about *Chung Kuo*, when he writes that "pour nous [aux *Cahiers*], il y avait autre chose en jeu dans la critique de *Chung Kuo*. Cela nous a fourni une occasion particulièrement commode pour réaffirmer notre méfiance envers le naturalisme" ("For us [at *Cahiers*] there are other important things at play in the critique of *Chung Kuo*. It provided us with a particularly convenient occasion to restate our mistrust of naturalism").[52] While obviously fully aware of the politicking behind this film, Daney's criticism points precisely to this presupposed innocence at the core of the "naturalistic" approach with which he defines Antonioni's haphazard style. Daney points to the lack of reversibility of the gaze present in the documentary model. He reminds us of the scene at the end of *The Passenger* in which the African chieftain grabs the camera to film Jack Nicholson—in China we witness a smuggling of images, the work of *contrebandiers*: "There exists no reversibility, no chance of becoming themselves *filmeurs*, no possibility of participating in the image which is made of them, no hold of the image. Mad people, children, primitives, the excluded, filmed without hope (for them) of reply, filmed 'for their own good' or for the sake of science or scandal: exoticism, philanthropy, horror."[53]

It is in particular this kind of folksy anthropology, which brings many travelers to compare what they see to what they know, that makes *Chung Kuo* promote a clear Western model, a golden standard of living that goes unchallenged.[54] As Antonioni states: "I arrive on location in a fixed state of 'virginity.' I do this because the best results are obtained by the 'collision' that takes place between the environment in which the scene is to be shot and my own particular state of mind at that specific moment. . . . So . . . improvisation comes directly from the rapport between the director and the people around him, both the usual professional collaborators and the people who just happen to be gathered in that particular area when the scene is being shot."[55]

This candid and abysmally simplistic understanding of the issue of representation of otherness in Italian culture is a matter with a long history rooted in the unprocessed violence of Italian colonialism and its racist legacies, which this book has already addressed. Though relatively brief and geographically limited, the Italian colonial "adventure," as it was defined at the time, left a profound impact on the national consciousness—a sense of cultural superiority that has marred the visual culture of Italy since the early twentieth century, a mindset that is still very much complicit in the structure of complacency that pervades the high/low spectrum of moving images and popular culture today.[56] The harsh rejection of postcolonial theory in Italian academia and its consequent lack of percolation in vernacular discourses has left the country with a repressed colonial unconscious.[57] It is a true visual pathology that affects Antonioni, making the Western traveler not see the Other—this is a colonial structure of seeing that allows the right to look without being looked at, the privilege of virginity in a ravaged land.

Karen Pinkus's assessment of Italian cinema in her essay "Empty Spaces: Decolonization in Italy" points to this very absence of colonial traces in the recoding of urban and neobourgeois spaces after World War II.[58] Pinkus's selection of case study seems at first unconventional: Antonioni's "alienation" symphony *L'eclisse* (*The Eclipse*, 1962), set mostly in the fascist-built space of EUR in Rome. The choice of Antonioni's high-modernist piece is significant as it has always been read as a world-cinema film avant la lettre in the way that it addresses modernity and its dire effects on the human condition. Choosing Antonioni, the living embodiment of the filmmaker of the atomic age, points to how deeply racial discourses are embedded and unnoticed in cultural products in postwar Italy. The scene analyzed by Pinkus, in which Vittoria (played by a diaphanous Monica Vitti) performs a mock African dance in blackface for the pleasure of two girlfriends, makes this point very clear. The apartment belongs to Marta, born in Kenya (even though we are not provided with any more details on this) and a native speaker of English, a language she often slips into. This scene has been read by critics, and obviously designed by Antonioni, to speak to women's alienation in the modern world. Marta and Vittoria, along with their third friend Anita, are just different embodiments of the new modern woman liberated from familial duty but left alone and deprived of affection by this new system. But, by wearing postcolonial lenses, we can read this scene symptomatically against the background of its location. EUR was one of the main expansion projects of the fascist regime and was strongly supported by the Duce himself. Meant to host the "Esibizione Universale di Roma," originally dubbed E42 in celebration of the 1942 World's Fair, this location has a lot in common with a similar fascist development in Addis Ababa.[59] Indeed, it is easy to think of EUR as a space filled with marches and triumphal crowds, precisely like the colonial capital of Ethiopia. This internal (domestic) colonialism is very much part of the fascist ethos of purging and acquiring new land for its own people. The African expansion was matched by an internal one, where the land was reconquered (in the military language preferred by the regime) for the people of Italy. This blackface scene right at the heart of both EUR and the film speaks to that racialized unconscious that sits in plain view in Italian cultural production then and now. It is finally her "Kenyan" friend Marta that puts an end to this pantomime with a drastic "basta fare i negri, per piacere" ("let's stop playing negros, please"), while clearly disturbed by this performance. Vittoria's blind spot to Italy's own postcolonial condition is at the core of what Angelo Restivo calls "the Cinema of the Economic Miracle," that is, the way in which art cinema promoted a vision of modernity and modernization domestically and abroad. My claim in this chapter is that this blind spot is very visible in Antonioni's project in China, starting from its very opening scene.[60]

In Tiananmen Square, as the opening song of the children's choir comes to an end, the camera frames a soldier and a couple with a baby all staring straight into the lens. The camera zooms in slightly to frame the group more tightly as they continue to return the camera's gaze. There is no fear or apprehension discernible in their looks. If anything, they exude a quiet confidence in the face of the foreigner's stare.[61] As Tom Gunning has argued, early nonfiction films are commonly "marked by the returned look of the people within the film, the gaze directed out at camera and viewer."[62] Paula Amad picked it up from there: "While direct address became increasingly prohibited in fiction films during the 1910s, it continued as a dominant stylistic feature of newsreels and documentary shorts at least until the early 1930s."[63] The "return of the gaze" thus performs a double response. On the one hand, it prevents the "entomologizing and zoologizing legacy" so much at the core of travel film, while on the other hand, "these returned gazes become the fetishized trace of our contemporary desire for—based on the historical lack of—the irrecoverable reverse shot of the Other's view of the world. . . . By offering evidence, whether empirical or textual, of subaltern scopic agency, the interpretation ultimately performs a form of visual ventriloquism: the colonized puppet might appear to be alive, but the strings are still being pulled by Western discourse's (now enlightened postcolonial) expectations and desires regarding the subject of the Other."[64]

Throughout *Chung Kuo*, we will be unwitting witness of this kind of "visual ventriloquism"—the desire of the Italian crew to make their subjects look alive is clear to see, in having them acquire a Western subjectivity somehow detached from the nation, the party, and the chairman. But what we gather now, reexamining the film from our privileged point of view as postcolonial, post-Said scholars, is precisely the act of violence perpetrated in stealing these "visual ripostes" (as Amad defines them) and giving them a phantasmatic agency that now looks more like stolen gazes.

The friendly voice that suddenly breaks the ambient sound we have heard so far is that of well-known dubber and voice actor Giuseppe Rinaldi. After all, this is the man who dubbed the most famous Hollywood stars, including in that same year Marlon Brando in *Last Tango in Paris* (Bernardo Bertolucci, 1972). This suave and friendly tone gained him a special place at the dinner table, so to speak, if one thinks of how pervasive dubbing still is as a practice of distributing foreign films and if one considers that until the 1980s Italy had but two state-controlled channels.[65] Rinaldi (reading the text prepared by Antonioni and Andrea Barbato, a well-known RAI journalist) explains to the audience that the song they just heard says, "I love Tiananmen Square" and "is sung in all schools in China." He continues: "this square is the center of the world for the Chinese, and so we decided to place here our cameras. This place is where most of the demonstrations for the Cultural Revolution happened, and now people are standing in line to have their photo taken." Rinaldi emphatically states: "it is them, the Chinese people, the real protagonists of these visual notes [*appunti filmati*]. We don't claim to want to represent China, we just want to observe." The introductory speech is given while the camera points to a street photographer, standing on a wooden box, giving instructions to the people preparing to be photographed. Funnily enough, I thought this man was Antonioni the first time I saw the film—of course he is not, he is just a middle-aged man with nice posture, white hair, and a bit of a stiff demeanor, who looks like he should be directing something bigger. I thought that maybe he was one of the artists punished at the height of the Cultural Revolution during one of the many waves of random purges (often based on personal acrimony and factious infighting rather than any real political disagreement) who never managed to get his job back.[66] If I were an artist of the caliber of Gustav Deutsch, I would do what he did in his masterpiece *Welt Spiegel Kino* (*World Mirror Cinema*, 2005) in which characters from the colonial archive are given new life through montage. In my film the unknown Chinese director would be seen directing a "model film" and some documentaries celebrating the chairman for the pleasure and enjoyment of large audiences.

According to Barbato and Antonioni, China is inaccessible and forbidden, and while we assume they are talking about the CCP policy of closure, the tone refers to a more mythical, ancestral closeness of the Land in the Middle that dates back, of course, to Marco Polo (who will appear shortly in the narrative). Right away, the voice-over comments on the very limited filming range allowed by careful minders. As the crew leaves the square on a bus, they are told not to shoot near Mao Zedong's house. "But we shot nonetheless," coyly muses Ruggeri, like a child that managed to sneak an extra cookie. As the camera shows men and women on their way to work in the morning, he claims, "the people are poor but not miserable, no luxury but no hunger . . . there's no anxiety or hurry."

The following scene in this first part of the film takes us under the old Tartar Walls where a group of old men are practicing tai chi, "a martial art and a dance." This leads to the next part, which is devoted to *guangbo ticao*, or "radio gymnastic exercise"; as the film explains, this is "a competing form of physical exercise, a form of group calisthenics institutionalized in primary and secondary schools all over the country from the early 1950s."[67] The contrast is stark: the tai chi practitioners move silently, with intense concentration and according to a slow, inner-directed rhythm; the young people in the guangbo ticao classes treat the exercise as an obligatory routine and go through the motions mechanically. The coexistence of old and new takes on additional significance in the context of the radical antitraditionalism of the Cultural Revolution. The guangbo ticao scenes also resonate with other scattered visual segments: preschool children singing revolutionary songs, kindergarteners making propaganda dance moves, a youth brigade en route to the fields, marching along while chanting slogans. Xiao Jiwei reads these scenes as direct Foucauldian interventions of the state into the mind and body of the youth, as opposed to the free flowing energy of the old tai chi practitioners. But there's no real sign of this contrast in the film, which instead points to a continuity between the two. While the Cultural Revolution started with the Red August campaign of 1966, it was fundamentally based on the rejection of the Four Olds, that is Old Ideas, Old Culture, Old Habits, and Old Customs, which brought along many of the excesses often mentioned with respect to the Cultural Revolution (such as Red Guards destroying old artifacts). Here in Antonioni's makeshift narrative the two seem to coexist peacefully, apparently both living well under an orientalist approach.[68]

The third scene of *Chung Kuo* opens with a child's exposed butt as a mother picks them up in her arms, an image which then leads to the portion of the film dedicated to the visit to the obstetrician. The crew, all men but for Enrica Fico, assistant director of the film and Antonioni's partner, stands in awe watching the procedure where a "worker in an electric valve factory is going to deliver her first child." This scene at the woman's clinic is a staple of all the films shot by Westerners traveling through Deng's China, and looking at how it is framed and structured in the narrative gives us a sense of the general approach of the film. The surprise that Antonioni's crew, like all the other Western crews, will experience lies in the use of acupuncture as an anesthetic for the mother delivering a baby—presumably, in the minds of the Chinese government officials in charge of handling the foreign visitors, this practice plays as a truly "Chinese" method, representing the country well in offering new strategies of medical discourse. As Pang Laikwan states: "The modernization of the Chinese traditional practices and the Sinicization of modernity could complement each other because they were carried out by the gentle and careful young woman" in the clinic.[69] It's an old traditional practice, it's indigenous, and it's low-tech, which means that it can be practiced anywhere and with little training. Let's not forget that the dissemination of medicine to the large rural masses was one of the aspirations (and occasional achievements) of the Cultural Revolution. These "barefoot doctors" are key figures in this process of mythopoesis, where young Red Guards, sometimes as young as high school age, would leave their towns to join medical practices in remote locations.[70] The mythology of acupuncture as a low-tech fully communist secret weapon is on full display in a 1968 official newsreel entitled *Mao Zedong Thoughts Opens the Forbidden Zones for the Deaf and Mute* (1971), which provides "cinematic testimony" to acupuncture's efficacy in conjunction with Mao Zedong thought as "revolutionary miracle medicine" that "cures" deaf-mute children. After teaching Mao's thought to them, children can fully participate in the revolution and each can shout "Long Live Chairman Mao" after their treatment.[71]

Antonioni looks at this bizarre scene with the detached eye of the entomologist looking at disappearing species. The camera is intrusive at the risk of being invasive, with dramatic close-ups of the needles and the face of the patient, and the narrative seems to repeat the official brochure of the party, asserting that these are simple and affordable techniques. During the crucial moment, as the doctors (all women) are performing a Cesarian section, we hear in Italian a series of questions directed at the woman. Is this her first child? Does she hope for a boy or a girl? The scene is one of the longest in *Chung Kuo*, almost eight minutes, and it ends with the delivering of the baby without any additional comments. "Antonioni's interest in the scene is twofold," writes Tom Waugh, "It's in the exotic significance of the needles and the 'human' drama of the woman giving birth, specific and concrete to be sure, but abstract in its divorce from societal context," which leaves the audience a bit lost, since the film seems to move on unmoved by this visually and politically complex scene.[72]

Shirley MacLaine and Claudia Weill's *The Other Half of the Sky*, which coincidentally starts with the same "I Love Beijing Tienanmen" song (it sounds like the same recording, but I could not verify) and deals with this same matter in a more organized manner. For example, one of the excuses Antonioni and his crew often used when talking about their trip to China was the short time of their stay—about five weeks. This is more or less the same time that MacLaine and her friends spent there, and yet the comparison is quite frankly detrimental to the Italians. The two films are interesting to compare for various reasons. They took place only two years apart, in 1972 and 1974, both shot after Richard Nixon's February 1972 visit, and both followed the same exact route organized by the party. But MacLaine and, mostly, Weill's vérité-style feminist film not only struck the right balance between participatory and observational but also captured more in only a few frames about the condition of women in China than Antonioni's prolonged scenes. In *The Other Half of the Sky*, the birth scene sits at the end of the film in an obvious symbolic position; it is part of a larger investigation about women's health, reproductive health, family planning, and the availability of doctors and medicine to women. It starts with one of the women having her shoulder treated with acupuncture, which then leads to the hospital where the C-section takes place. We see them and the filming crew getting dressed in hospital gear. This time the camera is located in an operation theater behind a glass dome, and the film includes reaction shots of the spectators as the operation proceeds. Rather than the silence of Antonioni's film, dictated ambiguously by respect for or speechlessness over the event, here we have the filmmakers commenting about the proceeding, asking questions to the doctors and the translators that accompany them. There's a general sense of stupor and joy that Weill's camera captures, and thanks to sync sound, in the final version we see a true participatory birth![73]

In the next scenes of Antonioni's film, the Italian crew is paraded around Beijing. First, we are in a kindergarten attached to a cotton mill factory with 6,400 workers (Cotton Mill no. 3), which has the function of educating the children about the "collectivized society" they will encounter. According to the commentary, the crew was also very surprised to find out that the children sing political songs, mostly in honor of President Mao.[74] Then we see an apartment next to that same cotton mill, where a couple is performing "gender equality." As always in the context of the Cultural Revolution, it is difficult to distinguish between performance for the Western camera and actual life performance for the sake of the party. The division of labor in the household is real, though, as both husband and wife share work inside and outside of the house. Antonioni does not see any of this, and the whole issue went unremarked. This is even more stunning after watching the monumental *Yukong*, where issues of gender equality are systematically dissected in long roundtable discussions with both women and men.

After the "model factory" visit, the first part of the film ends on a very touristy note: a trip to the Great Wall and then to the Ming Dynasty Tombs in the Changping Districts, right where Chris Marker lands in his short and dreamy *Sunday in Peking*. Antonioni and Barbato manage to sneak in a cheesy quote from Brecht ("Kings are remembered but not workers and slaves who built this wall") as they contemplate the snaking fortifications. Among the mix of banalities on the spread of Chinese civilization thanks to the wall, Antonioni adds: "the word Empire has no meaning for them anymore," pointing to the rewriting of history they think they have experienced, implicitly endorsing the idea that the revolution successfully erased the past.

Real China

The second part of *Chung Kuo* opens with a key scene. We are in an agricultural commune made up of both residents and students working in the fields. These model communes were often seen in the documentaries of foreign travelers through China and they are mockingly referred to as "Potemkin villages," fake or very artificial places highly curated by the local authority to look prosperous. The Chinese/Albanian agricultural commune visited by the Italian crew has all the signs of that model, as everybody seems particularly happy to take care of the pigs.[75] Students are depicted marching and singing with plows on their shoulders, held as if they were long guns, while surrounded by very healthy horses, as well as fat ducks, chickens, and more pigs. This scene leads us to the open market of Xinfadi (erroneously reported as Hsitan in the film), in the southern Beijing district of Fengtai, where Antonioni will be able to tell us that "beyond kindness and acute intellect the Chinese people have another prominent trait: *la ghiottoneria* (gluttony)." Chinese food for the Western traveler has always been historically a source of great surprise.[76]

The next step is the Forbidden City, where we finally have a mention of Marco Polo: "in questa città il gran cane ha un grande palagio" ("in this city the Gran Kahn has a big palace"), where the ancient spelling used by the Venetian traveler, *palagio*, and transliteration of the name of the Kahn as *cane* ("dog" in Italian) are left to trigger the exotic curiosity of the viewer. Antonioni continues, "we came here on a Sunday more to look at the people visiting this site rather than looking for memories of extinct dynasties," reinforcing the initial statement about the "virgin viewer" as the central trait of his approach. Unlike Rossellini, who in his reportage for Italian TV often notices how the camera and the crew are the real spectacle, here nobody acknowledges that they are the actual curiosity, the oddity that attracts attention as the people react to rarely seen foreigners. We notice, then, on the one hand this dream of invisibility, of being able to shoot vérité style or even worse, candid camera style, so as to capture reality, and on the other, the inability to acknowledge one's own Otherness and that of the cinematic apparatus, a rarely seen machine at this point in China.

Antonioni does not perceive his foreignness in the next scene either. In the old part of Beijing, in Liu Li Chang, Antonioni focuses on a woman with bound feet—a practice that the revolution has now completely abolished and a form of body mutilation that most travelers seem to be fascinated with as much as the Chinese authorities are ashamed of it. But Antonioni, as always, does not engage in depth, except for a short history of the practice narrated in the voice-over and some close-ups in which the woman is particularly annoyed by this attack on her privacy and asks them to leave her be. It is not a surprise that this is one of the scenes criticized by the *People's Daily's* article, as it was interpreted as a sign of Antonioni's desire to diminish the achievements of the revolution: "In order to defame the Chinese people, he racked his brains to present in a grotesque way various expressions of people sitting in tea-houses and restaurants, pulling carts, and strolling in the streets. He even did not stop at an old woman with bound feet."[77] The stupor of the reviewer in front of Antonioni's choices is well described by Jie Li. Antonioni is attacked for privileging the old and backward over the new and revolutionary aspects of China, for filming an old woman's bound feet and oxcarts rather than automobiles, donkey mills rather than tractors, boats rather than ships, straw houses rather than cement buildings, wooden bridges rather than railway bridges, weeds rather than crops. It seems to me that to the Chinese reviewers, these scenes are reminiscent of the iconography of the "feudal China" that featured so prominently in the anticommunist propaganda films that aimed at communicating the enduring backwardness of China despite the Communist Revolution.[78] The best known, *China: The Roots of Madness*, was a 1967 American Cold War propaganda piece widely shown in the West and was barely more than an extended anti-Maoist and anti-Chinese think piece. The film focuses on anti-Western sentiment in China from the Boxer Rebellion to the Cultural Revolution. It became clear that the *People's Daily*'s critique, as we have already seen, has to be read beyond factional inner fighting, as it was grounded in a deeper visual historical and national trauma that pivoted around issues of modernity and modernization. Since all government initiatives under Mao focused precisely on mechanization and the industrialization of production in both cities and the countryside, the strategy of the official documentaries of the time focused on this push toward modernity. Xin Liu points out that: "A direct reason that triggered the mass criticism against Antonioni in 1974 was the conflicts between China and the Soviet Union. While Antonioni was making his film in China, the Soviet Union was screening a documentary *Night over China—the Grandeur and Folly of China's Fallen Revolution*, produced in 1971 by its Central Studio for Documentary Film with the footage gathered before the Sino-Soviet split. After the release of *Chung Kuo*, the Soviet Union used some episodes in this Italian documentary as evidence to support its indictment of Mao Zedong."[79] *A Night over China* is a very powerful archive film directed by Alexander Medvedkin in 1971, as part of the post Sino-Soviet split that turned into an actual border dispute in 1969. Along with *Letter to a Chinese Friend* (1969), this Medvedkin film was widely shown on national television and, in border regions specifically, to alert the Soviet comrades of the crimes and failures of Maoism.[80] *A Night over China*'s deployment of massive and often unseen archival footage makes it even nowadays, and beyond the accusatory rhetorical intentions of the producers, an interesting insight into the violence of the Cultural Revolution as well as the backwardness of many rural areas. Both Soviet and American anti-Chinese propaganda had an obvious impact on the way the CCP members saw themselves being received around the world, and Antonioni's project, which was meant to rectify this kind of propaganda (along with all the other filmmakers, artists, and intellectuals traveling through China at this point in time), struck a chord when it didn't.

Sinologist Christian Sorace looks at another review of Antonioni's film which appeared in the *Guangming Daily* on February 13, 1974. While in many aspects it replicates the original review of the *People's Daily*, some parts focus even more on criticizing the actual rhetorical strategy deployed by the filmmakers. Here the reviewers write: "In the movie, the Chinese Revolution is missing, the extraordinary changes brought about by the Revolution are missing, the radiant glory of new China is missing; instead, all that people can see is only the old China of last century." The authors of the article, claims Sorace, accused Antonioni of *shi'erbujian*, which means to not see what is plainly there.[81] This is connected to a common practice of the Cultural Revolution, "According to the *People's Daily* editorial, in Antonioni's portrayal, 'it seems as if China's revolution has not changed the status of Chinese people and has not liberated them spiritually'—a direct challenge to the CCP's legitimating narrative that it freed China from its feudal past." Sorace continues: "During the Mao era, campaigns were organized in which people would 'speak bitterly' (*suku*) about the past, and 'recall past bitterness in order to savor the sweetness of the Present' (*yi ku si tian*). People were enjoined to remember and be thankful for their new lives provided to them by the Party. Antonioni's scenes of China's past haunting its present challenged this logic of legitimation."[82] "Speaking bitterly" is a mode of communication and a "speech act" that we see in most of the filmmakers' engagements with people during this period, but it dominates *Yukong* as it is an expected practice in communicating the successes of the present. The doctor in "The Fishing Village" episode praises the "barefoot doctors" after criticizing the old-fashioned bourgeois city doctors who overlooked rural patients, and the women confess to Marceline the hardships of women's health before the revolution. But it all ends on a positive note, a turn in the speech, facial expression, and tone toward praising the successes of the new China, the Cultural Revolution, and Chairman Mao.[83]

One interesting scene takes place in Wangfujing, a shopping street in Beijing, where Antonioni hides his cameras behind the curtains of a ground floor apartment, in that delusional hope of capturing real life that we have seen before. Quite astonishingly, the images are exactly the same as everything else we have seen so far. Everything is real and staged at once, as public and visible life in Cultural Revolution China is not terrain for "improvisation." This candid camera scene depicting children eating ice cream and adults going about their business triggered a comment in the voice-over about modesty and poverty—that universalist and fundamentally capitalist idea of poor people behaving well that in Beijing in 1972 seems truly out of place.[84] Probably the most exciting scene in this first part of Antonioni's documentary is the very last: we are at the Chang'an Grand Theater, where a puppet show with a full orchestra gives Antonioni the chance to present an actual theater, with patrons somewhat relaxed and enjoying the quite extraordinary performance. It goes without saying that the puppet show being edited in here points to the theatricality of Chinese life, as does the very last scene of the acrobats and jugglers at the end of the trip in Shanghai.[85]

Antonioni's Nonfiction Filmmaking: A Sympathy for the Modern

Antonioni started his career as a documentary filmmaker and a film critic in 1930s fascist Italy. His most celebrated early nonfiction short, *Gente del Po* (*People of the Po Valley*, 1943–45), is often hailed as a precursor to the neorealist movement that will occupy most of the film discourse in Italy in the postwar era.[86] It describes in eleven poetically intense minutes the life of people living and working along the banks of the river that runs through the northeast of the Italian peninsula. The film at the time of its release struck a chord with critics for its poetic realism, in which the harshness of the life of the characters blends with a lyrical tone both in the camera and editing style and in its micronarrative units, each focusing on vignettes of daily life. Young Michelangelo Antonioni, son of a well-to-do family from Ferrara, was one of the privileged, cosmopolitan filmmakers that during and in spite of the fascist regime managed to have a varied film career. In 1942, Antonioni cowrote the war film *Un pilota ritorna* (*A Pilot Returns*) with Roberto Rossellini and worked as assistant director on Enrico Fulchignoni's *I due Foscari* (*The Two Foscari*), an adaptation of Giuseppe Verdi's opera. In 1943, he traveled to France to assist Marcel Carné on *Les visiteurs du soir* (*The Devil's Envoy*, 1942). This allowed Antonioni to garner international filmmaking experience right in the middle of the war—quite a rare opportunity—which propelled him in 1943 to start his own career. In an essay published in the magazine *Cinema* in 1943, "Per un film sul fiume Po" ("For a Film on the River Po," a sort of preparatory text and photo piece for the film) Antonioni rejected both the voice-of-God expository mode embodied by the 1938 film *The River* (the Pare Lorenz classic on the Mississippi River financed by the Tennessee Valley Authority) and the narrative documentary à la Flaherty's *Elephant Boy* (1937, dubbed *La danza degli elefanti*, *The Dance of the Elephants* for the Italian market). This Flaherty/Korda film was shot partly on location in Mysore and was a true worldwide success, including in Italy where in 1937 it won the Best Film prize at the Venice Film Festival. Antonioni's refusal of the two most common approaches to nonfiction in the late '30s (didactic exposition and narrative nonfiction) pushed him toward a poetic and realistic style filled with great observational capacity able to capture the singularity of the locale and the people who inhabit it. Noa Steimatsky rightly comments that "'For a Film on the River Po' raises questions on the ways in which location shooting complicates the relation of fiction to documentary.... the relation of profilmic actuality to rhetoric and poetic functions, the relation of landscape and history, and the consciousness of place in the national imagination."[87] These concerns are visible in a dialectical approach to actuality/rhetoric, landscape/history, and place/national imagination that will pervade both Antonioni's fiction and nonfiction films to come.

A similar attitude is visible in Antonioni's second short film, *N.U. - Nettezza Urbana* (1948), which investigates the life of street cleaners in economically depressed postwar Rome, in many ways replicating the narrative and stylistic model already displayed in *Gente del Po*: an observational style that portrayed quick vignettes of daily life. Quite interestingly, Antonioni was also involved in commercial and sponsored nonfiction shorts like *L'amorosa menzogna* (*Lies of Love*, 1949), which was about the actors of the very popular Italian photoplays (*fotoromanzi*); also notable was the textile industry sponsored short *Sette canne, un vestito* (*Seven Weeds, One Suit*, 1949) on the production of rayon. *Sette canne* was commissioned by SNIA Viscosa, one of the largest chemical and textile plants in Italy, and this short film documents the work needed to produce this type of synthetic fabric.[88] The film describes the whole process: the collection of raw materials (the Giant Cane, or *Arundo* donax near Trieste), the incessant and monotonous work of the factory of Torviscosa between Udine and Trieste, and finally the display of the dress at a fashion show.[89] As Leonardo Quaresima writes, it's very evident that in early Antonioni "modernization is seen as a positive process, in correspondence with the people who traverse it . . . this 'sympathy for the modern' constitutes the backbone of Antonioni's early films with images of new mechanized mills, and in *N.U* with an image of a train and then focus on the novelty mechanized garbage truck."[90] The SNIA Viscosa plant of *Sette canne* is more of a space station, and the few humans we see are wearing protective gear that turns them into cosmonauts of modernity. *La funivia del faloria* (*The Funicular of Mount Faloria*, also known as *Vertigine*, or *Vertigo*, 1950) follows the gondolas' prodigious ascent to the alpine summit, and in the four minutes currently available of the film from the original eleven, people appear only at the very end. Stylistically, both Quaresima and Steimatsky point to the modernity of the content, frame, and composition of this nonfiction piece that resembles László Moholy-Nagy's Lichtrequisit or contemporaneous painting by Mario Sironi rather than any contemporary realist exercise.[91] As the earlier *Gente del Po*, which had a constant engagement with modernity (cranes, barges, etc.), *Sette canne* is not an elegy to riparian life but an essay on the old and the new, and more generally on the process of mechanization and modernization that will sweep through the country during the years of the economic boom.[92] The trip to China brings to the surface this "modernity imperative" of Antonioni's approach to filmmaking, as the notion of modernity itself is at the core of the discontent between the traveling film crew and the land they visited. In short, it is the notion of modernity that is challenged by the China project, as the ambivalence toward it that sits at the core of Antonioni's artistic practice grinds to a halt in Communist China.

Visual Entanglements

Rey Chow writes in her "China as Documentary" that "as bearers of specific attitudes and perspectives, so-called native informants and foreign observers are partners in a long historical relationship, the complexity of which lies not in either position alone but rather in their entanglement."[93] This "entanglement" became evident in part two, which starts off in the Henan province, in the Linzhou district, where in an agricultural commune we are given a bit of history of the Great Leap Forward that in 1958 initiated the program intended to create self-sufficient farming communities. This is followed by a trip to the Red Flag Canal, an engineering feat that Communist China was eager to show to the whole world. Antonioni lingers on the structure and on the tourists that visit the site. Of the many afterlives of *Chung Kuo*—that is, of the many critical and artistic works inspired by Antonioni's trip—*China Is Far Away: Antonioni in China* (2009), directed by Liu Haiping, stands out for its exciting "return to the crime scenes" moments.[94] While quite simple in its structure and its ambition, it can give contemporary audiences an interesting look at both China today and Antonioni's film. The most interesting aspects of Liu's film are the parts that follow in the original footsteps of Antonioni's crew who happily traveled through Cultural Revolution China while quite unprepared. Quite smartly, Liu Haiping stops in the locations that at the time were identified as more problematic by the Chinese censors—those that the *People's Daily* reviewers defined as the "vicious motives and despicable tricks" used by the Westerner to diminish the achievements of the revolution.[95]

Liu Haiping manages to retrace the steps of at least part of the Italian crew's trip and found some of the involuntary protagonists of that moment of West-East encounter that will have a great deal of resonance inside and outside of China. In Linzhou they find Tian Yongchang (director of the Fourth Hotel), who manages to dig out the guest log for May 27, 1972, in which seven Italian guests are registered (Antonioni, Fico, Barbato, DP Luciano Tovoli, RAI executive and journalist Furio Colombo, and sound person Giorgio Pallotta, plus one more traveler I was unable to identify). Quite interestingly, the manager reveals that they screened the documentary *Red Flag Canal* (1970) for Antonioni and Fico in the TV room of the hotel. This short film is a standard documentary production of the Cultural Revolution. Though in black and white, it manages to look and sound as loud and bombastic as possible in celebrating the accomplishments in water containment, as the canal would manage to provide water to a large part of the region and stimulate agricultural productions.[96]

What might the maestro have thought of this film? Nowhere during my research did I find anybody asking him if he had seen any Chinese films during his stay, which testifies to the sense of superiority attributed to the Western artist (why should he bother with minor art from a remote country?), and in doing so, our research misses an opportunity to hear from him and his crew if any actual filmic exchange ever happened. It is only thanks to Mr. Tian Yongchang, his good memory, and his impeccable bookkeeping that we know that Antonioni and Fico (whom he describes as being very much in love!) spend the evening at the hotel watching this film on television. While most scholars discuss this film as a typical revolutionary documentary that praises the achievement of the revolution in bringing water to the country-side, the visuals offer quite a stunning spectacle of the mountainous province to the new viewer (in this case, me). The film opens with a birds-eye view of the mountains as grandiose orchestral music accompanies the images, as a declarative and stertorous voice-over narrates the progress brought to this place by the revolution.

I am reminded of Antonioni's own passion for mountain peaks. In the early 1960s, Antonioni started painting miniature watercolors, which he called *Montagne incantate* (*Enchanted Mountains*). Although he never con-sidered himself a painter, he returned to them throughout his life. He would enlarge these tiny works, some barely a few centimeters across, into prints of up to two meters in length, revealing the arid or misty landscapes and colored deserts formed by his brush. This gesture echoes a scene in *Blow-Up* (1966) in which David Hemmings's character happens upon a dead body in his photograph, a discovery that drives the rest of the film in his maddening search for the truth. Antonioni's *Montagne incantate* series is one facet of a persistent engagement with the relationship between the visible and the in-visible. We see this at play, for instance, in the photographic apparition of the corpse in *Blow-Up*, the vanishing of a woman's sanity in *Deserto Rosso* (*Red Desert*, 1964), or in Antonioni's interest in the essence of photography itself.[97]

In the powerful opening of the film *Red Flag Canal*, these same mountains lead us to farmers working in a field, and finally to a group of young women reading and studying in a circle (as physical work had to match political awareness in Cultural Revolution China). There is one shot in particular that impressed me, a close-up of the leader of this group that zooms in on the face of this young woman reading a newspaper out loud; there's no sync sound here, but we see her mouth declaiming from a copy of the local paper, *Henan Daily*, whose title reads, "From poverty the desire for change." As the scene opens with a long shot of the group of "iron women" reading passionately together and ends with zooming in on the leader, this speaks to the three prominences rule we have already discussed, in which we move from the group to the leader; it also serves as an homage to the "iron women," the very first labor reserve of the revolution.[98] This close-up reminds me of similar camera movement in *Chung Kuo*, one of those authorial signature shots that I initially assigned to Antonioni's inquisitive gaze, but now I am left wondering if Antonioni noticed this zoom at all, or if he enjoyed it as much as I am doing now. This shot exists within the context of many close-ups of young women: in blue and red military-style outfits, with parted hair and stiff side braids carrying guns, plows, hoes and other agricultural tools on their shoulders, all shots that are in dialogue with the official portrait of the new "iron women" of the revolution. More notably, these opening sequences of *Red Flag Canal* are a clear attack on the vision of the rural areas as still being in the grip of patriarchy while promoting and elevating female workers with a very high political consciousness.[99]

Antonioni's trip continues with a visit to the Da Cai Yuan farm (Liu Haiping found Mr. Ma Dongsheng still in charge of the farm and able to remember the visit of Antonioni well), where we witness a Revolutionary Committee meeting. We also watch a visit to the school (which prompts a comment on the doubling of the population and the order demanding that many Chinese citizens must stay in the country) as well as a visit with an old couple, during which the only noticeable object in the setting is a poster of red-garbed Li Tiemei holding her father's lantern as she fights the Japanese invasion in *The Legend of the Red Lantern*, one of the eight party-approved model operas produced by the Beijing Opera and widely popularized by a filmed version in 1968.[100] This is indeed one of the few images, along with the omnipresent official portrait of Chairman Mao, that accompanies these voyages in Cultural Revolution China. For their style and placement, they look like images of saints in Catholic households, or of deities more generally, and they occupy a central space in the Cultural Revolution home. This can be viewed as a form of virtue signaling to the theater of everyday life as well as functioning as a thaumaturgic relic against the turbulence of the uncertain future. Since any act of speaking is in itself dangerous, repeating slogans and showcasing images became a safe way of expressing allegiance while also probably being a heartfelt talismanic gesture.[101]

The next scene stands out precisely because it breaks this communal performance, as the Italian crew manages to shoot an illegal farmer market in the Hunan province. The scene is short, and it simply depicts some poor products on display in the street, but it was one of the moments that triggered the *People's Daily*'s criticism as one of the treacherous attempts at depicting what is wrong in China. Once again we can note the excitement of the filmmakers in their engaging with candid camera moments. This continues with

Figure 4.1. Iron girls (*Red Flag Canal*).

another "illegal visit" to a remote village, which will feature prominently in the *People's Daily*'s review. The scene stands out as the most invasive so far. It is very clear that the oddest thing of all is the presence of the camera, but this goes unnoticed, as the crew convince themselves that they are real rebels in wanting to show what their minders did not want them to. The crew, in their desperate search for a real China, tries to capture life unhindered while clearly puzzling the locals. There's also a zoom in on a pig urinating that is difficult not to notice. Liu Haiping in his documentary manages to find this village. A few of the older folks remember Antonioni's visit and some even repeat the criticism of the film that must have formed part of their upbringing, even though none of the townsfolk had seen it. It is only at the very end of this scene that the voice-over acknowledges that "gli stranieri siamo noi, un colpo duro per il nostro orgoglio di europei" ("we are the foreigners here, a harsh blow to our European pride").

But this confessional mode, which could have become a very productive line of thought, is quickly abandoned and the film continues unhindered with its many close-ups and zoom-ins that Antonioni inflicts on reticent subjects with his hidden camera, filming market shoppers among the vegetable and poultry stalls. The less diplomatic Marceline Loridan went even further than me and the Chinese comrades in criticizing these stolen moments: "[Antonioni had] a look and also a behavior vis-a-vis the people he was filming that, for me, was very disagreeable. Because I don't like snatching [*piquer*] people like butterflies, whether it's in China, Japan, or Ardèche. It was camera-rape, and we wanted to do the opposite."[102]

As Tom Waugh clarifies, Ivens and Loridan in their own film alternate between the purely observational and more "catalytic" or "mise-en-présence" tactics, which facilitate the development of a particular situation. With the term *catalytic*, Waugh means the use of staged performances by local actors, who were asked to "perform" their actions and their speeches for the camera. This is particularly clear in the case of groups (or guilds as they were often referred in Communist China) where an individual is asked to speak for/by the group.[103] As Waugh explains:

> Sometimes the non-interactive approach might be called catalytic or "mise-en-présence." In the latter sense social actors and crew collaborate on facilitating an event that might not otherwise have happened there and then but which would then unfold spontaneously—a principle well known to the era's practitioners of direct cinema in the West. Sometimes the fine line between non-interventionist observation and collaborative mise-en présence is blurred: a case in point is the pharmacy staff's weekly meetings (a scene from *Yukong*) for criticism and improvement, which the by now familiar crew unobtrusively observed and which are marked by ranges of comfortable spontaneity alongside what one might call exemplary performances among certain participants. An engaging five-minute conversation where a dozen workers move from the advantages of having oxygen tanks in stock to the importance of courtesy and patience with all customers fluctuates among self-conscious ritual performances of prescribed self-criticism to interventions by individuals who have clearly forgotten the camera.[104]

What is striking about the village scene is precisely the radical difference in judgment it generated. In his documentary *China Is Far Away*, Liu Haiping interviews the DP Luciano Tovoli, who clearly remembers this as a highlight of the trip, precisely because it was one of the few moments of "freedom" granted to the foreign visitors—a true moment of cinema unhindered. The Chinese reviews of the film emphasize the commitment of the crew to

ANTONIONI IN CHINA

represent the old rather than the new and the comments captured by the village more than forty years later still repeat that kind of criticism. In play is the notion of freedom itself and how it was perceived by the two sides.

This aspect becomes even more evident as the film moves to Nanjing, with one scene that received particularly harsh criticism from the Chinese authorities and that Bertolucci would remember in his *Videocartolina*. It is the shot of the Nanjing bridge on the Yangtze River. The tone is laudatory, praising the massive effort that was required for its construction (length, number of workers involved, etc.), but the images are grainy and the day foggy while dust or pollution fills the shot that shows the structure from a distance. And, as Rinaldi's suave voice lists the engineering accomplishments, a wobbly electronic vibration emerges. It is the work of Italian avant-garde composer Luciano Berio, at the time employed by RAI's Studio di Fonologia Musicale (Musical Phonology Lab) in Milan, that provides this brief but striking obtrusion into the film narrative.[105] Quite interestingly, the sound of this short, two-minute-long sequence has not been mentioned by any reviewers either then or now, but I cannot imagine that it did not have an impact, maybe unconsciously, on the eager *People's Daily* reviewers when they wrote: "In photographing the Yangtze River Bridge at Nanking, the camera was intentionally turned on this magnificent modern bridge from very bad angles in order to make it appear crooked and tottering. A shot of trousers hanging to dry below the bridge is thrown in to mock the scene."[106]

Henri Roanne and Gérard Valet's *Chine*, made for Belgian television in 1971, is in many ways a more traditional expository documentary, with its very invasive and talkative voice-over that accompanies the spectator through every detail of every single image of China. The route they follow is more or less the same as every other traveler, but they do have a quite long segment on this bridge. Obviously, they perceived the keen interest of their handlers, and the scene starts with the tour (along with other tourists) where a guide gives a history of the heroic building of the bridge, followed by a montage of shots of the bridge from different locations. The voice-over cattily muses that "the Chinese are proud of this bridge on the Yangtze—it's their Tour Eiffel, their Statue of Liberty, their Tower of Pisa." Roanne and Valet understood that what was impressive about this structure was the fact that it actually existed—that it was completed against all odds—and not its appearance or its surroundings. Quite interestingly, Carlo Lizzani revealed in an interview how impossible it was to shoot something that was still under

146   TRAVELING AUTEURS

construction in China, such as a working site, which for the Chinese authorities emanated disorder. Instead, they wanted him to shoot the final product like a monument.[107]

But while Roanne and Valet and Lizzani "got the memo," so to speak, the treatment of this portion of the trip by Antonioni's foggy shots and Luciano Berio's wonky electronic recordings takes a weird turn. What happened? Is it just the Italian crew's childish search for freedom in the land of preorganized visits, or is it, as Umberto Eco reads it, a problem of cinematic translation? Umberto Eco, *maître à penser* of the Italian intelligentsia, did not miss this opportunity to chip in: "[The Chinese interpreted] the shot of the Nanking bridge as an attempt to make it appear distorted and unstable, because a culture which prizes frontal representation and symmetrical distance shots cannot accept the language of western cinema which, to suggest impressiveness, foreshortens and frames from below, prizing dissymmetry and tension over balance. And the shot of Peking's Tiananmen Square is seen as the denunciation of swarming mass disorder, while for Antonioni such a shot is the picture of life, and an ordered shot would be the picture of death, or would evoke the Nuremberg stadium."[108] Eco's point is well taken, but it shows a certain superficiality, since in this very chapter, we have seen the complexity, in spite of the strong central aesthetic directives, of what Chinese image culture promoted in those years. While to a distant observer "frontality and symmetry" are interesting points of access into Chinese visual culture, we already know at this point that these ideas are two among many factors that contributed to the creation of a visual revolution. Even a cursory look at political posters from the time shows an insistence on both "foreshortening and framing from below" the heroes, actions, and events. Also, there's a strong influence from folkloric nonperspectival art that the CCP maintained in its campaigns, as is clearly visible in the collection of Chinese propaganda posters.[109] It seems to me that the issue is not just related to interpretation or the semiotics of these images but to a more complex ideological and historical issue about the notion of modernity itself. Can we then say that Antonioni's modernism forced him toward an always ambivalent and articulated take on the modern, industrialized landscape, what Noa Steimatsky calls Antonioni's "modernist imperative"?[110] The problem, as often with films in "developing countries," is how the notion of modernity itself is conceived. In this case, we see this problem in the absolute refusal of the "uneven modernity" by the Chinese, that is, the unwillingness to accept the coexistence of a new and old China

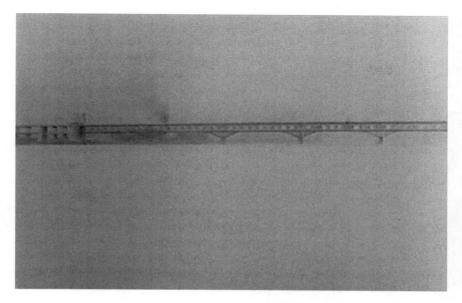

Figure 4.2. The Nanjing Bridge over the Yangtze River, "crooked and tottering" (*Chung Kuo*).

Figure 4.3. "Trousers hanging to dry" (*Chung Kuo*).

in the same shot. It goes against the performance of "speaking bitterly," for example, which must be followed by the sweetness of the present. This total rejection of the notion of "work in progress" in the representation of socialism is quite unique to the Chinese model, as socialist and Third-Worldist industrial films were very keen on showing labor in what John Mackay calls "disorganized noise"; he roots this mode of cinema in the avant-garde aim at not reifying the final product and its alienation by showing the process.[111] The idea of process is itself absent from both Chinese iconography and ideology—it is the final result, the accomplishment that is celebrated: the new versus the old, the present versus the past, and similar. This is probably the biggest and most visible difference in propaganda pieces, in both moving and nonmoving images: that statuary aspect of representation that the socialist modernity of the "developing country" was instead poignantly promoting. Even an engineering film like *Red Flag Canal* was focused mostly on the heroics of the workers rather than the process of the multitudes patiently building the structure, and a large portion of the film is devoted to celebrating the party officials at the inauguration ceremony.

This lack of interest in the process is at the core of the Cultural Revolution ethos, and it is visible in the way that narratives of political conversions, in which a hero finds his way into the party and the revolution, are replaced by sheer hagiography, as we have seen in the early moments of the Cultural Revolution when works of art that did not celebrate the leader were criticized. Probably the best case study is the figure of Lei Feng, the young revolutionary soldier lionized by the party as a role model for the youth, for both his dedication to the cause and his commitment to Mao's teaching. The 1965 eponymous black-and-white film *Lei Feng* (Zhaoqi Dong) is exemplary of this. Apart from a brief section devoted to "speaking bitterly," as Lei Feng tells his life story to schoolchildren, the rest of the film is a series of sketches that proves the high level of political consciousness of this young soldier through his reading of Mao's thought, which meant being loyal to one man and the party rather than your own revolutionary ideas. In the film there are dreamy sequences that show Lei Feng reading and taking notes on the multivolume opus. If earlier artistic preferences were devoted to "becoming a revolutionary," here it is about "being a revolutionary," following the party leadership. In the 2003 historical documentary *Morning Sun*, produced by the American educational media company Long Bow Group, there's a very interesting series of interviews with former Red Guards that explains the switch in party directives from inspirational stories, such as the widely successful Irish novel *The Gadfly* by Ethel Voynich, about a young Italian revolutionary in the 1840s who abandons the Catholic Church to devote himself to the cause (turned into a movie by the Soviets and widely distributed in China, dubbed in Chinese), to the new celebratory mode.[112] Antonioni's "bridge sequence" embodies in one shot the contradictions of a widely different understating of political art, and it signals well the new direction taken by the inflexibility of Cultural Revolution propaganda iconography.

Mao in Milan, or "Get Off the Horse in Order to Gather Flowers"

Inveterate Maoist Alain Badiou, collaborator of Ivens and Loridan for *Yukong*, writes as late as 1980 on the Cultural Revolution:

> Behind the enormous confusion about its various stages, the lines of force of the Cultural Revolution, the entrance on the stage of tens of millions of actors, and the blockage of its goal, all bear on what is essential: the reduction of the gap between intellectual and manual labor, between town and country; the subordination of the productive impetus to the institution of new social relations; the end of university elitism; the reduction of the insolence of cadres; the end of wage systems of inequality and stratification; the ideological opposition to the degenerate "Marxism" that rules in Moscow and in the "communist" parties pledging allegiance to it, and so on.[113]

Few now share Badiou's enthusiasm, but Maoism was a force to be reckoned with, inside and outside of China. Some of this bullet-point style list that he offers are indeed accomplishments of the late sixties and early seventies, which resonated widely through the ranks of the Western Left. While many of the slogans of the revolution were quickly adopted by the revolutionary literature of the time, the iconography that occupied the visual space of China's imaginary, and how it translated into the Western context, has not been properly addressed by scholars, beyond quick reference to some common "Chinese" fashion items popular among the *soixante-huitards* in Berlin, Paris, and Rome.[114]

While it is truly impossible to talk about a "Maoist cinema" with a set of coherent stylistic and narrative features, both in China and abroad, we do see Italian Maoists getting involved in proselytizing through media and at times imitating Cultural Revolution models. Of the large archipelago of groups very active at that time in Italy, what stands out is the Unione dei Comunisti Italiani (marxisti-leninisti), best known for their journal *Servire il popolo*.[115] The group, with bases in Rome and Milan, had some outreach in the countryside and aimed at re-creating the alliance between workers and peasants that was at the core of the Maoist credo. They were also the keenest to use images, and film specifically, to make their program known. For example, a political action (*azione*) that took place in Paola, a small city in Calabria, was filmed by Marco Bellocchio, at the time an active member of the group, who after the harsh critique of *La Cina è vicina* (*China Is Near*, 1967) seemed to have a rapprochement with Maoism. This revolutionary black-and-white film shot in March 1969 with DP Dimitri Nicolau, titled *Il popolo calabrese ha rialzato la testa* (*The People of Calabria Have Raised Their Heads*), describes the squatting by subproletariats in public housing under the leadership of the Unione. Another interesting work is *Viva il primo maggio rosso proletario* (*Long Live the Red and Proletarian May First*, 1969) on the celebration by the Unione in Rome and Milan on May 1, 1969, in which images of Maoist demonstrations through the streets of Milan and Rome are accompanied by a political lecture.

These two films can be thought of as potential ways to produce a Western Maoist film, certainly more in line with films produced in China in that period than the Brechtian modernism that Godard and his Dziga Vertov group were involved in and that produced works such as *Vent d'est, British Sounds* (1969), *Pravda, Lotte in Italia* (*Struggle in Italy*, 1971); *Jusqu'à la victoire* (*Until Victory*, 1970); *Vladimir et Rosa* (*Vladimir and Rosa*, 1971); *Tout va bien* (1972); and *Letter to Jane* (1972).[116] It also produced the infamous situationist approach of *Chinois, encore un effort pour être révolutionnaires* (*Peking Duck Soup*, 1977) by Rene Viénet and Ji Qingming, in which images of kung fu films are redubbed through the process of *détournement*: the resemantization of existing texts for political purposes.[117] For example, in *Il popolo calabrese* we have the voice-over of one of the leaders of the party, Enzo Lo Giudice, narrating the events in Paola. As a shot from the highway shows a group of children on an overpass looking down, Lo Giudice states: "I giovani dietro la rete guardano il benessere passare sotto di loro, e allontanarsi da loro, ma non sono rassegnati al carcere della società divisa in classi" ("The youth behind the net looks at prosperity going by under them, and moves away from them, but they are not resigned to the prison of society divided into classes"). The film continues with members of the Unione helping the people take

Figure 4.4. Mao in Piazza del Duomo (*Viva il primo maggio rosso proletario*).

Figure 4.5. Mao in the streets of Milan (*Viva il primo maggio rosso proletario*).

over the public housing apartments. This film is an excellent documentation of the tactics used by *Servire il popolo* and common among Marxist groups in Europe at the time: bringing the leadership of the party and the people together through a proper *enquête*. Marcelo Hoffman in *Militant Acts* has well researched the role of the enquête (in English translated as both inquiry and investigation), the process of collecting data, listening to the people, proselytizing among the masses, and more importantly contributing to "the production of forms of collective political subjectivity."[118] This *inchiesta* (as enquête is translated in Italian) was as well a very common form of grass-roots politics that had its basis in Mao's own "No investigation, no right to speak."[119] *Il popolo calabrese* is more affirmative and structured than some famous French counterparts, such as *La reprise du travail aux usines Wonder* (*The Return to Work at the Wonder Factory*, 1968), a ten-minute documentary shot by Jacques Willemont and Pierre Bonneau, two film students who had brought their camera for an enquête of sorts out to the industrial periphery of Paris in mid-June.[120] In Bellocchio's film, the listening part is matched by a clear celebration of the power of the party to act and solve real people's problems through the practice known as *établissement*, the placement of activists in hot spots in order to blend in with the population. As Kristin Ross states:

> The *enquête* (inquiry or investigation), initiated by Maoists in 1967 and conducted with workers and farmers door to door, in market places, in front of metro entrances, and in villages in *la France profonde* . . . originated in the refusal of one such representation, the mythic or transcendental one that made of "the Working Class" an undifferentiated united block. . . . What one did not know about the direct experience of workers—or small tenant farmers, for that matter—one could find out by "going to the people," learning from them—from practical action and close attention to local circumstances, that is, and not from theoretical texts. The Maoist model of Marxism placed greater emphasis on local conditions and historical circumstances—the situation—than on canonical texts. Mao's writings on the necessary link between theory and practice, the need, as he put it, to "get off the horse in order to gather flowers," provided one impetus out of the Latin Quarter, where his writings were read not so much as theoretical doctrine but more frequently as an invitation to leave the books and the city behind.[121]

The second film that is worth watching to understand this bizarre road to Maoist heaven is *Viva il primo maggio rosso proletario*, which stands out for its visualization of party directives.[122] It starts with a meeting in Corsico, a working-class town in the outskirts of Milan, with a worker condemning the revisionists of the Italian Communist Party (PCI) and their international allies while standing right in front of a poster that reads "Senza teoria nessuna rivoluzione" ("No Revolution without Theory"); then it moves to the Alfa Romeo car factory and a local high school to show dissemination of the newspaper *Servire il popolo* by activists. Finally, the last and longest portion of the film is devoted to the rally itself, in which activists are seen displaying flags of the Unione designed by Roman avant-garde artist Mario Schifano.[123] The key shot of this film is the image of Mao brought out on a palanquin by members of the party against the backdrop of the spires of the Duomo, the city's most iconic monument. This visual territorial occupation transliterates in the Italian context the many images of the Helmsman present at different locations, a prominent feature of Maoist documentaries.

Servire il popolo had a decisive advantage over their competitors as they managed to enlist many famous artists who actively contributed to the cause. It included sculptor Pino Spagnulo, who produced a massive hammer-and-sickle installation for *Servire il popolo* in 1972, as well as Mario Schifano, Tano Festa, and Franco Angeli, who each provided the group with financial support even though they were never active militants. As Jacopo Galimberti writes, "it is indeed possible to view Maoism also as the transmission belt for a strand of Marxist aesthetics, one predicated on figuration, intelligibility, anti-intellectualism and the national 'people' as the sole legitimate recipient of the work."[124] Galimberti rightly points out that this Maoist political art, which he defines as "militant orientalism," blended renewed interest for "the mysterious and unfathomable East" with political curiosity for the Chinese model.[125]

Alors, la Chine?

The moment of collision between Italian Maoists and Antonioni happened at the Venice Film Festival in 1974. After the Biennale's president Carlo Ripa di Meana was forced by pressure of the Chinese authority and the Italian government to move the screening to Venice proper from Lido, a group of militants physically attacked the guests. Carlo Di Carlo, one of Antonioni's closest collaborators throughout his entire life, remembers this episode well, especially as it triggered an intense debate on the boundary between arts and politics. The always eager Umberto Eco took inspiration from these events (which he witnessed) to comment on the matter: "Antonioni, nervous and troubled, was once again suffering his very personal and paradoxical drama—the antifascist artist who went to China inspired by affection and respect and who found himself accused of being a Fascist, a reactionary in the pay of the Soviet revisionism and American imperialism, hated by 800 million persons."[126] The zeal of the Italian Maoists (it's not clear which specific group was present) should not prevent us from understanding that the *People's Daily*'s reviewers on January 30, 1974, were mostly right in their accurate, almost shot-by-shot analysis of the film. I hope that in this chapter, I have shown how the general sense of superiority displayed by the crew was palpable; the orientalist gaze was the dominant note of this film as was that constant use of the word *freedom* in the voice-over. Likewise, the campaign launched by the party media against the film and its director was a total fabrication and a distortion of reality for sheer political gain.

Pang Laikwan in her acute *The Art of Cloning*, asks how criticism could be divorced from both the actual text and the claimed reality, while it was increasingly difficult to distinguish text from reality. From this campaign, we realize that representations were never understood as naive reflections of reality during the Cultural Revolution, but different people could produce different views of the same reality. *The People's Daily* commentary did accuse a scene of being staged, but the main body of the criticism did not—or dared not—counteract Antonioni by charging him with fabricating the footage, and there was no dispute that the documentary images presented were indexical to Shanghai's city view and the people's everyday lives. The whole campaign against *Chung Kuo* was not directed at Antonioni's "constructions"; the filmmaker was attacked for the "realities" he chose to record: he deliberately depicted a backward reality of China against the blissful and progressive reality that his host wanted him to present and the world to consume. Laikwan's claim to indexicality is very useful in the middle of this political and ideological mess that *Chung Kuo*, in spite of everybody's best intentions, has become, in that it points to a key element of the film: its absolute faithfulness to indexical reality and its total detachment from political and ideological elements that imbued the reality that was shown.

When Carlo Di Carlo was finally able to bring *Chung Kuo* back to China in 2004, what he discovered was that the new China was very happy to welcome back Antonioni's film, mostly because few remembered it and even fewer cared about it. Gone was the Gang of Four and the Cultural Revolution as

ANTONIONI IN CHINA

well as the censorship that followed the few public screenings of the film. The reportage on the event that was included in the French version of the DVD does a good job at showing the enthusiasm of the very young audience at the screening. It took place at the Beijing Film Academy and particularly notable was the excitement of these young people in being able to see life during the Cultural Revolution "indexically." Since autochthonous images have been removed and doctored over time, this foreign(er) incursion into China and its brutal attempt at showing reality is now a unique document.[127]

An American Coda

Antonioni's film was picked up by ABC and broadcast on December 10 and 11, 1973, at 10:00 p.m. with a commentary by the now legendary Ted Koppel. The film had been split into two parts of one hour each (including ads) and was retitled *Highlights from Michelangelo Antonioni's Chung Kuo: China Special*, Parts 1 and 2.[128] This American broadcast, which I was able to access thanks to the Media Collection of the Richard Nixon Presidential Library in Yerba Buena, is a stunning document for contemporary media scholars. First, the voice-over is done by Antonioni himself. He speaks fluently in English and his commentary is more direct and less exoticizing than the Italian version's. I am actually surprised that no scholar has written about this version before, because this is one of the more real, more Antonioni-esque I want to say, versions of the film to appear. The very spare commentary is matched by totally different sound mixing. Ambient sound is louder and everything becomes more audible and in consequence more visible. Luciano Berio's noisy intrusions are gone. The film has not just been shortened—it includes segments that are not in the Italian version. For example, in the second part there's a long scene at a Buddhist temple in which the issues of removal of statues and religion is discussed; also added was a long section in a kindergarten in Nanjing (during which we hear "I Love Beijing Tiananmen" sung live by the children) that shows a day in the life of children.

What is also of great interest is the way in which the American broadcast entirely removed the authorial aura that surrounds this film. This functions to turn it into what my colleagues Charles Acland and Haidee Wasson would define as "useful cinema": in this case a document that provides the average evening viewer with a peephole into a hidden world.[129] In short, this version of *Chung Kuo* is catered toward a more worldly, aware, and sophisticated midcentury American man, as the show's target audience is obviously gendered. It goes without saying that the discovery of this tape at the Nixon library makes a lot of sense politically. The American journalist Ted Koppel punctuates the film with comments, underlining its importance in being able to understand China. Nixon's visit in February 1972 had opened up a new phase in Sino-American relations, and it is clear that ABC promoted the series as a spy film of sorts, a look into the belly of the beast. This, accompanied by constant advertisements for GM cars, Aetna insurance company, Vlasic pickles, and ABC's own shows make this a very interesting piece for historians of 1970s American media in a global context.[130] For Antonioni scholars, this is a kind of alternative reality moment, that is to say, a glimpse into how the film should have looked and sounded if the auteur actually had more control over his product. In a bizarre loop, the pragmatic use of this footage by ABC had obviously given Antonioni more freedom to toy with the raw footage and make this a more interesting film.

Antonioni's *Chung Kuo* is a paradigmatic traveling cultural object, in the sense defined by James Clifford, as its own very existence, its multiple readings and interpretations, its own function and meaning, have traversed a good part of both the globe and twentieth century modernity.

Notes

1. Rayns, "Model Citizen."
2. Hatton, "Wham!"
3. Baschiera, "Beijing." See also Zhang, *Chinese National Cinema*, 238.
4. Cahill and Holland, "Double Exposures."
5. Said, "Traveling Theory," 180.
6. Wang, *Sublime Figure*, 208, 209.
7. Li, *Utopian Ruins*, 168.
8. Li, 167. I would like to thank Jie Li, who has been one the first readers and supporters of this work. She provided historical contextualization to my research and refocused parts of my writing.
9. Dalla Gassa, Zecca, and Neri, *Reinventing Mao*, 13; see also Leese, *Mao Cult*, and Lovell, *Maoism*.
10. Wolin, *Wind*, 3. Following Lovell, we can say that "there is perhaps a story to be told about the expansion of Maoism that also led to the dissemination of ideas such as 'serving the people,' 'consciousness-raising,' and 'cultural revolution' in education, which have had an impact on feminist, gay rights, racial equality, environmental and academic movements outside China" (Lovell, *Maoism*, 61).

11. I use the term icon in the way envisioned by Bishnupriya Ghosh "as magical technologies, cultural mechanisms that facilitate articulations of collective aspiration" (Ghosh, *Icons*, p. 3).

12. See Macciocchi, *Dalla Cina*, or the English version, Macciocchi, *Daily Life*. For a survey of French intellectuals traveling through China, see Hourmant, *Avenir radieux*.

13. For a summary of Italian travelers' memoires, see Basilone, "Impressions."

14. Available in English as Barthes, "Well, and China."

15. See the posthumously published Barthes, *Carnets*, 32 and Barthes, *Travels*, 18.

16. There's now a large bibliography that is often critical of these Maoist intellectuals. See for example Hollander, *Political Pilgrims*; Bourseiller, *Maoïstes*; and Hayot, *Chinese Dreams*.

17. A nice critical anthology of twentieth-century Italian writers in China can be found in Soscia, *In Cina*; Marinelli, *Viaggiatori*; Yang, *Cina*; and Benvenuti, *Viaggiatore*. See also the recent Basilone, *Distance*.

18. Benvenuti, "Diarismo."

19. In English, see Moravia, *Red Book*.

20. Brunetta, *Umberto Barbaro*.

21. Umberto Barbaro's article was originally published in the journal *Il ponte* and was recently rereleased in a special issue edited by Silvia Calamandrei. See Barbaro, "Paradosso," 108, my translation.

22. Said, *Orientalism*, 156.

23. Clò, "Mondo Exotica," and Adinolfi, *Mondo Exotica*. For a survey of Italian filmmakers in China, see the very recent Carolan, *Orienting Italy*.

24. In *Orienting Italy*, Carolan points out that the film was originally screened in New York in AromaRama, an olfactory cinematic system that provided the "smell of China" to the audience. Stefano Bona, in a forthcoming article, has patiently reconstructed the production history of the film.

25. Lupton, *Chris Marker*, 50.

26. See King, *Lost in Translation*, in particular "The Shanghai Gesture" (44–74), which analyzes orientalist representations of crime in Hollywood films.

27. Both these films are available in the digital archives of the NFB/ONF website. In a similar vein is the more traditional expository medium-length film *Thunderbirds in China* (Les Rose, 1974), which narrates the travel of the members of the University of British Columbia's Thunderbirds hockey team to China.

28. This film is available on the Dutch television VPRO digital archive and, as I write, on YouTube with English subtitles.

29. See the chapter "Acting to Play Oneself" (71–92) in Waugh, *Right to Play Oneself*.

30. The *New York Times* review of the film states the obvious, "Nowhere, however, is there an indication of crime, poverty, deprivation or unhappiness among

China's 800 million people," apparently a requirement for films about China, particularly for the reviewer, a Russian-born *émigré* with obviously very little patience for both ladies and commies. See Weiler, "MacLaine."

31. Minami, "Transnational Feminism."

32. My gratitude to Claudia Weill, who generously provided me with the film, which is otherwise, sadly, not available on the market.

33. I would like to thank the Cinematek (the Royal Belgian Film Archive) and the film director Henri Roanne for providing me with a copy of the film and some extra material. Also, in spite of my attempts, I have not been able to locate *Awakening Giant: China* by Danish anthropologist Jens Bjerre (1970), a film often mentioned in the contemporaneous literature as being extremely successful.

34. Waugh, Conscience, 584.

35. This is why, for me, Antonioni's *Chung Kuo* is a far more honest work, despite its openly declared position of detachment from what it frames. Ivens and Loridan's film is no doubt an honest document of what they saw and heard during their protracted stay in China, but we now know far more about what was happening outside the purview of their camera, throwing much of what they show into question. Antonioni was conscious that he was seeing only the surface reality of Mao's China and he made a film about his encounter with that surface, foregrounding his limited viewpoint. (Edwards, "Critical Reflection")

36. A thorough comparison between Chung Kuo and Yukong is in Sun, "Two Chinas?"

37. Liu, "Reception," 26.

38. See Xiao, "Traveler's Glance," and the Chinese sources she quotes: Chen, "Incident."

39. Chatman, *Antonioni*, 135, 170.

40. I managed to match the actual trip of the crew and the diegetic temporality of the film thanks mostly to *China Is Far Away: Antonioni in China* (2009), the documentary directed by Liu Haiping.

41. As Xiao reminds us, "the most important piece of non-diegetic music, this numbingly repetitive and bombastic children's song blares over the opening and closing titles of each of the film's three sections, and formed part of the daily routine in Chinese primary schools at the time" (Xiao, "Traveler's Glance," 113).

42. The article in now available online on massline.org. See "Renmin Ribao" Commentator, "Vicious Motive."

43. "In a word, the massive criticism campaign against Antonioni was partly a scene created by the Gang of Four as part of their plot against Premier Zhou Enlai, which went far beyond the film itself" (Liu, "Reception," 29).

44. Berry, "Red Poetics," 30. See also McGrath, "Cultural Revolution."

45. Clark, "Model Theatrical Works."

46. Clark, 110.

47. Berry, "Red Poetics."

48. On the "Theory of the Three Prominences," see Berry, "Red Poetics."

49. This is, for example, the case analyzed by Chris Berry of the cinematic versions of *Taking Tiger Mountain by Strategy*, in which the main hero Yang Zirong has infiltrated the bandits' hideout. Berry writes: "At 50 minutes into the film, the scene of Yang's arrival at their lair uses the theory of the three prominences to put the spotlight on him—literally. . . . The lighting, music, and the bright colors all clearly demarcate him from the bandits. Where the bandits have an unhealthy pale greenish pallor, Yang's face is bright and shining, his wide and intense eyes outlined with black mascara" (Berry, "Red Poetics," 37).

50. Chu, *Chinese Documentaries*, 62.

51. Antonioni, *Architecture of Vision*, 51.

52. Daney, "Remise en scene." The translation is from Caughie, *Television Drama*, 112.

53. Caughie, *Television Drama*, 112. This issue is well described by Waugh in his comparison between *Yukong* and *Chung Kuo*:

> In *Chung Kuo*, Antonioni felt no such compunction or friendship. Repeatedly violating the ethical right of the subject, whether national or individual, to control his or her own image, Antonioni seems perversely to have insisted on filming whatever his hosts requested him not to. For example, the things he was asked not to film and did, included the following: a gunboat in Shanghai Harbor, a free-enterprise peasant market on a rural road, even a burial caught in telephoto when his hosts suggested that the filming of a burial would offend the Chinese sense of privacy. As he and Ivens/Loridan demonstrated, it is easy to shoot film in China. But it is far more difficult and a far greater achievement to receive and honor people's trust. For Ivens and Loridan, their first responsibility was to their subjects, and Antonioni was not so motivated. (Waugh, Conscience, 583)

54. Jennifer Barker offers a captivating reading of the film in which she claims that *Chung Kuo* "engages in a fascinating negotiation of the terms and conventions of ethnography as a Western scientific enterprise and of the narrative strategies on which that enterprise depends." See Barker, "Bodily Irruptions," 57.

55. Antonioni, *Architecture of Vision*, 28–29.

56. Giuliani, *Race*.

57. Of the ample research that addresses the colonial visual unconscious, I recommend De Franceschi, *L'Africa*; Bullaro, *Terrone*; O'Healy, *Migrant Anxieties*; Andall and Duncan, *National Belongings*; Grechi and Gravano, *Presente imperfetto*.

58. Pinkus, "Empty Spaces."

59. Fuller, "Fascist Plans."

60. Restivo, *Economic Miracles.*

61. Edwards, "Critical Reflection."

62. Gunning, "Before Documentary."

63. Amad, "Visual Riposte," 56. See also Vernet, "Look."

64. Amad, "Visual Riposte," 56.

65. For more info on Rinaldi, see *Enciclopedia del doppiaggio.* On Italian television, see Padovani, *Fatal Attraction.*

66. Paul Clark, in his essential *Chinese Cinema,* describes the sudden lack of expertise in the Chinese industry due to this constant reshuffling and "reorganization of the ranks," which often meant harsh criminal punishments that were at times difficult to understand (137–45).

67. Xiao, "Traveler's Glance," 110.

68. Xiao, 110–11.

69. Laikwan, *Art of Cloning,* 294.

70. An enlightening conversation about barefoot doctors takes place in the episode "The Fishing Village (Shantoung)" in Ivens and Loridan's *Yukong,* where a real doctor in a fishing village describes with a certain dubiousness the policy of sending young people in the countryside. In "Pharmacy (Pharmacie)" the acupunctural ministrations of the young pharmacists have a political as well as a dramatic and visual meaning. See Waugh, Conscience, 585.

71. Li, *Utopian Ruins.* I would like to thank Concordia's doctoral student Xin Zhou, who provided me with an accurate translation and some background information on this famous film.

72. Waugh, Conscience, 585.

73. Another very popular documentary at the time was *From Mao to Mozart: Isaac Stern in China* (1979) by Murray Lerner, which follows the famous violinist's first tour in China. Also worth noting is *Shanghai New Wind* (1978) by Junichi Ushiyama.

74. The factory is now Beijing Jingmian Textile Group in Shi Li Pu, Chaoyang District, Beijing, China. As of time of writing, it's still visible on Google Maps.

75. This scene was singled out for criticism by the *People's Daily,* since unwittingly the film shows these animals while the loudspeaker is blasting the famous aria *Ode of the Dragon River,* one of the "revolutionary operas" engineered during the Cultural Revolution by Jiang Qing. For more on this, see Liu, "Reception," 30.

76. While all commentators I encountered had something to say about Chinese cooking and eating, of the bunch I have been engaging with around the time of Antonioni's visit, only the uber-gourmand Giorgio Manganelli seemed to really appreciate the complexity and subtlety of Chinese cuisine. See Manganelli, *Cina.*

77. "Renmin Ribao" Commentator, "Vicious Motive," iii.

78. Li, *Utopian Ruins,* 17.

ANTONIONI IN CHINA

79. Liu, "Reception," 25. By Xin Liu see also Liu, *Travelogues*, for an insightful analysis of Italian travellers in China through a mobility perspective.

80. Urbansky, "Unfathomable Foe."

81. Sorace, "Aesthetics," 14.

82. Sorace, 13.

83. I see in this narrowing of focus onto praise an echo of the "three prominences," the formula coined by Jiang Qing for artists to follow in their creative work: give prominence to positive characters among all the characters; give prominence to main heroes among the positive characters; and give prominence to the central character among the main heroes.

84. Merrilyn Fitzpatrick found detailed criticisms of this scene in an article in *China Reconstructs* (June 1974):

> "Written by two clerks working in a bank in Beijing's busy Wangfujing shopping street, the article admits from the outset that Antonioni was open about his stylistic intentions. But, say the clerks, his methods show that he was really 'looking for pictures with which to vilify our capital and the Chinese people.' Refusing the bank's offer for him to shoot the street scene from the roof of the bank building, Antonioni eventually chose the view from a window on the ground floor 'from which one can see only the entrance to a side street and a small section of the Wangfuching street.' More enraging was the fact that he drew the curtains and cut two 30-centimeter slits in them with a pair of scissors. Then he poked the lens through a slit and started to take sneak shots. He hid behind those curtains for a long time, racking his brains for ways in which he could attack and denigrate our great capital. Truly contemptible to the extreme!" (Fitzpatrick, "China Images Abroad," 89)

85. As pointed out by Homay King in her *Lost in Translation*, "the acrobat sequence retroactively codes the entire film . . . as a recording of a series of performances and displays rather than as a 'documentary' per se" (106).

86. See Leavitt, *Italian Neorealism*, and Pitassio, *Neorealist Film Culture* for a thorough analysis of the pervasiveness of neorealist discourses in postwar Italian culture.

87. Steimatsky, *Italian Locations*, 2.

88. On the Italian phenomenon of *fotoromanzi* see the recent Bonifazio, *Photoromance*.

89. Alain Resnais and Raymond Queneau would take this a step (or two) further with their plastic molding epic, *Le Chant du Styrène* (1958).

90. Quaresima, "Making Love."

91. Steimatsky, *Italian Locations*, 1–33; Quaresima, "Making Love," 130–33.

92. For an analysis of the cinema of the "boom," see Restivo, *Economic Miracles*.

93. Chow, "China as Documentary," 16.

94. A very similar more recent film, *Seeking Chung Kuo* (Liu Weifu and Zhu Yun, 2019), follows Italian journalist Gabriele Battaglia in search of places and characters encountered by Antonioni in his film.

95. "Renmin Ribao" Commentator, "Vicious Motive."

96. Hongqi Canal is located in Linzhou City (formerly Lin County) in Henan Province. Linzhou City is located at the junction of the Henan, Shanxi, and Hebei Provinces of Hongqi Canal.

97. See the catalog Païni, Bergala, and Pacelli, *Sguardo*.

98. Jin, "'Iron Girls.'" I would like to thank my colleague Joshua Neves for his help in analyzing this scene.

99. Useful in terms of comparison of the elevation of female workers to iron women ready to replace men's jobs in the new China are the March 8 all-women fishermen crew of "The Fishing Village (Shantoung)" in Ivens and Loridan's *Yukong*. To Loridan's questions they respond proudly that "the East wind is still blowing. . . . We are now independent women working in a cooperative."

100. The signalman's lantern became an instantly recognizable icon for the opera, and a stand-alone symbol that represented revolution. It is often associated with Yan'an (as with the examples shown here). Yan'an was the Communist headquarters during the second United Front against the Japanese and was the location for Mao's speech on art and literature, which was Jiang Qing's inspiration and justification for the creation of revolutionary model works.

101. Popular reaction to the volatile political situation took on many different forms. Since passive endurance was perceived as coterminous with harboring hidden resentment toward the CCP chairman's policies, the active expounding of the cult became an omnipresent phenomenon. One possible consequence engendered by the dominant rhetoric and rituals of worship was Mao's inclusion in the local pantheon. The quasi-religious confessions before Mao's portrait were thus turned into divine worship. Although similar phenomena had already been observed in the 1950s, they now spread more widely in rural areas, where Mao came to replace other deities on the house altar, a custom that continues to the present. But even in urban Shanghai, citizens could be observed conducting the rituals of the "Three Loyalties" in private. Many brigade headquarters established "loyalty chambers" (*zhongzi shi*) or "loyalty halls" (*zhongzi tang*), which were clearly modeled on ancestral temples (Leese, *Mao Cult*, 210). See also Landsberger, "Deification."

102. Ivens et al., *Yukong*, 605.

103. "A social actor's identity is defined by his or her relation to a group, rather than through a distinctive individual psychology. His or her first alliance is not to the self or the state, but to the immediate community, on whom rests the responsibility for responding collectively to an outside threat and for working out a

solution. . . . In the talking group convention, allowing oneself to be filmed is not a private affair but a participation in collective speech, in group identification and affirmation. . . . The processes of oral culture create a catalytic dialectical tension among different groups and enter into community consolidation and problem solving. Group speech operates on a collective scale with a transformative power that is analogous to that of the individual subject's access to language in the psychoanalytic process." (Waugh, *Right to Play Oneself*, 248–52)

104. Waugh, *Conscience*, 607.

105. Luciano Berio briefly describes the work he did for this film in "La danza del cinese" ("The Dance of the Chinese Man"), which is mostly devoted to his admiration for public kinesthetic practices. He wonders if it would be possible to have Italian factory workers do the same. See Berio, *Scritti sulla musica*, 144–48.

106. "Renmin Ribao" Commentator, "Vicious Motive," iv.

107. In Santi, "Comunismo," 290.

108. Eco, "Interpretatione," 11.

109. Min, Duo, and Landsberg, *Posters*.

110. Steimatsky, *Italian Locations*, 1.

111. MacKay, "Disorganized Noise."

112. *The Gadfly* (Aleksandr Faintsimmer, 1955).

113. Badiou, "Triumphant Restoration," 660. This intervention appeared originally in the "Idées" section of the newspaper *Le Monde* on December 9, 1980.

114. On Italian Maoism, see Niccolai, *Rivoluzione*; Lumley, *States of Emergency*; and Ferrante, *Cina non era vicina*.

115. For an interesting assessment of Italian Maoism and the dissemination of Mao's Little Red Book, see Reill, "Partisan Legacies."

116. For a good assessment of avant-garde Maoism in cinema, see Leung, "Two Fronts."

117. See the witty critique of the film by Haski, "Kung-Fu."

118. See Hoffman, *Militant Acts*, 3. Hoffman states: "The investigation is not an activity between two ready-made subjects who simply exchange questions and answers (or information more generally) with no further consequences. It is an act that harbors the potential to produce a collective political subject, a new 'we' among the various participants in the investigations, not to mention many others" (16).

119. The best known of these activist investigations is probably UCFML's *Livre*. On the role of the *enquête*, see Ross, *May '68*.

120. Ross, *May '68*, 231.

121. Ross, 184.

122. The film was produced by Maurizio Cacciaguerra with Marco Bellocchio in Rome and Elda Tattoli in Milan and it showcased a text written by the leader Aldo Brandirali. Brandirali, who was then at the center of a grotesque cult of personality,

164 TRAVELING AUTEURS

subsequently joined Silvio Berlusconi's party and a right-wing lay ecclesiastic movement called Comunione e Liberazione (Community and Liberation).

123. On Schifano's political involvement see Caminati, "Anticolonial Cinema."

124. Galimberti, "Maoism," 219. In the latter part of the 1960s, the number of periodicals claiming a Maoist line increased, including *Vento dell'Est* (*Wind from the East*) and *Lavoro Politico* (*Political Work*).

125. Galimberti, 224.

126. Eco, "Interpretatione."

127. Alice Xiang has scouted Chinese webpages to collect some interesting comments about these screenings: Xiang, "Ordinary Seeing."

128. A screening planned at MOMA (Museum of Modern Art) in New York "on Tuesday, December 26, at 5:30 p. m., as part of the Museum's series of films made for RAI Radiotelevisione Italiana, will not be shown, it was announced today by Adrienne Mancia, Associate Curator of the Department of Film. The screening has been cancelled because the film is not yet ready for a public showing." See "Screening of 'China' Cancelled."

129. Acland and Wasson, *Useful Cinema*.

130. I would like to thank Regina Longo, media archivist at Brown University, for locating this film, and A. Mackenzie Roberts, audiovisual preservation specialist at Richard Nixon Presidential Library and Museum, for allowing me access to the film.

Bibliography

Acland, Charles R., and Haidee Wasson. *Useful Cinema*. Durham, NC: Duke University Press, 2011.

Adinolfi, Francesco. *Mondo Exotica: Sounds, Visions, Obsessions of the Cocktail Generation*. Edited and translated by Karen Pinkus and Jason Vivrette. Durham, NC: Duke University Press, 2008.

Adorno, Theodor. "The Essay as Form." *New German Critique* 32, no. 1 (1984): 151–71.

Amad, Paula. "Visual Riposte: Looking Back at the Return of the Gaze as Postcolonial Theory's Gift to Film Studies." *Cinema Journal* 52, no. 3 (Spring 2013): 49–74.

Andall, Jacqueline, and Derek Duncan, eds. *National Belongings: Hybridity in Italian Colonial and Postcolonial Cultures*. New York: Peter Lang, 2010.

Andrew, Dudley. "An Atlas of World Cinema." *Framework: The Journal of Cinema and Media* 45, no. 2 (Fall 2004): 9–23.

———. *What Cinema Is! Bazin's Quest and Its Charge*. Hoboken, NJ: Wiley-Blackwell, 2010.

Antonioni, Michelangelo. *The Architecture of Vision: Writings and Interviews on Cinema*. Venice: Marsilio, 1996.

———. *Chung Kuo, Cina*. Turin: Giulio Einaudi, 1974.

———. "Il fatto e l'immagine." *Cinema nuovo* 164 (July 1963): 249–50.

Anzoino, Tommaso. *Pier Paolo Pasolini*. Florence: La Nuova Italia, 1974.

Aristarco, Guido. *Sciolti dal giuramento: Il dibattito critico-ideologico sul cinema negli anni Cinquanta*. Bari: Dedalo, 1981.

Askari, Kaveh. *Relaying Cinema in Midcentury Iran: Material Cultures in Transit*. Oakland: University of California Press, 2022.

Astourian, Laure. "Jean Rouch's *Moi, un Noir* in the French New Wave." *Studies in French Cinema* 18, no. 3 (2018): 252–66.

Astruc, Alexandre. "Du stylo à la caméra et de la caméra au stylo." *L'Écran Français* 144 (March 30, 1948): np.

———. "Renaissance du cinéma en Italie: Rome, ville ouverte." *Combat* (November 16, 1946), np.

Azoulay, Ariella Aïsha. *Potential History: Unlearning Imperialism*. London: Verso, 2019.

Badiou, Alain. "The Triumphant Restoration." *Positions: East Asia Cultures Critique* 13, no. 3 (Winter 2005): 659–62.

Barański, Zygmunt G. "Pier Paolo Pasolini: Culture, Croce, Gramsci." In *Culture and Conflict in Postwar Italy: Essays on Mass and Popular Culture*, edited by Zygmunt G. Barański and Robert Lumley, 139–59. London: Palgrave Macmillan, 1990.

Barattoni, Luca. *Italian Post-Neorealist Cinema*. Edinburgh: Edinburgh University Press, 2012.

Barbaro, Umberto. "Paradosso sulla fotogenia della Cina di Mao." *Il Ponte* 76, no. 5 (2020): 107–12.

Barker, Jennifer M. "Bodily Irruptions: The Corporeal Assault on Ethnographic Narration." *Cinema Journal* 34, no. 3 (Spring 1995): 57–76.

Barthes, Roland. *Carnets du voyage en Chine*. Edited by Anne Herschberg-Pierrot. Paris: Christian Bourgois Editeur, 2009.

———. *Travels in China*. Edited by Anne Herschberg-Pierrot. Translated by Andrew Brown. Cambridge: Polity, 2012.

———. "Well, and China?" *Discourse* 8, no. 1, translated by Lee Hildreth (1986): 116–22.

Baschiera, Stefano. "From Beijing with Love: The Global Dimension of Bertolucci's *The Last Emperor*." *Journal of Italian Cinema & Media Studies* 2, no. 3 (September 2014): 399–415.

Basilone, Linetto. *The Distance to China: Twentieth-Century Italian Travel Narratives of Patriotism, Commitment and Disillusion (1898–1985)*. Oxford: Peter Lang, 2023.

———. "Impressions, Allegories and Disillusionment: Italian Travel Writing on Twentieth Century China (1925–1985)." PhD diss., University of Auckland, 2019.

Bazin, André. "Difesa di Rossellini." *Cinema Nuovo* 65 (August 1955): 147–49.

———. *What Is Cinema?* Vol. 1. Berkeley: University of California Press, 1967.

Bedjaoui, Ahmed. *Cinema and the Algerian War of Independence: Culture, Politics, and Society*. London: Palgrave Macmillan, 2020.

Benedetti, Carla. *Pasolini contro Calvino: Per una letteratura impura*. Turin: Bollati Boringhieri, 1998.

Ben-Ghiat, Ruth. *Italian Fascism's Empire Cinema*. Bloomington: Indiana University Press, 2015.

Benjamin, Walter. *Reflections: Essays, Aphorisms, Autobiographical Writings.* Edited by Peter Demetz. Translated by Edmund Jephcott. San Diego: Harcourt, 1978.

Benvenuti, Giuliana. "Il diarismo in 'Asia Maggiore' di Franco Fortini." In *Memorie, autobiografie e diari nella letteratura italiana dell'Ottocento e del Novecento,* edited by Anna Dolfi, Nicola Turi, and Rodolfo Sacchettini, 497–507. Pisa: ETS, 2008.

———. *Il viaggiatore come autore: L'India nella letteratura italiana del Novecento.* Bologna: Il Mulino, 2008.

Berio, Luciano. *Scritti sulla musica.* Turin: Giulio Einaudi, 2013.

Berry, Chris. "Red Poetics: The Films of the Chinese Cultural Revolution Revolutionary Model Operas." In *The Poetics of Chinese Cinema,* edited by Gary Bettinson and James Udden, 29–49. London: Palgrave Macmillan, 2016.

Berthe, Jamie. "Beyond the Entomological Critique: Re-Thinking Rouch and African Cinema." *Studies in French Cinema* 18, no. 3 (2018): 267–77.

Bertozzi, Marco. *Storia del documentario italiano. Immagini e culture dell'altro cinema.* Venice: Marsilio, 2008.

Bhabha, Homi K. *The Location of Culture.* London: Routledge, [1994] 2012.

———. "Notes on Globalization and Ambivalence." In *Cultural Politics in a Global Age: Uncertainty, Solidarity, and Innovation,* edited by David Held and Henrietta L. Moore, 36–47. Oxford: Oneworld Publications, 2008.

Blunt, Alison, and Cheryl McEwan, eds. *Postcolonial Geographies.* London: Continuum, 2002.

Boarini, Vittorio, and Pietro Bonfiglioli, eds. *La mostra internazionale del cinema libero 1960–1980.* Venice: Marsilio, 1981.

Bonifazio, Paola. *The Photoromance: A Feminist Reading of Popular Culture.* Cambridge, MA: MIT Press, 2020.

Boone, Joseph A. *The Homoerotics of Orientalism.* New York: Columbia University Press, 2014.

Bourgeois, Nathalie, Bernard Bénoliel, and Alain Bergala. *India: Rossellini et les animaux.* Paris: Cinémathèque Française, 1997.

Bourseiller, Christophe. *Les Maoïstes: La folle histoire des gardes rouges français.* Paris: Plon, 1996.

Brennan, Timothy. *At Home in the World: Cosmopolitanism Now.* Cambridge, MA: Harvard University Press, 1997.

Brioni, Simone, and Shimelis Bonsa Gulema, eds. *The Horn of Africa and Italy: Colonial, Postcolonial and Transnational Encounters.* Oxford: Peter Lang, 2018.

Brunetta, Gian Piero. *Umberto Barbaro e l'idea di neorealismo (1930–1943).* Padua: Liviana, 1969.

Brunette, Peter. "Just How Brechtian Is Rossellini?" *Film Criticism* 3, no. 2 (Winter 1979): 30–42.

Bruno, Giuliana. "The Body of Pasolini's Semiotics: A Sequel Twenty Years Later." In *Pier Paolo Pasolini: Contemporary Perspectives*, edited by Patrick Rumble and Bart Testa, 88–105. Toronto: University of Toronto Press, 1994.

———. "Heresies: The Body of Pasolini's Semiotics." *Cinema Journal* 30, no. 3 (Spring 1991): 29–42.

Bullaro, Grace Russo., ed. *From Terrone to Extracomunitario: New Manifestations of Racism in Contemporary Italian Cinema: Shifting Demographics and Changing Images in a Multi-Cultural Globalized Society*. Leicester: Troubador Publishing, 2010.

Cahill, James Leo. *Zoological Surrealism: The Nonhuman Cinema of Jean Painlevé*. Minneapolis: University of Minnesota Press, 2019.

Cahill, James Leo, and Luca Caminati, eds. *Cinema of Exploration: Essays on an Adventurous Film Practice*. New York: Routledge, 2020.

Cahill, James Leo, and Timothy Holland. "Double Exposures: Derrida and Cinema, an Introductory Séance." *Discourse* 37, nos. 1–2 (Winter/Spring 2015): 3–21.

Caillois, Roger. *Les jeux et les hommes: Le masque et le vertige*. Paris: Gallimard, 1958.

Caminati, Luca. *Cinema as Happening: Pasolini's Primitivism and the Sixties Italian Art Scene*. Milan: Postmedia, 2010.

———. "A Culture of Reality: Neorealism, Narrative Non-Fiction, and Roberto Rossellini (1930s–1960s)." In *A Companion to Documentary Film History*, edited by Joshua Malitsky, 239–54. Hoboken, NJ: Wiley-Blackwell, 2021.

———. "Italian Anti-Colonial Cinema: Global Liberation Movements and the Third-Worldist Films of the Long '68." *Screen* 63, no. 2 (Summer 2022): 139–57.

———. "Italian Cinema and the World Cinema Stress Test." *Canadian Journal of Film Studies/Revue Canadienne d'Études Cinématographiques* 29, no. 2 (2020): 25–36.

———. *Orientalismo eretico: Pier Paolo Pasolini e il cinema del Terzo Mondo*. Milan: Bruno Mondadori, 2007.

———. "Pasolini's Southward Quest(ion)." *Estetica: Studi e Ricerche* 7, no. 2 (2017): 273–92.

———. *Roberto Rossellini documentarista: Una cultura della realtà*. Rome: Carocci, 2012.

Camon, Ferdinando. "Conversazione con Pasolini." In *Il mestiere di scrittore: Conversazioni critiche*, 94–122. Milan: Garzanti, 1973.

Carles, Philippe, and Jean-Louis Comolli. *Free Jazz / Black Power*. Edited and translated by Giorgio Merighi and Patricia De Millo. Turin: Giulio Einaudi, [1971] 1973.

———. *Free Jazz Black Power*. Paris: Éditions Champ Libre, 1971.

Carolan, Mary Ann McDonald. *Orienting Italy: China through the Lens of Italian Filmmakers*. Albany: State University of New York Press, 2022.

BIBLIOGRAPHY

Casarino, Cesare. "The Southern Answer: Pasolini, Universalism, Decolonization." *Critical Inquiry* 36, no. 4 (2010): 673–96.

Cassarini, Maria Carla. *Miraggio di un film: Carteggio de Castro-Rossellini-Zavattini*. Venice: Edizioni Erasmo, 2017.

Castello, Giulio Cesare, and Claudio Bertieri. *Venezia 1932–1939: Filmografia critica*. Rome: Edizioni di Bianco e Nero, 1959.

Castro, Josué de. *Geografia della fame*. Bari: Leonardo Da Vinci Editrice, 1954.

Caughie, John. *Television Drama: Realism, Modernism, and British Culture*. Oxford: Oxford University Press, 2004.

Caves, Roger W., ed. *Encyclopedia of the City*. London: Routledge, 2005.

César, Filipa. "Meteorisations: Reading Amílcar Cabral's Agronomy of Liberation." *Third Text* 32, no. 2–3 (2018): 254–72.

Chakrabarty, Dipesh. *Provincializing Europe: Postcolonial Thought and Historical Difference*. Princeton, NJ: Princeton University Press, 2008.

Chatman, Seymour. *Antonioni: or, the Surface of the World*. Berkeley: University of California Press, 1985.

Chen, Donglin. "The Incident of Chung Kuo." *Dangshi Bolan* 6 (2006): 4–10.

Chen, Kuan-Hsing. *Asia as Method: Toward Deimperialization*. Durham, NC: Duke University Press, 2010.

Chiesi, Roberto, ed. *La rabbia di Pier Paolo Pasolini*. Bologna: Cineteca di Bologna, 2009.

———. "Lo sguardo di Pasolini: La forma della città, un film di Pier Paolo Pasolini e Paolo Brunatto." *Parol*. Accessed March 1, 2023. http://www.parol.it/articles/pasolini.htm.

Choe, Youngmin. *Tourist Distractions: Traveling and Feeling in Transnational Hallyu Cinema*. Durham, NC: Duke University Press, 2016.

Chow, Rey. "China as Documentary: Some Basic Questions (Inspired by Michelangelo Antonioni and Jia Zhangke)." *European Journal of Cultural Studies* 17, no. 1 (February 2014): 16–30.

Christiansen, Samantha, and Zachary Scarlett, eds. *The Third World in the Global 1960s*. Oxford: Berghahn, 2012.

Chu, Yingchi. *Chinese Documentaries: From Dogma to Polyphony*. London: Routledge, 2007.

Clark, Paul. *Chinese Cinema: Culture and Politics since 1949*. Cambridge: Cambridge University Press, 1988.

———. "Model Theatrical Works and the Remodelling of the Cultural Revolution." In *Art in Turmoil: The Chinese Cultural Revolution, 1966–76*, edited by Richard King, 167–87. Vancouver: UBC Press, 2010.

Clark, Steve, ed. *Travel Writing and Empire: Postcolonial Theory in Transit*. London: Zed Books, 1999.

Clifford, James. "Museums as Contact Zones." In *Routes: Travel and Translation in the Late Twentieth Century*, edited by James Clifford, 188–219. Cambridge, MA: Harvard University Press, 1997.

———. *The Predicament of Culture: Twentieth-Century Ethnography, Literature, and Art*. Cambridge, MA: Harvard University Press, 1988.

———. "Traveling Cultures." In *Cultural Studies*, edited by Lawrence Grossberg, Cary Nelson, and Paula Treichler, 96–116. Oxfordshire: Routledge, 1992.

Clò, Clarissa. "Mondo Exotica: Ethnography, Eros, and Exploitation in Italian Cinema of the 1960s and 1970s." In *Cinema of Exploration: Essays in Adventurous Film Practice*, edited by James Leo Cahill and Luca Caminati, 247–65. New York: Routledge, 2021.

Peretti, Luca, and Paola Scarnati. Con le mani libere. *Algeria, internazionalismo e cinema Italiano*. Rome: Effigi edizioni, 2023.

Costa, Antonio. "Effetto dipinto." *Cinema e Cinema* 54, no. 5 (1989): 37–48.

Cramer, Michael. "Rossellini's History Lessons." *New Left Review* 78 (November/December 2012): 115–34.

———. *Utopian Television: Rossellini, Watkins, and Godard Beyond Cinema*. Minneapolis: University of Minnesota Press, 2017.

Crawshaw, Carol, and John Urry. "Tourism and the Photographic Eye." In *Touring Cultures: Transformations of Travel and Theory*, edited by Chris Rojek and John Urry, 176–95. New York: Routledge: 1997.

Crouch, David, Rhona Jackson, and Felix Thompson, eds. *The Media and Tourist Imagination: Converging Cultures*. New York: Routledge, 2005.

Dainotto, Roberto. *Europe (in Theory)*. Durham, NC: Duke University Press, 2007.

Dalla Gassa, Marco. *Orient (to) Express: Film di viaggio, etno-grafie, teoria d'autore*. Milan: Mimesis, 2016.

Dalla Gassa, Marco, Federico Zecca, and Corrado Neri, eds. *Reinventing Mao: Maoisms and National Cinemas*. Special issue of *Cinéma & Cie* 18, no. 30 (2018).

Daney, Serge. "La remise en sceène." In *La rampe: Cahier critique 1970–1982*, 54–63. Paris: Gallimard, 1983.

———. "L'Écran du fantasme (Bazin et les bêtes)." In *La rampe: Cahier critique 1970–1982*, 34–38. Paris: Gallimard, 1983.

———. "The Screen of Fantasy." In *Rites of Realism: Essays on Corporeal Cinema*, edited by Ivone Margulies, translated by Mark A. Cohen, 32–41. Durham, NC: Duke University Press, 2003.

Daniélou, Alain. *The Way to the Labyrinth: Memories of East and West*. Translated by Marie-Claire Cournand. New York: New Directions Publishing, 1987.

Daulatzai, Sohail. *Fifty Years of "The Battle of Algiers": Past as Prologue*. Minneapolis: Minnesota University Press, 2016.

De Andrade, Mario, and Léonard Sainville, eds. *Letteratura negra*. Vols. 1–2. Rome: Editori Riuniti, 1961.

Debord, Guy. *The Society of the Spectacle*. Translated by Donald Nicholson-Smith. New York: Zone Books, [1967] 1995.

De Franceschi, Leonardo, ed. *L'Africa in Italia: Per una controstoria postcoloniale del cinema italiano*. Rome: Aracne, 2013.

———. *Lo schermo e lo spettro: Sguardi postcoloniali su Africa e afrodiscendenti*. Milan: Mimesis, 2017.

De Giuseppe, Massimo. "Il 'Terzo Mondo' in Italia: Trasformazioni di un concetto tra opinione pubblica, azione politica e mobilitazione civile (1955–1980)." *Ricerche di storia politica* 14, no. 1 (April 2011): 29–52.

De Groof, Matthias, ed. *Lumumba in the Arts*. Leuven: Leuven University Press, 2020.

de Lauretis, Teresa. "Language, Representation, Practice: Re-Reading Pasolini's Essays on Cinema." *Italian Quarterly* 21–22, no. 1 (Fall 1980–Winter 1981): 159–66.

Del Boca, Angelo. *Italiani, brava gente? Un mito duro a morire*. 5th ed. Venice: Neri Pozza, 2011.

Deleuze, Gilles. *Cinema 2: The Time-Image*. Translated by Hugh Tomlinson and Robert Galeta. Minneapolis: University of Minnesota Press, 1989.

de Luca, Tiago. *Planetary Cinema: Film, Media and the Earth*. Amsterdam: Amsterdam University Press, 2022.

de Luca, Tiago, and Nuno Barradas Jorge, eds. *Slow Cinema*. Edinburgh: Edinburgh University Press, 2016.

de Martino, Ernesto. *Magic: A Theory from the South*. Translated by Dorothy Louise Zinn. Chicago: HAU Books, 2015.

———. *Morte e pianto rituale nel mondo antico: Dal lamento funebre antico al pianto di Maria*. Edited by Marcello Massenzio. Turin: Giulio Einaudi, [1958] 2021.

De Santi, Pier Marco. "Il comunismo in contropiede: *La Muraglia Cinese*." In *Carlo Lizzani: un lungo viaggio nel cinema*, edited by Vito Zagarrio, 281–90. Venice: Marsilio, 2010.

Deplano, Valeria, and Alessandro Pes, eds. *Quel che resta dell'impero: La cultura coloniale degli italiani*. Milan: Mimesis, 2014.

Deprez, Camille. "The Films Division of India, 1948–1964: The Early Days and the Influence of the British Documentary Film Tradition." *Film History* 25, no. 3 (2013): 149–73.

Dickie, John. *Darkest Italy: The Nation and Stereotypes of the Mezzogiorno, 1860–1900*. New York: St. Martin's, 1999.

Dickinson, Kay. *Arab Cinema Travels: Transnational Syria, Palestine, Dubai and Beyond*. London: British Film Institute, 2016.

Djagalov, Rossen. *From Internationalism to Postcolonialism: Literature and Cinema between the Second and the Third Worlds*. Montreal: McGill-Queen's University Press, 2020.

Djagalov, Rossen, and Masha Salazkina. "Tashkent '68: A Cinematic Contact Zone." *Slavic Review* 75, no. 2 (Summer 2016): 279–98.

Duncan, Derek. "Italy's Postcolonial Cinema and Its Histories of Representation." *Italian Studies* 63, no. 2 (2008): 195–211.

Eaton, Mick, ed. *Anthropology, Reality, Cinema: The Films of Jean Rouch*. London: British Film Institute, 1979.

Eco, Umberto. "De Interpretatione, or the Difficulty of Being Marco Polo [On the Occasion of Antonioni's China Film]." *Film Quarterly* 30, no. 4 (Summer 1977): 8–12. https://doi.org/10.2307/1211577.

———. *The Open Work*. Translated by Anna Cancogni. Cambridge, MA: Harvard University Press, [1962] 1989.

Edwards, Dan. "Looking at / Looking in Antonioni's *Chung Kuo, Cina*: A Critical Reflection Across Three Viewings." *Senses of Cinema*, no. 74 (March 2015). http://www.sensesofcinema.com/2015/feature-articles/looking-at-looking-in-antonionis-chung-kuo-cina-a-critical-reflection-across-three-viewings/.

Elias, Amy J., and Christian Moraru, eds. *The Planetary Turn: Relationality and Geoaesthetics in the Twenty-First Century*. Evanston, IL: Northwestern University Press, 2015.

Enciclopedia del doppiaggio. "Pagina principale." Last modified February 20, 2020. http://www.enciclopediadeldoppiaggio.it/.

Eshun, Kodwo, and Ros Gray, eds. "Special Issue: The Militant Image: A Ciné-Geography." *Third Text* 25, no. 1 (2011): 1–138.

Fabian, Johannes. *Time and the Other: How Anthropology Makes Its Object*. New York: Columbia University Press, 1983.

Fanon, Frantz. *Les damnés de la terre*. Paris: François Maspero, 1961.

———. *The Wretched of the Earth*. Translated by Richard Philcox. New York: Grove, 2007.

Ferrante, Stefano. *La Cina non era vicina*. Milan: Sperling & Kupfer, 2008.

Fidotta, Giuseppe. "Ruling the Colonies with Sound: Documentary, Technology and Noise in *Cronache dell'Impero*." *Journal of Italian Cinema and Media Studies* 4, no. 1 (January 2016): 111–25.

Figge, Maja. "(Post)Koloniale Beziehungen: Fritz Langs Indienfilme Zwischen Abstraktion und Orientalismus." In *Total.—Universalismus und Partikularismus in Post_kolonialer Medientheorie*, edited by Ulrike Bergermann and Nanna Heidenreich, 189–206. Bielefeld: Transcript, 2015.

Fitzpatrick, Merrilyn. "China Images Abroad: The Representation of China in Western Documentary Films." *Australian Journal of Chinese Affairs* 9, no. 1 (January 1983): 87–98.

BIBLIOGRAPHY

Fogu, Claudio. *The Fishing Net and the Spider Web: Mediterranean Imaginaries and the Making of Italians*. London: Palgrave Macmillan, 2020.

Fortini, Franco. *Attraverso Pasolini*. Milan: Einaudi, 1993.

Foster, Hal. *The Return of the Real: The Avant-Garde at the End of the Century*. Cambridge, MA: MIT Press, 1996.

Fuller, Mia. "Wherever You Go, There You Are: Fascist Plans for the Colonial City of Addis Ababa and the Colonizing Suburb of EUR '42." *Journal of Contemporary History* 31, no. 2 (1996): 397–418.

Gadducci, Fabio, Leonardo Gori, and Sergio Lama. *Eccetto Topolino: Lo scontro culturale tra l fascismo e fumetti*. Battipaglia: Nicola Pesce Editore, 2011.

Galimberti, Jacopo. "Maoism, Dadaism and Mao-Dadaism in 1960s and 1970s Italy." In *Art, Global Maoism and the Chinese Cultural Revolution*, edited by Jacopo Galimberti, Noemi de Haro García, and Victoria H. F. Scott, 213–32. Manchester: Manchester University Press, 2019.

———. "A Third-Worldist Art? Germano Celant's Invention of Arte Povera." *Art History* 36, no. 2 (April 2013): 418–41.

Gallagher, Tag. *The Adventures of Roberto Rossellini: His Life and Films*. Boston: Da Capo, 1998.

Gandhi, Leela. *Affective Communities: Anticolonial Thought, Fin-de-Siècle Radicalism, and the Politics of Friendship*. Durham, NC: Duke University Press, 2006.

Garga, Bhagwan Das. *The Art of Cinema: An Insider's Journey through Fifty Years of Film History*. New York: Viking, 2005.

Gatto, Marco. "Una sineciosi ideologica: Pasolini, Fortini e la razionalità dialettica." *Annali d'Italianistica* 40, no. 1 (2022): 251–61.

Geertz, Clifford. *Works and Lives: The Anthropologist as Author*. Stanford, CA: Stanford University Press, 1988.

Ghatak, Ritwik. "Documentary: The Most Exciting Form of Cinema." In *Cinema and I*, 46–59. Kolkata: Ritwik Memorial Trust, 1987.

Ghosh, Bishnupriya. *Global Icons: Apertures to the Popular*. Durham: Duke University Press, 2011.

Giovacchini, Saverio, and Robert Sklar, eds. *Global Neorealism: The Transnational History of a Film Style*. Jackson: University Press of Mississippi, 2012.

Giuliani, Gaia, ed. *Il colore della nazione*. Milan: Le Monnier, 2016.

———. *Race, Nation and Gender in Modern Italy: Intersectional Representations in Visual Culture*. London: Palgrave Macmillan, 2019.

———. "Razza Cagna: *Mondo* Movies, the White Heterosexual Male Gaze, and the 1960s–1970s Imaginary of the Nation." *Modern Italy* 23, no. 4 (2018): 429–44.

Glynn, Ruth. "Porosity and Its Discontents: Approaching Naples in Critical Theory." *Cultural Critique* 107, no. 1 (Spring 2020): 63–98.

Godard, Jean-Luc. *Godard on Godard*. Edited by Jean Narboni and Tom Milne. Translated by Tom Milne. Boston: Da Capo, 1986.

Gokulsing, K. Moti, and Wimal Dissanayake. *Indian Popular Cinema: A Narrative of Cultural Change*. Stoke-on-Trent: Trentham Books, 2004.

Goodall, Mark. "Shockumentary Evidence: The Perverse Politics of the Mondo Film." In *Remapping World Cinema: Identity, Culture and Politics in Film*, edited by Stephanie Dennison and Song Hwee Lim, 118–28. London: Wallflower, 2006.

Gramsci, Antonio. *Tesi di Lione*. Rome: Sinapsi Editore, 2018.

Grechi, Giulia. *Decolonizzare il museo: Mostrazioni, pratiche artistiche, sguardi incarnati*. Milan: Mimesis, 2021.

Grechi, Giulia, and Viviana Gravano, eds. *Presente imperfetto. Eredità coloniali e immaginari razziali contemporanei*. Milan: Mimesis, 2016.

Greene, Naomi. *Pier Paolo Pasolini: Cinema as Heresy*. Princeton, NJ: Princeton University Press, 1990.

Greene, Shelleen. *Equivocal Subjects: Between Italy and Africa—Constructions of Racial and National Identity in the Italian Cinema*. London: Continuum, 2012.

Griffiths, Alison. *Wondrous Difference: Cinema, Anthropology, and Turn-of-the-Century Visual Culture*. New York: Columbia University Press, 2002.

Grimshaw, Anna, and Amanda Ravetz. *Observational Cinema: Anthropology, Film, and the Exploration of Social Life*. Bloomington: Indiana University Press, 2009.

Groupe pour la fondation de l'Union des Communistes de France marxiste-léniniste (UCFML) and Éditions Maspero. *Le livre des paysans pauvres: 5 années de travail maoïste dans une campagne française*. Paris: Maspero, 1976.

Guha, Malini. *From Empire to the World: Migrant London and Paris in the Cinema*. Edinburgh: Edinburgh University Press, 2015.

Gunning, Tom. "Before Documentary: Early Nonfiction Films and the 'View' Aesthetic." In *Uncharted Territory: Essays on Early Nonfiction Film*, edited by Daan Hertogs and Nico de Klerk, 9–25. Amsterdam: Filmmuseum, 1997.

———. *The Films of Fritz Lang: Allegories of Vision and Modernity*. London: British Film Institute, 2000.

Hadouchi, Olivier. "'African Culture Will Be Revolutionary or Will Not Be': William Klein's Film of the First Pan-African Festival of Algiers (1969)." *Third Text* 25, no. 1 (2011): 117–28.

Haski, Pierre. "Kung-fu et cul politique: Dans les années 70, mashups jubilatoires." *Rue89/L'Obs*, March 20, 2015. http://www.nouvelobs.com/rue89/rue89-cinema/20150320.RUE8342/kung-fu-et-cul-politique-dans-les-annees-70-mashups-jubilatoires.html.

Hatton, Celia. "When China Woke Up to Wham!" *BBC News*, April 1, 2015. http://www.bbc.com/news/blogs-china-blog-32229596.

Hay, James. "Placing Cinema, Fascism, and the Nation in a Diagram of Italian Modernity." In *Re-Viewing Fascism: Italian Cinema, 1922–1943*, edited by Jacqueline Reich and Piero Garofalo, 105–38. Bloomington: Indiana University Press, 2002.

———. *Popular Film Culture in Fascist Italy: The Passing of the Rex*. Bloomington: Indiana University Press, 1987.

Hayot, Eric. *Chinese Dreams: Pound, Brecht, Tel Quel*. Ann Arbor: University of Michigan Press, 2004.

Hegel, G. W. Friedrich. *The Philosophy of History*. Mineola, NY: Dover, [1837] 1956.

Herman, Jean. "Rossellini tourne India '57." *Cahiers du Cinéma* 73 (July 1957): 1–9.

Hoffman, Marcelo. *Militant Acts: The Role of Investigations in Radical Political Struggles*. Albany: SUNY Press, 2019.

Hollander, Paul. *Political Pilgrims: Travels of Western Intellectuals to the Soviet Union, China, and Cuba 1928–1978*. Oxford: Oxford University Press, 1981.

Hom, Stephanie Malia. *Empire's Mobius Strip: Historical Echoes in Italy's Crisis of Migration and Detention*. Ithaca, NY: Cornell University Press, 2019.

Sun, Hongyun. "Two Chinas? Joris Ivens' Yukong and Antonioni's China." *Studies in Documentary Film* 3, no. 1 (2009): 45–59.

Houcke, Anne-Violaine. "Affinités électives entre Cecilia Mangini et Pier Paolo Pasolini." *Trafic* 89, no. 1 (Spring 2014): 52–62.

———. "Ignoti, banditi, dimenticati: Le (hors-)champ de l'Italie (post-)fasciste/la fracture interne." In *Eisenstein, leçons mexicaines: Cinéma, anthropologie, archéologie dans le mouvement des arts*, edited by Laurence Schifano and Antonio Somaini, 263–78. Nanterre: Presses Universitaires de Paris Ouest, 2016.

Hourmant, François. *Au pays de l'avenir radieux: Voyages des intellectuels français en URSS, à Cuba et en Chine populaire*. Paris: Aubier, 2000.

Hoveyda, Fereydoun, and Jacques Rivette. "Entretien avec Roberto Rossellini." *Cahiers du Cinéma* 94 (April 1959): 1–11.

Huggan, Graham. *The Postcolonial Exotic: Marketing the Margins*. London: Routledge, 2001.

Hughes, John. "Recent Rossellini." *Film Comment* 10, no. 4 (July–August 1974): 16–21.

Humphrey, Daniel. *Archaic Modernism: Queer Poetics in the Cinema of Pier Paolo Pasolini*. Detroit: Wayne State University Press, 2020.

Ivens, Joris, Marceline Loridan-Ivens, Jean-Marie Doublet, and Jean-Pierre Sergent. *Comment Yukong déplaça les montagnes: Introduction au voyage*. Paris: Imprimerie S.I.M, 1976.

Jaikumar, Priya. *Where Histories Reside: India as Filmed Space*. Durham, NC: Duke University Press, 2019.

Jameson, Fredric. *The Prison-House of Language: A Critical Account of Structuralism and Russian Formalism*. Princeton, NJ: Princeton University Press, 1972.

Jian, Guo, Yongyi Song, and Yuan Zhou. *Historical Dictionary of the Chinese Cultural Revolution*. Lanham: Scarecrow Press, 2006.

Jin, Yihong. "Rethinking the 'Iron Girls': Gender and Labour during the Chinese Cultural Revolution." *Gender & History* 18, no. 3, translated by Kimberley Ens Manning and Lianyun Chu (November 2006): 613–34.

Kahin, George McTurnan. *The Asian-African Conference: Bandung, Indonesia, April 1955*. Ithaca, NY: Cornell University Press, 1955.

Kalter, Christoph. *The Discovery of the Third World: Decolonization and the Rise of the New Left in France, c.1950–1976*. Cambridge: Cambridge University Press, 2016.

Kaplan, Caren. *Questions of Travel: Postmodern Discourses of Displacement*. Durham, NC: Duke University Press, 1996.

King, Homay. *Lost in Translation: Orientalism, Cinema, and the Enigmatic Signifier*. Durham, NC: Duke University Press, 2010.

Kracauer, Siegfried. *Theory of Film: The Redemption of Physical Reality*. Princeton, NJ: Princeton University Press, [1960] 1997.

Kwon, Nayoung Aimee, Takushi Odagiri, and Moonim Baek, eds. *Theorizing Colonial Cinema: Reframing Production, Circulation, and Consumption of Film in Asia*. Bloomington: Indiana University Press, 2022.

Laikwan, Pang. *The Art of Cloning: Creative Production during China's Cultural Revolution*. London: Verso, 2017.

Landecker, Hannah. "Microcinematography and the History of Science and Film." *Isis* 97, no. 1 (March 2006): 121–32.

Landsberger, Stefan R. "The Deification of Mao: Religious Imagery and Practices during the Cultural Revolution and Beyond." In *China's Great Proletarian Cultural Revolution: Master Narratives and Post-Mao Counternarratives*, edited by Woei Lien Chong, 139–84. Lanham: Rowman & Littlefield, 2002.

Landy, Marcia. "Genre, Politics, and the Fascist Subject in the Cinema of Italy (1922–1945)." In *A Companion to Italian Cinema*, edited by Frank Burke, 65–81. Hoboken, NJ: John Wiley & Sons, 2017.

Leavitt, Charles L. *Italian Neorealism: A Cultural History*. Toronto: University of Toronto Press, 2020.

Lee, Christopher J., ed. *Making a World after Empire: The Bandung Moment and Its Political Afterlives*. Athens: Ohio University Press, 2010.

Leese, Daniel. *Mao Cult: Rhetoric and Ritual in China's Cultural Revolution*. Cambridge: Cambridge University Press, 2011.

Le Sueur, James D. *Uncivil War: Intellectuals and Identity Politics during the Decolonization of Algeria*. 2nd ed. Lincoln: University of Nebraska Press, 2005.

Leung, Man-tat Terence. "Struggling between Two Fronts: Godard, Dziga Vertov Group and the Ethical Predicaments of Post-1968 French Maoism." *Cinéma & Cie: Film and Media Studies Journal* 18, no. 30 (2018): 21–40.

BIBLIOGRAPHY

Li, Jie. *Utopian Ruins: A Memorial Museum of the Mao Era*. Durham, NC: Duke University Press, 2020.

Licheri, Paolo. *Rossellini dal grande al piccolo schermo: Per una televisione tra divulgazione e spettacolo*. Naples: Liguori Editore, 2016.

Limbrick, Peter. *Arab Modernism as World Cinema: The Films of Moumen Smihi*. Oakland: University of California Press, 2020.

————. "Pasolini in Morocco: Cinematic Space and the Poetics and Politics of the Reprise." Paper presented at PPP/RRR: Pier Paolo Pasolini/Riprese Reprises Retakes, Montreal, September 28–30, 2022.

Lisle, Debbie. *The Global Politics of Contemporary Travel Writing*. Cambridge: Cambridge University Press, 2006.

Liu, Xin. "China's Reception of Michelangelo Antonioni's Chung Kuo." *Journal of Italian Cinema & Media Studies* 2, no. 1 (March 2014): 23–40.

————. "Italian Travelogues on Maoist China (1950s–1970s) through the Lens of Mobilities Studies." In *Cultural Mobilities between China and Italy*, edited by Valentina Pedone and Gaoheng Zhang, 171–99. London: Palgrave Macmillan, 2023.

Lombardi, Giancarlo, and Christian Uva, eds. *Italian Political Cinema: Public Life, Imaginary, and Identity in Contemporary Italian Film*. New York: Peter Lang, 2016.

Lombardi-Diop, Cristina, and Caterina Romeo. "Italy's Postcolonial 'Question': Views from the Southern Frontier of Europe." *Postcolonial Studies* 18, no. 4 (October 2015): 367–83.

————, eds. *L'Italia postcoloniale*. Milan: Mondadori, 2014.

Love, Rachel E. "Anti-Fascism, Anticolonialism and Anti-Self: The Life of Giovanni Pirelli and the Work of the Centro Frantz Fanon." *Interventions: International Journal of Postcolonial Studies* 17, no. 3 (2015): 343–59.

Lovell, Julia. *Maoism: A Global History*. New York: Vintage Books, 2019.

Lumley, Robert. *States of Emergency: Cultures of Revolt in Italy from 1968 to 1978*. London: Verso, 1990.

Lupton, Catherine. *Chris Marker: Memories of the Future*. London: Reaktion Books, 2005.

MacCannell, Dean. *The Tourist: A New Theory of the Leisure Class*. Oakland: University of California, [1976] 1999.

Macciocchi, Maria Antonietta. *Daily Life in Revolutionary China*. Translated by Alfred Ehrenfeld and Frank Kehl. New York: Monthly Review Press, 1972.

————. *Dalla Cina: Dopo la rivoluzione culturale*. Milan: Feltrinelli, 1971.

MacDougall, David. *Transcultural Cinema*. Edited by Lucien Taylor. Princeton, NJ: Princeton University Press, 1998.

MacKay, John. "Disorganized Noise: *Enthusiasm* and the Ear of the Collective." *KinoKultura* 7 (January 2005). http://www.kinokultura.com/articles/jan05-mackay.html.

Maggi, Armando. "Pasolini's *The Walls of Sana'a*: Its Sublime Ruins, and the Demands of Its Images." *Studi Pasoliniani* 14, no. 1 (2020): 11–24.

Mahler, Anne Garland. *From the Tricontinental to the Global South: Race, Radicalism, and Transnational Solidarity.* Durham, NC: Duke University Press, 2018.

———. "Global South." *Oxford Bibliographies*: Literary and Critical Theory. Oxford University Press. Last modified October 25, 2017. https://www .oxfordbibliographies.com/display/document/obo-9780190221911/obo -9780190221911-0055.xml.

Mancini, Michele, and Giuseppe Perrella, eds. *Pier Paolo Pasolini: Corpi e luoghi.* Rome: Theorema, 1981.

Mancosu, Gianmarco. *Vedere l'impero: L'Istituto Luce e il colonialismo fascista.* Milan: Mimesis, 2022.

Manganelli, Giorgio. *Cina e altri Orienti.* Milan: Adelphi, 2014.

Maraschin, Donatella. *Pasolini: Cinema e antropologia.* London: Peter Lang, 2014.

———. "Ricerche sul campo nel periodo 1950–60: Pasolini antropologo?" *Italianist* 24, no. 2 (2004): 169–207.

Marinelli, Maurizio. *La Cina dei viaggiatori: Lettere, diari, descrizioni di viaggio degli occidentali in Cina tra '800 e '900; Materiali esistenti nelle biblioteche di Bologna.* Bologna: Il Nove, 1994.

Mariniello, Silvestra. "Temporality and the Culture of Intervention." *Boundary 2* 22, no. 3 (Autumn 1995): 111–39.

Marx, Karl. "The British Rule in India." *New-York Daily Tribune,* June 10, 1853.

McGrath, Jason. "Cultural Revolution Model Opera Films and the Realist Tradition in Chinese Cinema." *Opera Quarterly* 26, nos. 2–3 (Spring–Summer 2010): 343–76.

Mende, Tibor. *Conversations with Mr. Nehru.* London: Secker & Warburg, 1956.

Mennel, Barbara. "Returning Home: The Orientalist Spectacle of Fritz Lang's *Der Tiger von Eschnapur* and *Das Indische Grabmal.*" In *Framing the Fifties: Cinema in a Divided Germany,* edited by John Davidson and Sabine Hake, 28–43. Oxford: Berghahn Books, 2009.

Merjian, Ara H. *Against the Avant-Garde: Pier Paolo Pasolini, Contemporary Art, and Neocapitalism.* Chicago: University of Chicago Press, 2020.

Mestman, Mariano. "*L'ora dei forni* e il cinema politico italiano prima e dopo il '68." *Imago: Studi di cinema e media* 15, no. 1 (2017): 37–453.

Mezzadra, Sandro, and Federico Rahola. "The Postcolonial Condition: A Few Notes of the Quality of Historical Time in the Global Present." *Postcolonial Text* 2, no.1 (2006): 36–54.

Mignolo, Walter D. *Local Histories/Global Designs: Coloniality, Subaltern Knowledges, and Border Thinking.* Princeton, NJ: Princeton University Press, 2000.

BIBLIOGRAPHY

Min, Anchee, Duo Duo, and Stefan R. Landsberg. *Chinese Propaganda Posters*. Los Angeles: Taschen America, 2011.

Minami, Kazushi. "'How Could I Not Love You?': Transnational Feminism and US-Chinese Relations during the Cold War." *Journal of Women's History* 31, no. 4 (Winter 2019): 12–36.

Mirzoeff, Nicholas. *The Right to Look: A Counterhistory of Visuality*. Durham, NC: Duke University Press, 2011.

Moe, Nelson. *The View from Vesuvius: Italian Culture and the Southern Question*. Oakland: University of California Press, 2006.

Moravia, Alberto. *The Red Book and the Great Wall: An Impression of Mao's China*. Translated by Ronald Strom. London: Secker and Warburg, 1968.

Moro, Margherita. "Roberto Rossellini tra Cile e Brasile." *Mosaico Italiano* 20, no. 214 (2022): 10–15.

Moynagh, Maureen. *Political Tourism and Its Texts*. Toronto: University of Toronto Press, 2008.

Mulay, Vijaya. *From Rajahs and Yogis to Gandhi and Beyond: Images of India in International Films of the Twentieth Century*. Kolkata: Seagull Books, 2010.

Mundell, Ian. "'Rouch Isn't Here, He Has Left': A Report on Building Bridges: The Cinema of Jean Rouch." *Senses of Cinema*, Festival Reports no. 34, February 2005. http://www.sensesofcinema.com/2005/festival-reports /jean_rouch_conference/.

Nagib, Lúcia. *Realist Cinema as World Cinema: Non-Cinema, Intermedial Passages, Total Cinema*. Amsterdam: Amsterdam University Press, 2020.

Naldini, Nico. *Pasolini, una vita*. Milan: Einaudi, 1989.

Nash, Mark, ed. *Red Africa: Affective Communities and the Cold War*. London: Black Dog Press, 2016.

Nehru, Jawaharlal. *The Discovery of India*. New Delhi: Penguin Books India, 2004.

Niccolai, Roberto. *Quando la Cina era vicina: La rivoluzione culturale e la sinistra extraparlamentare italiana negli anni '60 e '70*. Rome: BFS Edizioni, 1998.

Nijland, Dirk. "Jean Rouch: A Builder of Bridges." In *Building Bridges: The Cinema of Jean Rouch*, edited by Joram ten Brink, 21–35. London: Wallflower Press, 2007.

O'Healy, Aine. *Migrant Anxieties: Italian Cinema in a Transnational Frame*. Bloomington: Indiana University Press, 2019.

O'Leary, Alan. *The Battle of Algiers*. Milan: Mimesis, 2019.

———. "The Phenomenology of the *Cinepanettone*." *Italian Studies* 66, no. 3 (2011): 431–43.

———. "What Is Italian Cinema?" *California Italian Studies* 7, no. 1 (2017): 1–26.

Osborne, Richard. "India on Film, 1939–1945." In *Film and the End of Empire*, edited by Lee Grieveson and Colin MacCabe, 55–72. London: British Film Institute, 2011.

Ottolini, Tullio. "Giovanni Pirelli e la guerra d'indipendenza algerina: Tra attivismo intellettuale e soutien concreto." In *Giovanni Pirelli intellettuale del Novecento*, edited by Mariamargherita Scotti, 85–110. Milan: Mimesis, 2016.

Padgaonkar, Dileep. *Under Her Spell: Roberto Rossellini in India*. New Delhi: Penguin Viking, 2008.

Padovani, Cinzia. *A Fatal Attraction: Public Television and Politics in Italy*. Lanham, MD: Rowman & Littlefield, 2004.

Païni, Dominique, Alain Bergala, and M. Luisa Pacelli. *Lo sguardo di Michelangelo Antonioni e le arti*. Ferrara: Fondazione Ferrara Arte, 2013.

Palomino, Pablo. "On the Disadvantages of 'Global South' for Latin American Studies." *Journal of World Philosophies* 4, no. 2 (Winter 2019): 22–39.

Panvini, Guido. "Third Worldism in Italy." In *Marxist Historical Cultures and Social Movements during the Cold War: Case Studies from Germany, Italy and Other Western European States*, edited by Stefan Berger and Christoph Cornelissen, 289–308. London: Palgrave Macmillan, 2019.

Pasolini, Pier Paolo. "Bandung Man/L'uomo di Bandung." In *The Scandal of Self-Contradiction: Pasolini's Multistable Subjectivities, Traditions, Geographies*, edited by Luca Di Blasi, Manuele Gragnolati, and Christoph F. E. Holzhey, 279–301. Vienna: Turia + Kant, 2012.

———. "Frammento alla morte/To Death: A Fragment." In *The Selected Poetry of Pier Paolo Pasolini*, edited and translated by Stephen Sartarelli, 295–98. Chicago: University of Chicago Press, 2014.

———. *Heretical Empiricism*. Edited by Louise K. Barnett. Translated by Ben Lawton and Louise K. Barnett. Bloomington: Indiana University Press, 1988.

———. "Il teatro di parola." In *Saggi sulla politica e sulla società*. Edited by Walter Siti, 1521–25. Milan: Mondadori, 1999.

———. "La Guinea." In *Poesia in forma di rosa*, 13–19. Milan: Garzanti, 1964.

———. *Le belle bandiere: Dialoghi 1960–65*. Rome: Editori Riuniti, 1978.

———. *Lettere 1955–1975*. Milan: Giulio Einaudi, 1988.

———. "L'uomo di Bandung." In *Tutte le poesie*, edited by Walter Siti, vol. 1, 1305–13. Milan: Mondadori, 2003.

———. *Lutheran Letters*. Translated by Stuart Hood. Manchester, UK: Carcanet Press, 1987.

———. "Mamma Roma." In *Saggi sulla politica e sulla società*, edited by Walter Siti, 1315–19. Milan: Mondadori, 1999.

———. *Per il cinema*. Milan: Mondadori, 2001.

———. "Profezia/Prophecy." In *The Selected Poetry of Pier Paolo Pasolini*, edited and translated by Stephen Sartarelli, 362–75. Chicago: University of Chicago Press, 2014.

———. *Saggi sulla letteratura e sull'arte*. Milan: Mondadori, 1999.

BIBLIOGRAPHY

————. *Saggi sulla politica e sulla società*. Milan: Mondadori, 1999.

————. "Studio sulla rivoluzione antropologica in Italia." In *Scritti corsari*, 38–45. Milan: Garzanti, 1975.

Patriarca, Silvana. *Italian Vices: Nation and Character from the Risorgimento to the Republic*. Cambridge: Cambridge University Press, 2010.

————. *Race in Post-Fascist Italy: "War Children" and the Color of the Nation*. Cambridge: Cambridge University Press, 2022.

Perniola, Ivelise. "Documentari fuori regime." In *Storia del cinema italiano*, edited by Orio Caldiron, 372–80. Venice: Marsilio, 2006.

Peterson, Jennifer Lynn. *Education in the School of Dreams: Travelogues and Early Nonfiction Film*. Durham, NC: Duke University Press, 2013.

Pezzini, Isabella. "Asia teatro dell'immaginario: Viaggi letterari, avventure, gusto e divulgazione fra ottocento e novecento." In *L'oriente: Storie di viaggiatori italiani*, edited by Gino Benzoni, 38–55. Milan: Nuovo Banco Ambrosiano, 1985.

Pinkus, Karen. *Clocking Out: The Machinery of Life in 1960s Italian Cinema*. Minneapolis: Minnesota University Press, 2020.

————. "Empty Spaces: Decolonization in Italy." In *A Place in the Sun: Africa in Italian Colonial Culture from Post-Unification to the Present*, edited by Patrizia Palumbo, 299–320. Berkeley: University of California Press, 2003.

Pitassio, Francesco. *Neorealist Film Culture, 1945–1954: Rome, Open Cinema*. Amsterdam: Amsterdam University Press, 2019.

Piva, Anna. "Pasolini traduttore di Eschilo: Appunti sull'Orestiade del 1960." *Studi Pasoliniani* 14, no. 1 (2020): 37–50.

Ponzanesi, Sandra. "Beyond the Black Venus: Colonial Sexual Politics and Contemporary Visual Practices." In *Italian Colonialism: Legacy and Memory*, edited by Jacqueline Andall and Derek Duncan, 165–89. Oxford: Peter Lang, 2005.

Ponzanesi, Sandra, and Adriano José Habed, eds. *Postcolonial Intellectuals in Europe: Critics, Artists, Movements, and Their Publics*. London: Rowman & Littlefield International, 2020.

Prashad, Vijay. *Poorer Nations: A Possible History of the Global South*. London: Verso, 2013.

Pratt, Mary Louise. *Imperial Eyes: Travel Writing and Transculturation*. Oxfordshire: Routledge, 1992.

Quaresima, Leonardo. "'Making Love on the Shores of the River Po': Antonioni's Documentaries." In *Antonioni: Centenary Essays*, edited by Laura Rascaroli and John David Rhodes, 115–33. London: BFI, 2011.

Raban, Jonathan. *For Love & Money: Writing, Reading, Travelling, 1969–1987*. London: Collins Harvill, 1987.

Rahola, Federico. *Zone definitivamente temporanee: I luoghi dell'umanità in eccesso*. Verona: Ombre Corte, 2005.

Raizen, Karen T. "Voicing the Popular in *Appunti per un'Orestiade Africana*." In *Pier Paolo Pasolini, Framed and Unframed: A Thinker for the Twenty-First Century*, edited by Luca Peretti and Karen T. Raizen, 79–97. London: Bloomsbury, 2018.

Rancière, Jacques. "Democracy Means Equality." *Radical Philosophy* 82, no. 1 (March/April 1997): 29–35.

———. *The Emancipated Spectator*. Translated by Gregory Elliott. London: Verso, 2011.

Rascaroli, Laura. *The Personal Camera: Subjective Cinema and the Essay Film*. London: Wallflower, 2009.

Rascaroli, Laura, and John David Rhodes, eds. *Antonioni: Centenary Essays*. London: British Film Institute/Palgrave Macmillan, 2011.

Rayns, Tony. "Model Citizen: Bernardo Bertolucci on Location in China." *Film Comment* 23, no. 6 (November–December 1987): 31–36.

Reill, Dominique Kirchner. "Partisan Legacies and Anti-Imperialist Ambitions: The Little Red Book in Italy and Yugoslavia." In *Mao's Little Red Book: A Global History*, edited by Alexander C. Cook, 185–205. Cambridge: Cambridge University Press, 2014.

"Renmin Ribao" Commentator. "A Vicious Motive, Despicable Tricks: A Criticism of M. Antonioni's Anti-China Film 'China.'" *Peking Review* 17, no. 5 (February 1, 1974): 7–10. https://www.massline.org/PekingReview/PR1974/PR1974-05h.htm.

Renov, Michael. *The Subject of Documentary*. Minneapolis: University of Minnesota Press, 2004.

Resmini, Mauro. *Italian Political Cinema: Figures of the Long '68*. Minneapolis: University of Minnesota Press, 2023.

Restivo, Angelo. *The Cinema of Economic Miracles: Visuality and Modernization in the Italian Art Film*. Durham, NC: Duke University Press, 2002.

Rhodes, John David. *Stupendous, Miserable City: Pasolini's Rome*. Minneapolis: Minnesota University Press, 2007.

Rohdie, Sam. *The Passion of Pier Paolo Pasolini*. Bloomington: Indiana University Press, 1996.

Rondolino, Gianni. *Roberto Rossellini*. Turin: UTET Libreria, 2006.

Rony, Fatimah Tobing. *The Third Eye: Race, Cinema, and Ethnographic Spectacle*. Durham, NC: Duke University Press, 1996.

Ross, Kristin. *May '68 and Its Afterlives*. Chicago: University of Chicago Press, 2002.

Rossellini, Roberto. "Il mio dopoguerra." *Cinema Nuovo* 70 (November 1955): 346–51.

———. *Il mio metodo: Scritti e interviste*. Edited by Adriano Aprà. Venice: Marsilio Editori, 1987.

————. *My Method: Writings and Interviews*. Edited by Adriano Aprà. Venice: Marsilio Editori, 1992.

Rouch, Jean. *Ciné-Ethnography*. Edited and translated by Steven Feld. Minneapolis: University of Minnesota Press, 2003.

Rouch, Jean, and Roberto Rossellini. "La ricerca della verità." In *Roberto Rossellini: Il cinema, la televisione, la storia, la critica*, edited by Edoardo Bruno, 39–51. Sanremo: Casabianca, 1980.

Rouch, Jean, and Ousmane Sembène. "A Historic Confrontation between Jean Rouch and Ousmane Sembène in 1965: 'You Look at Us as If We Were Insects.'" In *Modern Art in Africa, Asia and Latin America: An Introduction to Global Modernisms*, edited by Elaine O'Brien, Everlyn Nicodemus, Melissa Chiu, Benjamin Genocchio, Mary K. Coffey, and Roberto Tejada, 94–97. Hoboken, NJ: Wiley Blackwell, 2013.

Roy, Srirupa. "Moving Pictures: The Films Division of India and the Visual Practices of the Nation-State." In *Beyond Belief: India and the Politics of Postcolonial Nationalism*, 32–65. Durham, NC: Duke University Press, 2007.

Rozsa, Irene. "On the Edge of the Screen: Film Culture and Practices of Noncommercial Cinema in Cuba (1948–1966)." PhD diss., Concordia University, 2020.

Ruberto, Laura E., and Kristi M. Wilson, eds. *Italian Neorealism and Global Cinema*. Detroit: Wayne State University Press, 2007.

Rumble, Patrick. "Contamination and Excess: *I racconti di Canterbury* as a 'struttura da farsi.'" In *Pasolini Old and New: Surveys and Studies*, edited by Zygmunt G. Barański, 345–62. Dublin: Four Courts Press, 1999.

————. "Ideas vs. Odors of India: Third Worlds in Moravia and Pasolini, with a Post-Script on Manganelli." In *Scrittori, tendenze letterarie e conflitto delle poetiche in Italia (1960–1990)*, edited by Massimo Ciavolella, 193–204. Ravenna: Longo, 1993.

Ruoff, Jeffrey, ed. *Virtual Voyages: Cinema and Travel*. Durham, NC: Duke University Press, 2006.

Russell, Catherine. *Experimental Ethnography: The Work of Film in the Age of Video*. Durham, NC: Duke University Press, 1999.

Rutherford, Jonathan. "Interview with Homi Bhabha: The Third Space." In *Identity: Community, Culture, Difference*, edited by Jonathan Rutherford, 207–21. London: Lawrence and Wishart, 1990.

Said, Edward. *Culture and Imperialism*. New York: Vintage, 1994.

————. *Orientalism*. New York: Vintage, 1978.

————. "Traveling Theory." In *The World, the Text, and the Critic*, 226–47. Cambridge, MA: Harvard University Press, 1983.

Salazkina, Masha. "World Cinema as Method." *Canadian Journal of Film Studies* 29, no. 2 (Fall 2020): 10–24.

BIBLIOGRAPHY

———. *World Socialist Cinema: Alliances, Affinities, and Solidarities in the Global Cold War.* Oakland: University of California Press, 2023.

Sartre, Jean-Paul. "Les grenouilles qui demandent un roi." *Situations vol 5, Colonialisme et néo-colonialisme,* 89–144. Paris: Gallimard, 1964.

Schneider, Jane, ed. *Italy's "Southern Question": Orientalism in One Country.* Oxford: Berg, 1998.

"Screening of 'China' Cancelled." *Museum of Modern Art* 139, December 22, 1972. https://www.moma.org/docs/press_archives/4928/releases/MOMA_1972_0157_139.pdf.

Shedde, Meenakshi, and Vinzenz Hediger, "Come On, Baby, Be My Tiger: Inventing India on the German Screen in *Der Tiger von Eschnapur* and *Das indische Grabmal.*" In *Import Export: Cultural Transfer/India, Germany, Austria,* edited by Angelika Fitz, Merle Kröger, Alexandra Schneider, and Dorothee Wenner, 99–107. Berlin: Parthas, 2005.

Shepard, Todd. *The Invention of Decolonization: The Algerian War and the Remaking of France.* Ithaca, NY: Cornell University Press, 2006.

Sieg, Katrin. *Ethnic Drag: Performing Race, Nation, Sexuality in West Germany.* Ann Arbor: University of Michigan Press, 2002.

Sillanpoa, Wallace P. "Pasolini's Gramsci." *MLN* 96, no. 1 (January 1981): 120–37.

Sorace, Christian. "Aesthetics." In *Afterlives of Chinese Communism,* edited by Christian Sorace, Ivan Franceschini, and Nicholas Loubere, 11–16. Canberra: Anu Press, 2019.

Sørenssen, Bjørn. "Digital Video and Alexander Astruc's Caméra-Stylo: The New Avant-Garde in Documentary Realized?" *Studies in Documentary Film* 2, no. 1 (March 2008): 47–59.

Soscia, Danilo, ed. *In Cina: Il grand tour degli italiani verso il centro del mondo 1904–1999.* Pisa: ETS, 2010.

Spivak, Gayatri Chakravorty. "Can the Subaltern Speak?" In *Can the Subaltern Speak? Reflections on the History of an Idea,* edited by Rosalind Morris, 21–78. New York: Columbia University Press, 2010.

Srivastava, Neelam. "Frantz Fanon in Italy: Or, Historicizing Fanon." *Interventions: International Journal of Postcolonial Studies* 17, no. 3 (2015): 309–28.

———. *Italian Colonialism and Resistances to Empire, 1930–1970.* London: Palgrave Macmillan, 2018.

Stark, Trevor. "'Cinema in the Hands of the People': Chris Marker, the Medvedkin Group, and the Potential of Militant Film." *October* 139, no. 1 (Winter 2012): 117–50.

Steimatsky, Noa. *Italian Locations: Reinhabiting the Past in Postwar Cinema.* Minneapolis: University of Minnesota Press, 2008.

Stjernholm, Emil. "Visions of Post-Independence India in Arne Sucksdorff's Documentaries." *BioScope: South Asian Screen Studies* 8, no. 1 (June 2017): 81–102.

BIBLIOGRAPHY

Stoler, Ann Laura, ed. *Imperial Debris: On Ruins and Ruination*. Durham, NC: Duke University Press, 2013.

Strain, Ellen. *Public Places, Private Journeys: Ethnography, Entertainment, and the Tourist Gaze*. New Brunswick, NJ: Rutgers University Press, 2003.

Subini, Tomaso. "Pasolini e la Pro Civitate Christiana: Un carteggio inedito." *Bianco & Nero* 64, nos. 1–3 (2003): 253–62.

Surugue, Bernard. "Jean Rouch and the Sacred Cattle." In *Building Bridges: The Cinema of Jean Rouch*, edited by Joram ten Brink, 9–20. London: Wallflower Press, 2007.

Sutoris, Peter. *Visions of Development: Films Division of India and the Imagination of Progress, 1948–75*. Oxford: Oxford University Press, 2016.

Thomas, Rosie. *Bombay before Bollywood: Film City Fantasies*. Albany: SUNY Press, 2015.

Todorov, Tzvetan. *On Human Diversity: Nationalism, Racism, and Exoticism in French Thought*. Cambridge, MA: Harvard University Press, 1993.

Tosi, Virgilio. *Cinema before Cinema: The Origins of Scientific Cinematography*. London: British Universities Film & Video Council, 2005.

Trento, Giovanna. *Pasolini e l'Africa, l'Africa di Pasolini: Panmeridionalismo e rappresentazioni dell'Africa postcoloniale*. Milan: Mimesis, 2010.

——— . "Pier Paolo Pasolini in Eritrea: Subalternity, Grace, Nostalgia, and the 'Rediscovery' of Italian Colonialism in the Horn of Africa." In *Postcolonial Italy: Challenging National Homogeneity*, edited by Cristina Lombardi-Diop and Caterina Romeo, 139–55. London: Palgrave Macmillan, 2012.

Truffaut, François. "Rossellini: Je ne suis pas le père du néoréalisme." *Arts*, June 1954, np.

——— . "Une certaine tendance du cinéma français." *Cahiers Du Cinéma* 31 (January 1954): 15–29.

Urbansky, Sören. "The Unfathomable Foe. Constructing the Enemy in the Sino-Soviet Borderlands, ca. 1969–1982." *Journal of Modern European History* 10, no. 2 (May 2012): 255–79.

Uva, Christian. *L'immagine politica: Forme del contropotere tra cinema, video e fotografia nell'Italia degli anni Settanta*. Milan: Mimesis, 2015.

Vázquez-Arroyo, Antonio Y. "Universal History Disavowed: On Critical Theory and Postcolonialism." *Postcolonial Studies* 11, no. 4 (2008): 451–73.

Verdicchio, Pasquale. "Colonialism as a 'Structure That Wants to Be Another Structure.'" In *The Savage Father*, by Pier Paolo Pasolini, 51–64. Translated by Pasquale Verdicchio. Hamilton, ON: Guernica, 1999.

Verdone, Mario. *Roberto Rossellini*. Paris: Seghers, 1963.

Vernet, Marc. "The Look at the Camera." *Cinema Journal* 28, no. 2 (Winter 1989): 48–63.

"A Vicious Motive, Despicable Tricks: A Criticism of M. Antonioni's Anti-China Film *China*." *Chinese Law & Government* 7, no. 3 (1974): 110–20.

Walker, Gavin. "The Postcolonial and the Politics of the Outside: Return(s) of the National Question in Marxist Theory." *Viewpoint Magazine*, February 1, 2018. https://www.viewpointmag.com/2018/02/01/postcolonial-politics-outside-returns-national-question-marxist-theory/.

———. "Postcoloniality in Translation: Historicities of the Present." *Postcolonial Studies* 14, no. 1 (February 2011): 111–26.

Wang, Ban. *The Sublime Figure of History: Aesthetics and Politics in Twentieth-Century China*. Redwood, CA: Stanford University Press, 1997.

Wark, McKenzie. "Pasolini: Sexting the World." *Public Seminar*, July 15, 2015. https://publicseminar.org/2015/07/pasolini-sexting-the-world/.

Waugh, Thomas. *The Conscience of Cinema: The Works of Joris Ivens 1912–1989*. Amsterdam: Amsterdam University Press, 2017.

———. *The Right to Play Oneself: Looking Back on Documentary Film*. Minneapolis: University of Minnesota Press, 2011.

Weaver-Hightower, Rebecca, and Peter Hulme, eds. *Postcolonial Film: History, Empire, Resistance*. New York: Routledge, 2014.

Weiler, A. H. "Film: MacLaine in China." *New York Times*, March 13, 1975. https://www.nytimes.com/1975/03/13/archives/film-maclaine-in-china.html.

White, Robert G. *An Atonal Cinema: Resistance, Counterpoint and Dialogue in Transnational Palestine*. New York: Bloomsbury Academic, 2023.

Wolfe, Charles. "Historicizing the 'Voice of God': The Place of Vocal Narration in Classical Documentary." *Film History* 9, no. 2 (1997): 149–67.

Wolin, Richard. *The Wind from the East: French Intellectuals, the Cultural Revolution, and the Legacy of the 1960s*. Princeton, NJ: Princeton University Press, 2010.

Wollen, Peter. *Reading and Writings: Semiotic Counter-Strategies*. London: Verso, 1985.

Xiang, Alice. "'When Ordinary Seeing Fails': Reclaiming the Art of Documentary in Michelangelo Antonioni's 1972 China Film *Chung Kuo*." *Senses of Cinema*, July 5, 2013. http://www.sensesofcinema.com/2013/feature-articles/when-ordinary-seeing-fails-reclaiming-the-art-of-documentary-in-michelangelo-antonionis-1972-china-film-chung-kuo/.

Xiao, Jiwei. "A Traveler's Glance: Antonioni in China." *New Left Review* 79, no. 1 (January/February 2013): 103–20.

Yang, Lin. "L'immaginario della Cina nei reportage di viaggio degli scrittori italiani (1955–1980)." PhD diss., University of Chicago, 2012.

Zavattini, Cesare. *Neorealismo ecc.* Milan: Bompiani, 1979.

Zhang, Yingjin. *Chinese National Cinema*. New York: Routledge, 2004.

Zuelow, Eric G. E. *A History of Modern Tourism*. Basingstoke: Palgrave Macmillan, 2016.

Index

12 dicembre (*December 12*) (Pasolini, 1972), 84

Acland, Charles, 155
Adorno, Theodor W., 84
Africa: Pasolini and, 68–69, 75–76, 86–94, 99–100, 109–10. *See also* postcolonialism and postcolonial theory
Algerian War, 70
Al-Ma'mal Foundation for Contemporary Art (Jerusalem), 99
"Alors, la Chine?" (Barthes), 115
Álvarez, Santiago, 10
Amad, Paula, 128
Amado, Jorge, 49
Amico, Gianni, 20n28; *Appunti per un film sul jazz* (*Notes for a Film on Jazz*, 1965), 95; *Tropici* (*Tropics*, 1968), 94–95
L'amorosa menzogna (*Lies of Love*) (Antonioni, 1949), 138
Anastas, Ayreen: *Pasolini Pa* Palestine* (2005), 16, 98–100, *101*, 102
Andrew, Dudley, 31
Angeli, Franco, 153
Aniene Film, 38

animals: in *India: Matri Bhumi* (Rossellini, 1959), 40, 41–44, *43*, 47–48, 56–57; in *L'India vista da Rossellini* (Rossellini, 1959), 55, 56–57; in Rossellini's early documentaries, 31–33
anti-Chinese propaganda films, 135–36
anticolonialism, 2–8. *See also* solidarity
anticommunist propaganda films, 135
Antonelli, Carlo, 61
Antonioni, Michelangelo: China and, 6. *See also Chung Kuo, Cina* (Antonioni, 1972); documentary films and, 137–39; miniature watercolors and, 141; neorealism and, 137; orientalism and, 122–23, 125–26, 128–35, 154; as traveling auteur, 4–8
Antonioni, Michelangelo—films: *L'amorosa menzogna* (*Lies of Love*, 1949), 138; *Blow-Up* (1966), 141; *Deserto Rosso* (*Red Desert*, 1964), 141; *L'eclisse* (*The Eclipse*, 1962), 127–28; *La funivia del faloria* (*The Funicular of Mount Faloria*, 1950),

INDEX

Antonioni, Michelangelo—films
(*cont.*)
139; *Gente del Po* (*People of the
Po Valley,* 1943–45), 137, 139;
N. U. - Nettezza urbana (1948), 138;
Professione: reporter (*The Passenger,*
1975), 126; *Sette canne, un vestito*
(*Seven Weeds, One Suit,* 1949),
138–39. See also *Chung Kuo, Cina*
(Antonioni, 1972)
Aoula-Syad, Daoud: *Waiting for
Pasolini* (2007), 16, 98, 100–102
Appunti per un film sul jazz (*Notes for a
Film on Jazz*) (Amico, 1965), 95
Appunti per un film sull'India (*Notes for
a Film on India*) (Pasolini, 1968), 51,
75, 77, 92, 96
Appunti per un'Orestiade africana
(*Notes Towards an African Orestes*)
(Pasolini, 1969), 15, 75, 86–94,
89–90, 96, 99–100, 109–10
Appunti per un poema sul Terzo Mondo
(*Notes for a Poem on the Third World*)
(Pasolini, 1968), 76, 82–85, 91
Arab Cinema Travels (Dickinson), 9
Army Film Center (AFC), 28
art cinema: Aoula-Syad and, 100–
101; Pasolini and, 88, 98, 100;
postcolonial world and, 6, 7–8;
Rossellini and, 14–15, 25,
30–31
arte povera, 85
The Art of Cloning (Laikwan), 154
ashramas (stages of life), 40
*Asia Maggiore: Viaggio nella Cina e
altri scritti* (Fortini), 115
Asif, K.: *Mughal-e-Azam* (1960), 29
Askari, Kaveh, 2–3
Astruc, Alexandre, 34
Atelier Collectif de Création, 35
Atti degli Apostoli (Rossellini,
1969), 59

Au Pays des mages noirs (Rouch,
1947), 35
Avoir 20 ans dans les Aurès (*To Be
Twenty in the Aures*) (Vautier,
1972), 85
Awakening Giant: China (Bjerre,
1970), 158n33
Azoulay, Ariella, 12, 18, 78

Badiou, Alain, 149
Baldi, Gian Vittorio, 95
Baldwin, James, 94
I bambini ci guardano (*The Children
Are Watching Us*) (De Sica,
1943), 32
Bandung Conference (Afro–Asian
Conference, 1955), 3, 14, 69–70,
109–10
Ban Wang, 113
Barbaro, Umberto, 116–17
Barbato, Andrea, 129–30, 133, 140
Barbieri, Gato, 94–95
Barker, Jennifer, 159n54
Barthes, Roland, 76, 114–15
The Battle of Algiers (Pontecorvo,
1966), 16, 79
Bazin, André, 31, 33, 46–47
Beauvoir, Simone de, 114, 116
Bellocchio, Marco, 2, 16–17, 163n122;
La Cina è vicina (*China Is Near,*
1967), 150; *Il popolo calabrese
ha rialzato la testa* (*The People of
Calabria Have Raised Their Heads,*
1969), 150–52; *Viva il primo maggio
rosso proletario* (*Long Live the Red
and Proletarian May First,* 1969),
150, *151*, 152–53
Benedetti, Carla, 106n56
Benjamin, Walter, 27
Benvenuti, Giuliana, 115
Bergala, Alain, 36, 41,
58–59

INDEX

Bergman, Ingrid, 34, 58, 61
Berio, Luciano, 145–46, 155
Berlusconi, Silvio, 163n122
Berry, Chris, 159n49
Bertolucci, Bernardo: *L'ultimo
imperatore* (*The Last Emperor*,
1987), 109; *Ultimo tango a Parigi*
(*Last Tango in Paris*, 1972), 94–95,
129; *Videocartolina dalla Cina*
(*Videopostcard from China*, 1985),
109–11, 145
Bertolucci, Giuseppe, 97
Bettetini, Gianfranco, 76
Bhabha, Homi, 12, 21n41, 81, 98
Bhakra Nangal (Thapa, 1958), 45
Bhownagary, Jehangir "Jean," 38
biennio rosso (Two Red Years, 1967–
69), 70
"Birth of a New Avant-Garde: The
Camera as a Pen" (Astruc), 34
Bjerre, Jens: *Awakening Giant: China*
(1970), 158n33
blackness, 97–98
Black Panthers (Varda, 1968), 85
Blasetti, Alessandro: *Europa di notte*
(*European Nights*, 1958), 117
Blow-Up (1966), 141
Bonneau, Pierre: *La reprise du travail
aux usines Wonder* (*The Return to
Work at the Wonder Factory*) (with
Willemont, 1968), 152
Boone, Joseph Allen,
104n28
Borkar brothers, 65n57
Bradley, Harold, 95
Brancati, Vitaliano, 58
Brandirali, Aldo, 163n122
Brecht, Bertolt, 83, 133
Brecht and Method (Jameson), 30
Brennan, Timothy, 21n37
British Sound (Dziga Vertov Group,
1969), 150

Brunatto, Paolo: *Pasolini e . . . "La forma
della città"* (1973), 80, 84, 105n43
Brunette, Peter, 62n4
Buddhism, 47, 55–56
Bull, Lucien, 33
Burton, Richard, 20n31

Cacciaguerra, Maurizio, 163n122
Cahiers du Cinéma (journal), 31, 33–
34, 36, 66n77, 126
Cahill, James Leo, 60, 110–11
caméra-stylo, 34
La canta delle marane (Mangini,
1952), 72
"Can the Subaltern Speak?" (Spivak),
86–87
Caplan, Karen, 13
Carles, Philippe, 94
Carné, Marcel: *Les visiteurs du soir*
(*The Devil's Envoy*, 1942), 137–38
Carolan, Mary Ann McDonald,
157n24
Carrière, Marcel: *Images de Chine*
(*Images of China*, 1974), 119; *Ping
Pong* (1974), 119
Casarino, Cesare, 72–73
Castro, Josué de, 48–49
Cavalcanti, Alberto, 34; *Rien que
l'heur* (*Nothing but the Time*,
1926), 118
Central Newsreel and Documentary
Film Studio, 125
Central Studio for Documentary
Film, 135
Centro Sperimentale di
Cinematografia (Rome), 38
"A Certain Tendency in French
Cinema" (Truffaut), 34
Césair, Aimé, 107n82
César, Filipa, 10; *Spell Reel* (2017), 16
Cesarini Sforza, Marco, 50–57
Chahine, Youssef, 10

190 INDEX

Chakrabarty, Dipesh, 5, 78
Chaplin, Charlie: *The Circus* (1928), 46–47; *The Immigrant* (1917), 66n86
Chatman, Seymour, 122
"Che fare?" ("What Is to Be Done?") (Lenin), 83
Chiesi, Roberto, 105n43
China: Antonioni and, 6. See also *Chung Kuo, Cina* (Antonioni, 1972); Bertolucci and, 109–11, 145; modernization and, 135, 139, 146–48; Moravia and, 115–16; orientalism and, 110–11, 115–16, 117–18, 125–26, 128–35, 154; visual culture and politics in, 112–13, 123–25, 148–49; Western travelers and filmmakers in, 109–11, 114–22
China: The Roots of Madness (Stuart, 1967), 135
"China as Documentary" (Chow), 139
China Is Far Away: Antonioni in China (Liu, 2009), 140–41, 142, 143, 144
Chine (Valet and Roanne, 1971), 121, 145–46
Chinese Cinema (Clark), 160n66
Chinese Documentaries (Chu), 125
Chinois, encore un effort pour être révolutionnaires (*Peking Duck Soup*) (Viénet and Ji, 1977), 150
Chow, Rey, 139
Chu, Yingchi, 125
Chung Kuo, Cina (Antonioni, 1972): afterlives of, 140–41, 142, 143, 144; aftermath and political repercussions of, 111–12; American broadcast (1973) of, 155–56; Chinese reception of, 16, 123, 125, 134–35, 136, 140, 142–43, 144–45, 154–55, 160n75; Italian Maoism and, 16–17, 153–54; orientalism and, 122–23, 125–26, 128–35, 154;

production and structure of, 15–16, 122–23, 128–35, 137, 139–48, *147*
Cina e altri orienti (Manganelli), 116
La Cina è vicina (*China Is Near*) (Bellocchio, 1967), 150
Cinema (journal), 64n43, 138
Cinema nuovo (journal), 33, 37
cinéma vérité: Antonioni and, 134; Bertolucci and, 109; *Comment Yukong déplaça les montagnes* (*How Yukong Moved the Mountains*) (Ivens and Loridan, 1976) and, 121; Pasolini and, 15, 84, 85, 109; Rossellini and, 30–31; Weill and, 132
The Circus (Chaplin, 1928), 46–47
Citti, Sergio, 91
civiltà dei consumi (consumption culture), 80–81
Clark, Paul, 124, 160n66
Cleaver, Eldridge, 3
Clifford, James, 8–9, 30, 36, 95–96, 156
Clouzot, Henri-Georges, 34
Colombo, Furio, 140
colonialism: anticolonialism and, 2–8. See also solidarity; cinema and, 4; Italy and, 4, 126–28. See also postcolonialism and postcolonial theory
Coltrane, John, 94–95
Comandon, Jean, 33
Comizi d'amore (*Love Meetings*) (Pasolini, 1964), 84
Comment Yukong déplaça les montagnes (*How Yukong Moved the Mountains*) (Ivens and Loridan, 1976), 111, 121–22, 144, 149, 160n70, 162n99
commodity fetishism, 113
Comolli, Jean-Louis, 94
comparative ethnography, 79–80

INDEX

Comunione e Liberazione (Community and Liberation), 163n122

La conquista de Mexico (Rivera), 103n8

contemplative cinema, 42

Convention Concerning the Protection of the World Cultural and Natural Heritage (1972), 78

Conversations with Mr. Nehru (Mende), 53, 58

Corriere della Sera (newspaper), 115

cosmopolitanism, 21n37

Costa, Pedro, 42

Cramer, Michael, 30, 59

Culture and Imperialism (Said), 17, 98

Dainotto, Roberto, 26–27

Dalai Lama, 55–56

Dalla Cina: Dopo la rivoluzione culturale (Macciocchi), 116

Dalla Gassa, Marco, 11

Daney, Serge, 47, 126

Daniélou, Alain, 43–44

"La danza del cinese" ("The Dance of the Chinese Man") (Berio), 163n105

Daphne (unfinished) (Rossellini, 1939), 32–33

DasGupta, Sonali Sen Roy, 16, 37–38, 39, 47, 56, 60

Daulatzai, Sohail, 69–70

Debord, Guy, 80, 113

debunking, 66n86

The Decameron (*Il Decameron*) (Pasolini, 1971), 77

decolonization. *See* solidarity

De Franceschi, Leonardo, 18

Deleuze, Gilles, 86

Delli Colli, Tonino, 77

de Martino, Ernesto, 71–72

De Menil family, 67n97

Deng Xiaoping, 110

Deng Yingchao (Madam Zhou Enlai), 120

Derrida, Jacques, 110

De Santis, Giuseppe: *Italiani brava gente* (1964), 21n49

Deserto Rosso (*Red Desert*) (Antonioni, 1964), 141

De Sica, Vittorio: *I bambini ci guardano* (*The Children Are Watching Us*, 1943), 32

détournement, 150

Deutsch, Gustav: *Welt Spiegel Kino* (*World Mirror Cinema*, 2005), 129

Dia, Lam Ibrahim, 35

Di Carlo, Carlo, 153, 154–55

Dickinson, Kay, 9

"Difesa di Rossellini" (Bazin), 33

Di Giammatteo, Fernando, 64n36

Dimanche à Peking (*Sunday in Peking*) (Marker, 1956), 118, 133

The Discovery of India (Nehru), 53, 58

documentary films: in Fascist Italy, 30–32, 137–38; travel and, 8–11. *See also specific directors and films*

Dong Zhaoqi: *Lei Feng* (1965), 148

double exposure, 110–11

Du Bois, W. E. B., 18, 73

I due Foscari (*The Two Foscari*) (Fulchignoni, 1942), 137

Dulac, Germaine, 33

Duncan, Derek, 18

Dziga Vertov Group, 150

L'eclisse (*The Eclipse*) (Antonioni, 1962), 127–28

Eco, Umberto, 76, 83, 146, 153–54

Edipo re (*Oedipus Rex*) (Pasolini, 1967), 75

Eisenstein, Sergei, 34

Eldridge Cleaver, Black Panther (Klein, 1970), 85

Elephant Boy (Flaherty and Korda, 1937), 138

"Empty Spaces: Decolonization in Italy" (Pinkus), 127

L'Esprit (magazine), 118

"Essay as Form" (Adorno), 84

L'età di Cosimo de Medici (Rossellini, 1972–73), 67n96

ethnographic cinema, 30–31, 35–37, 44, 71–73, 79–80, 82, 85. *See also* visual ethnography

ethnography, 29, 79–80, 88

Europa '51 (Europe '51) (Rossellini, 1952), 14, 25, 26, 31, 47–48

Europa di notte (European Nights) (Blasetti, 1958), 117

Fabian, Johannes, 26

Fanon, Frantz, 3, 71, 93

Fantasia sottomarina (Undersea Fantasy) (Rossellini, 1938), 31, 32–33

Farocki, Harun, 96

Fascist Italy: colonialism and, 3, 127–28; documentary films in, 30–32, 137–38

Ferranti, Gastone, 97

Festa, Tano, 153

Festival del Cinema Latino-Americano (Latin American Film Festival) (Santa Margherita Ligure and Sestri Levante), 7

Festival panafricain d'Alger (Klein, 1969), 85

Fico, Enrica, 131, 140–41

Figge, Maja, 28–29, 63n15

Films Division of India, 28, 45–46

Il fiore delle mille e una notte (Arabian Nights) (Pasolini, 1974), 75, 77, 96, 104n28

Fitzpatrick, Merrilyn, 161n84

Flaherty, Robert, 32, 34, 35; *Elephant Boy* (with Korda, 1937), 138

Flaubert, Gustave, 20n31

Fogu, Claudio, 27

Folkstudio jazz club, 95

Food and Agriculture Organization (FAO), 48

Fortini, Franco, 115

Foster, Hal, 30, 82

Francesco, giullare di Dio (The Flowers of Saint Francis) (Rossellini, 1950), 14, 25

Freddi, Luigi, 31

free indirect discourse (*discorso libero indiretto*), 85–86

Free Jazz/ Black Power (Carles and Comolli), 94

Freud, Sigmund, 12

From Mao to Mozart: Isaac Stern in China (Lerner, 1979), 160n73

From the Tricontinental to the Global South (Mahler), 6

Fulchignoni, Enrico, 35; *I due Foscari (The Two Foscari*, 1942), 137

La funivia del faloria (The Funicular of Mount Faloria, a.k.a. *Vertigo)* (Antonioni, 1950), 139

The Gadfly (Voynich), 148–49

Galeazzi, Marco, 103n8

Galimberti, Jacopo, 2–3, 153

Gallagher, Tag, 37, 40, 65n57

Gandhi, Leela, 10

Gandhi, Mohandas Karamchand, 37, 55

García Espinosa, Julio, 10

Garga, B. D., 27–28

Gassman, Vittorio, 106n73

Geertz, Clifford, 36, 95

INDEX

Genet, Jean, 71

Gente del Po (*People of the Po Valley*) (Antonioni, 1943–45), 137, 139

Geography of Hunger (de Castro), 48–49

Germania anno zero (*Germany, Year Zero*) (Rossellini, 1948), 26, 31, 49

Ghatak, Ritwik, 63n20

Ghosh, Bishnupriya, 157n11

Giannarelli, Ansano, 20n28

Il Giorno (newspaper), 116

Giuliani, Gaia, 11, 13, 18, 79

Global South. *See* solidarity

Godard, Jean-Luc, 33, 150; *Letter to Jane* (with Gorin, 1972), 150; *Loin du Vietnam* (*Far from Vietnam*) (with Ivens et al., 1967), 85

Godden, Rumer, 29

Goffredo, Giuseppe, 26–27

Golden River (Pathy, 1954), 45–46

Gomes, Miguel, 10

Gorin, Jean-Pierre: *Letter to Jane* (with Godard, 1972), 150

gradualismo (gradualism), 103n8

Gramsci, Antonio, 3–4, 71, 73

Gravano, Viviana, 22n70

Grechi, Giulia, 22n70

Greene, Shelleen, 18, 92, 93–94

Griffiths, Alison, 13

Grimshaw, Anne, 30

Gruppo '63, 85

Guadagnino, Luca: *Inconscio italiano* (*Italian Unconscious*, 2011), 18

Guangming Daily (newspaper), 136

Guareschi, Giovannino, 97

Guevara, Che, 3

Gunning, Tom, 28–29, 128

Gupta, Hari San, 38

Hai Rui Dismissed from Office, 124

Heath, Stephen, 76

Hemmings, David, 141

Henan Daily (newspaper), 141

heretical orientalism, 70, 96

Herman, Jean (Jean Vautrin), 37–38, 66n76

Hinton, Carma: *Morning Sun* (2003), 148–49

Hirakud Dam, 40, *41*, 44, 45, 55

Hoffman, Marcelo, 152

Holland, Timothy, 110–11

Hom, Stephanie Malia, 18

Hondo, Med, 10

Houcke, Anne-Violaine, 103n18

Hoveyda, Fereydoun, 37

Humphrey, Daniel, 104n28

hunger, 48–49

Un'idea dell'India (An Idea of India) (Moravia), 95–96, 115

Idea di un isola (*Idea of an Island*) (Rossellini, 1967), 30

IDHEC (Institut des hautes études cinématographiques, Paris), 37–38

Ignoti alla città (Mangini, 1958), 72, 103n18

"I Love Beijing Tiananmen" ("Wo ai Beijing Tiananmen") (song), 122–23, 129, 132, 155

Images de Chine (*Images of China*) (Carrière, 1974), 119

The Immigrant (Chaplin, 1917), 66n86

Imperial Eyes (Pratt), 12, 13

Impressions of China (McWilliams, 1976), 118–19

INCOM (Industrie Corto Metraggi), 31

Inconscio italiano (Guadagnino, 2011), 18

India: Marx on, 26; modernization of, 23–29, 42, 44, 45–46, 52–56, 60; Moravia and, 95–96, 115; orientalism and, 24–29, 44–45, 47–48, 50–52, 57, 60; Pasolini and, 28–29, 81–82, 115; postwar filming in, 28–29, 45–46; Rossellini and, 6, 13–15, 16, 23–27, 37, 58–61, 109–10. See also *India: Matri Bhumi* (Rossellini, 1959); *L'India vista da Rossellini* (1959); *J'ai fait un beau voyage* (1959)

India: Matri Bhumi (Rossellini, 1959): animals in, 40, 41–44, *43*, 47–48, 56–57; production of, 23–29; sound and narrator's voice in, 36; structure and episodes of, 13–14, 38–48, 51; writing and production of, 37–38, *39, 41, 43*

India National Congress Party, 24

Indian Films Development (IFD), 38

Indian News Parade (INP), 28

Indian Village (Sucksdorff, 1951), 28

L'India vista da Rossellini (Rossellini, 1959), 13–14, 23–24, 45, 48–57

Das indische Grabmal (*The Indian Tomb*) (Lang, 1958/59), 28–29

Information Films of India (IFI), 28

Intervista a Salvador Allende (*Interview with Salvador Allende*) (Rossellini, 1973), 30

irrealtà (unreality), 80

Istituto LUCE (L'Unione Cinematografica Educativa), 31–32

Italian Communist Party (Partito Comunista Italiano, PCI): China and, 116–18; Pasolini and, 84–85; solidarity and, 3–4, 70–71

Italiani brava gente (De Santis, 1964), 21n49

Italian Socialist Party (Partito Socialista Italiano, PSI), 70

Ivens, Joris, 10, 144; *Comment Yukong déplaça les montagnes* (*How Yukong Moved the Mountains*) (with Loridan, 1976), 111, 121–22, 144, 149, 160n70, 162n99; *Loin du Vietnam* (*Far from Vietnam*) (1967), 85

I Wish I Knew (Jia, 2010), 111–12

Jacopetti, Gualtiero, 10; *Mondo Cane* (*A Dog's World*, 1962), 10, 117

Jaguar (Rouch, 1971), 35–36

J'ai fait un beau voyage (Rossellini, 1959), 13–14, 23–24, 48–50, 57–58

Jaikumar, Priya, 16, 24, 29, 40

Jameson, Fredric, 30

Jarman, Derek, 85

jazz, 94–95

Jiang Qing, 123–25, 161n83

Jia Zhangke: *I Wish I Knew* (2010), 111–12

Ji Qingming: *Chinois, encore un effort pour être révolutionnaires* (*Peking Duck Soup*) (with Viénet, 1977), 150

Julien, Isaac, 96

Jusqu'à la victoire (*Until Victory*) (Dziga Vertov Group, 1970), 150

Kaul, Mani, 60

Kezich, Tullio, 64n36

Khan, Mehboob: *Mother India* (1957), 38

Khandpur, K. L.: *Rivers in Harness* (1949), 45–46

Khrushchev, Nikita, 33

Kiers, Roelof: *Toerist in China* (*Tourists in China*, 1972), 119

King, Homay, 161n85

Kittu (M. V. Krishnaswamy), 38, 47

INDEX

Klein, William, 10, 96; *Eldridge Cleaver, Black Panther* (1970), 85; *Festival panafricain d'Alger* (1969), 85; *Loin du Vietnam* (*Far from Vietnam*) (with Ivens et al., 1967), 85
Koppel, Ted, 155–56
Korda, Zoltan: *Elephant Boy* (with Flaherty, 1937), 138
Kracauer, Siegfried, 66n86
Krishnaswami, M. V. (Kittu), 38, 47

Laikwan, Pang, 131, 154
Lalou, Étienne, 57–58
Landecker, Hannah, 67n98
Lang, Fritz, 27, 28–29; *Das indische Grabmal* (*The Indian Tomb*, 1958/59), 28–29; *Der Tiger von Eschnapur* (*The Tiger of Eschnapur*, 1958), 28–29
The Legend of the Red Lantern (model opera), 142
Lei Feng, 148
Lei Feng (Dong, 1965), 148
Lelouch, Claude: *Loin du Vietnam* (*Far from Vietnam*) (with Ivens et al., 1967), 85
Lenin, Vladimir, 83
Lerner, Murray: *From Mao to Mozart: Isaac Stern in China* (1979), 160n73
Lettera aperta a un giornale della sera (*Open Letter to the Evening News*) (Maselli, 1970), 1–2
Letter to a Chinese Friend (Medvedkin, 1969), 135
Letter to Jane (Godard and Gorin, 1972), 150
Levi, Carlo, 49
Li, Jie, 113, 117, 135
Lichtrequisit, 139
The Life of Wu Xun (Sun Yu, 1950), 124
Liu, Xin, 135

Liu Haiping: *China Is Far Away: Antonioni in China* (2009), 140–41, 142, 143, 144
Liu Weifu: *Seeking Chung Kuo* (2019), 162n94
Lizzani, Carlo, 145–46; *La muraglia cinese* (*Behind the Great Wall*, 1957), 117–18
Lo Giudice, Enzo, 150
Loin du Vietnam (*Far from Vietnam*) (Ivens et al., 1967), 85
Lombardi-Diop, Cristina, 62n11
La longe marche (*The Long March*) (Beauvoir), 114
Lorenz, Pare: *The River* (1938), 138
Loridan, Marceline, 10, 144; *Comment Yukong déplaça les montagnes* (*How Yukong Moved the Mountains*) (with Ivens, 1976), 111, 121–22, 144, 149, 160n70, 162n99
Lost in Translation (King), 161n85
La lotta dell'uomo per la sopravvivenza (*Man's Struggle for Survival*) (Rossellini, 1970), 49
Lotte in Italia (*Struggle in Italy*) (Dziga Vertov Group, 1971), 150
Lovell, Julia, 114
A Love Supreme (Coltrane), 94–95
Lui (magazine), 114

Macciocchi, Maria Antonietta, 116
MacDougall, David, 30
MacLaine, Shirley, 111; *The Other Half of the Sky: A China Memoir* (with Weill, 1975), 119–21, 132–33
Ma Dongsheng, 142
Magnani, Anna, 61
Mahler, Anne Garland, 6, 79
Maldoror, Sarah, 10
Malle, Louis, 10, 28–29
Manganelli, Giorgio, 116, 160n76

INDEX

Mangini, Cecilia, 72; *La canta delle marane* (1952), 72; *Ignoti alla città* (1958), 72, 103n18; *Stendalì* (1960), 72

Maoism, 16–17, 113–15, 149–54

Mao Zedong, 110, 123–24, 131

Mao Zedong Thoughts Opens the Forbidden Zones for the Deaf and Mute (newsreel, 1971), 131

Maraini, Dacia, 115

Maraschin, Donatella, 72

Marey, Étienne-Jules, 33

Mariniello, Silvestra, 97, 106n72

Marker, Chris, 10, 19n6, 37, 85; *Dimanche à Peking (Sunday in Peking*, 1956), 118, 133; *Loin du Vietnam (Far from Vietnam)* (with Ivens et al., 1967), 85

Marx, Karl, 26

Marxism: de Castro and, 48; Pasolini and, 6, 15, 71, 83–85, 95–96

Maselli, Citto: *Lettera aperta a un giornale della sera (Open Letter to the Evening News*, 1970), 1–2

McWilliams, Don: *Impressions of China* (1976), 118–19

Medea (Pasolini, 1969), 87

Medvedkin, Alexander: *Letter to a Chinese Friend* (1969), 135; *Night over China* (1971), 135–36

Mekas, Jonas, 84

Melio, Marcello, 94–95

Mende, Tibor, 53, 58

Il messia (The Messiah) (Rossellini, 1975), 59

Mestman, Mariano, 4

Metz, Christian, 76

Mezzadra, Sandro, 17, 69

Miccichè, Lino, 7

Middle East, 98–100; Pasolini and, 76–81, 82–83

Mignolo, Walter, 26

Militant Acts (Hoffman), 152

militant orientalism, 2–3

Mirzoeff, Nicholas, 73, 74–75, 106n46

modernism: Pasolini and, 72, 85; Rossellini and, 30–31

modernity and modernization: Antonioni and, 127–28, 135, 139, 146–48; China and, 135, 139, 146–48; India and, 23–29, 42, 44, 45–46, 52–56, 60; Pasolini and, 73, 76, 77–78, 79–81; in postwar Italy, 5–6, 79–81; Rossellini and, 23–27, 42, 52–56, 60

Moholy-Nagy, László, 139

Moi un noir (Rouch, 1958), 35, 36

Le Monde (newspaper), 115

Mondo cane (A Dog's World) (Jacopetti et al., 1962), 10, 117

Mondo films, 10–11

Mondo Libero (newsreel), 97

"Montage interdit" (Bazin), 46–47, 66n77

Morante, Elsa, 81, 115

Moravia, Alberto, 81, 95–96, 115–16

Morning Sun (Hinton, 2003), 148–49

Moro, Margherita, 38

Morte e pianto rituale nel mondo antico (De Martino), 72

Mostra Internazionale del Cinema Libero in Porretta Terme (Porretta Terme Free Cinema Festival), 7

Mostra Internazionale del Nuovo Cinema (Pesaro), 7

Mother India (Khan, 1957), 38

Mouzourane, Tallou, 35

Moye, Don, 94–95

Moynagh, Maureen, 9–10

Mughal-e-Azam (Asif, 1960), 29

Le mura di Sana'a (The Walls of Sana'a) (Pasolini, 1971), 15, 75, 77–81

INDEX

La muraglia cinese (*Behind the Great Wall*) (Lizzani, 1957), 117–18
Murray, Yvonne, 94
"Museums as Contact Zones" (Clifford), 8–9

Nagib, Lucia, 7
Naples, 26, 27, 58
La nave bianca (*The White Ship*) (Rossellini, 1941), 32
Nehru, Jawaharlal: de Castro and, 49; modernization of India and, 23–29, 44, 45–46, 55–56; Rossellini and, 14, 16, 37, 49–50, 53, 55–56, 58, 66n87
neorealism: Antonioni and, 137; Lizzani and, 117; postcolonial world and, 7–8; Rossellini and, 14, 25–26, 29–31, 33, 47, 61
New York Times (newspaper), 157n30
Nicholson, Jack, 126
Night over China (Medvedkin, 1971), 135–36
Nixon, Richard, 132, 156
Non-Aligned Movement (NAM), 3, 5, 6–7, 70, 109–10
"Notes on Globalization and Ambivalence" (Bhabha), 98
N. U. - Nettezza urbana (1948), 138

Octobre à Paris (*October in Paris*) (Panijel, 1962), 85
O'Healy, Áine, 18
O'Leary, Alan, 10–11, 79
Omegna, Roberto, 33
On Human Diversity (Todorov), 9
Onorati, Marino, 64n36
opera, 123–24
Opera aperta (Eco), 83

Organization of Solidarity with the People of Asia, Africa and Latin America (OSPAAAL), 6
orientalism: Antonioni and, 122–23, 125–26, 128–35, 154; China and, 110–11, 115–16, 117–18, 122–23, 125–26, 128–35, 154; India and, 24–29; as "militant" (Galimberti), 2–3; Moravia and, 115–16; Pasolini and, 70, 75–76, 79, 88–96, 125–26; Rossellini and, 24–27, 44–45, 47–48, 50–52, 57, 60, 125–26; Said on, 9, 11–13, 17, 20n31, 26–27, 98, 112, 117; travel essay films and, 8–9
Orientalism (Said), 11–12, 13, 20n31, 26–27
oriental sublime, 24
Orsini, Valentino, 20n28
Osborne, Richard, 28
Ossessione (*Obsession*) (Visconti, 1943), 32
The Other Half of the Sky: A China Memoir (MacLaine and Weill, 1975), 119–21, 132–33

Padgaonkar, Dileep, 38, 47, 59–60, 65n59
Il padre selvaggio (*The Savage Father*) (Pasolini, 1975), 75
Painlevé, Jean, 32–33
Paisan (*Paisà*) (Rossellini, 1946), 31
Palestine, 82–83, 98–100
Pallavicini, Sandro, 31
Pallotta, Giorgio, 140
Panijel, Jacques: *Octobre à Paris* (*October in Paris*, 1962), 85
"Paradosso sulla fotogenia della Cina di Mao" ("Paradox on the *photogenie* of Mao's China") (Barbaro), 116–17
participatory ethnography, 88

198   INDEX

Pasolini, Pier Paolo: in Africa and the Middle East, 15, 68–69, 75–81, 82–83, 86–94, 98–100, 109–10; blackness and, 97–98; contemporary responses to, 16, 98–102; in India, 28–29, 81–82, 115; literature of decolonization and, 71; Moravia and, 115; orientalism and, 70, 75, 79, 88–96, 125–26; Rossellini and, 66n87; semiotic counter-strategies and, 73–76; sexualization of black and brown bodies and, 13; solidarity and, 68–73, 79–80, 88–96; as traveling auteur, 4–8

Pasolini, Pier Paolo—films: *12 dicembre* (*December 12*, 1972), 84; *Appunti per un film sull'India* (*Notes for a Film on India*, 1968), 51, 75, 77, 92, 96; *Appunti per un'Orestiade africana* (*Notes Towards an African Orestes*, 1969), 15, 75, 86–94, 89–90, 96, 99–100, 109–10; *Appunti per un poema sul Terzo Mondo* (*Notes for a Poem on the Third World*, 1968), 76, 82–85, 91; *Comizi d'amore* (*Love Meetings*, 1964), 84; *The Decameron* (*Il Decameron*, 1971), 77; *Edipo re* (*Oedipus Rex*, 1967), 75; *Il fiore delle mille e una notte* (*Arabian Nights*, 1974), 75, 77, 96, 104n28; *Medea* (1969), 87; *Le mura di Sana'a* (*The Walls of Sana'a*, 1971), 15, 75, 77–81; *Il padre selvaggio* (*The Savage Father*, 1975), 75; *La rabbia* (*Anger*, 1963), 75, 84, 96–98; *Sopralluoghi in Palestina per il Vangelo secondo Matteo* (*Location Scouting in Palestine*, 1964), 15, 75, 82, 99–100; *Teorema* (1968), 85

Pasolini, Pier Paolo—writings: "Apologia" (Apology), 71; *La Divina*

Mimesis, 106n56; *Gramsci's Ashes*, 71; *Heretical Empiricism*, 81, 86; *Letteratura negra* (Black literature), 93; *Lettere luterane* (*Lutheran Letters*), 74–75; "Il PCI ai giovani" (Poem to young communist students), 71, 102n6; *Petrolio*, 106n56; "Profezia" ("Prophecy"), 68–69, 70; *Ragazzi di vita* (*The Ragazzi*, 1955), 75; *La resistenza negra* (The Black resistance), 93; "Sviluppo e progresso" ("Development and Progress"), 81; "L'uomo di Bandung" (Bandung Man), 22n61; *Una vita violenta* (*A Violent Life*, 1959), 75

Pasolini e . . . "La forma della città" (Brunatto, 1973), 80, 84, 105n43

Pasolini Pa* Palestine (Anastas, 2005), 16, 98–100, *101*, 102

Pathy, Pittamandalam Venktatachalapathy: *Golden River* (1954), 45–46

Patriarca, Silvana, 18

Peretti, Luca, 4, 18

personal camera mode, 14, 24

"Per un film sul fiume Po" ("For a Film on the River Po") (Antonioni), 138

Petri, Elio, 2

Peuple en marche (Vautier, 1963), 85

Pezzini, Isabella, 47

Piano, Renzo, 67n97

Un pilota ritorna (*A Pilot Returns*) (Rossellini, 1942), 32, 137

Ping Pong (Carrière, 1974), 119

Pinkus, Karen, 127

Pirelli, Giovanni, 71

political travelers, 9–10

Polo, Marco, 130, 134

Pontecorvo, Gillo, 2, 10, 20n28; *The Battle of Algiers* (1966), 16, 79

INDEX 199

Ponzanesi, Sandra, 18
Il popolo calabrese ha rialzato la testa
  (*The People of Calabria Have Raised*
  Their Heads) (Bellocchio, 1969),
  150–52
postcolonial condition, 17
postcolonialism and postcolonial
  theory: anticolonialism and, 2–8;
  Italian academia and, 127; Pasolini
  and, 70, 73–76; travel cinema and,
  8–11; uncanny and, 11–13, 24–25.
  See also Bandung Conference
  (Afro–Asian Conference, 1955);
  orientalism; solidarity
postmodernity, 84–85
Potential History: Unlearning
  Imperialism (Azoulay), 12
Pratt, Mary Louise, 8–9, 12
Pravda (Dziga Vertov Group, 1969),
  150
The Predicament of Culture (Clifford),
  95–96
La prise de pouvoir par Louis XIV
  (*The Taking of Power by Louis XIV*)
  (Rossellini, 1966), 30
Pro Civitate Christiana, 82
Professione: reporter (*The Passenger*)
  (Antonioni, 1975), 126
Prosperi, Franco, 10
Provincializing Europe (Chakrabarty), 78
Puyi, 109

Quaderni piacentini (journal), 115
Quaresima, Leonardo, 139
Qu'est-ce que le cinéma? (Bazin), 66n77
A Question of People (Rossellini,
  1974), 49
Questions of Travel (Caplan), 13

La rabbia (*Anger*) (Pasolini, 1963), 75,
  84, 96–98

Rabinow, Paul, 95
Rahola, Federico, 17, 69
Raizen, Karen T., 94
Rancière, Jacques, 83, 106n52
Rascaroli, Laura, 14, 22n60, 24,
  64n43, 85
Ravetz, Amanda, 30
Red Flag Canal (documentary, 1970),
  140, 141–42, *143*, 148
"Le réel et l'imaginaire" (Bazin),
  66n77
reflexivity, 95–96
relay, 2–3
Renmin Ribao (*People's Daily*)
  (newspaper), 123, 124, 125, 134–35,
  136, 140, 142–43, 154, 160n75
Renoir, Jean, 10, 27, 28–29, 35, 38; *The*
  River (1956), 29, 54
La reprise du travail aux usines Wonder
  (*The Return to Work at the Wonder*
  Factory) (Willemont and Bonneau,
  1968), 152
Resnais, Alain, 37; *Loin du Vietnam*
  (*Far from Vietnam*) (with Ivens et al.,
  1967), 85
Restivo, Angelo, 128
Return to the Real (Foster), 82
reverse ethnography, 29
revolutionary pedagogy, 83–84
Rien que l'heur (*Nothing but the Time*)
  (Cavalcanti, 1926), 118
The Right to Look (Mirzoeff), 74–75
Rinaldi, Giuseppe, 129
Rinascita (journal), 103n8
Ripa di Meana, Carlo, 153
Rive Gauche group, 37
The River (Lorenz, 1938), 138
The River (Renoir, 1956), 29, 54
Rivera, Diego, 103n8
Rivers in Harness (Khandpur, 1949),
  45–46

INDEX

Rivette, Jacques, 33–34

La rivoluzione culturale in Cina ovvero il Convitato di pietra (Moravia), 115–16

Roanne, Henri: *Chine* (with Valet, 1971), 121, 145–46

Rocha, Glauber, 48

Rome, Open City (Rossellini, 1945), 14, 25, 31, 47

Romeo, Caterina, 62n11

Rony, Fatimah Tobing, 13, 30

Rosaldo, Renato, 95

Rose, Les: *Thunderbirds in China* (1974), 157n27

Rosi, Francesco, 2

Ross, Kristin, 2, 152

Rossellini, Franco, 77

Rossellini, Renzo, 38, 49, 61

Rossellini, Roberto: Das Gupta and, 16, 37–38, 39, 60; documentaries and, 29–33; documentary films and, 29–33; India Project and, 6, 13–15, 16, 23–27, 37, 58–61, 109–10. See also *India: Matri Bhumi* (Rossellini, 1959); *L'India vista da Rossellini* (1959); *J'ai fait un beau voyage* (1959); made-for-television historical dramas and, 30–31, 59; narrative themes in filmography by, 25; neorealism and, 14, 25–26, 29–31, 33, 47, 61; orientalism and, 24–27, 44–45, 47–48, 50–52, 57, 60, 125–26; Rouch and, 30–31, 35–37; as traveling auteur, 4–8

Rossellini, Roberto—films: *Atti degli Apostoli* (1969), 59; *Daphne* (unfinished, 1939), 32–33; *L'età di Cosimo de Medici* (1972–73), 67n96; *Europa '51* (*Europe '51*, 1952), 14, 25, 26, 31, 47–48; *Fantasia sottomarina* (*Undersea Fantasy*, 1938), 31, 32–33; *Francesco, giullare di Dio* (*The Flowers of Saint Francis*, 1950), 14, 25;

Germania anno zero (*Germany, Year Zero*, 1948), 26, 31, 49; *Idea di un isola* (*Idea of an Island*, 1967), 30; *L'India vista da Rossellini* (1959), 13–14, 23–24, 45, 48–57; *Intervista a Salvador Allende* (*Interview with Salvador Allende*, 1973), 30; *J'ai fait un beau voyage* (1959), 13–14, 23–24, 48–50, 57–58; *La lotta dell'uomo per la sopravvivenza* (*Man's Struggle for Survival*, 1970), 49; *Il messia* (*The Messiah*, 1975), 59; *La nave bianca* (*The White Ship*, 1941), 32; *Paisan* (*Paisà*, 1946), 31; *Un pilota ritorna* (*A Pilot Returns*, 1942), 32, 137; *La prise de pouvoir par Louis XIV* (*The Taking of Power by Louis XIV*, 1966), 30; *A Question of People* (1974), 49; *Rome, Open City* (1945), 14, 25, 31, 47; *Il ruscello di Ripa Sottile* (*The Brook of Ripasottile*, 1940), 32–33; *Socrates* (1971), 59; *Stromboli* (1950), 14, 25, 31, 35, 42, 47–48; *Il tacchino prepotente* (*The Bullying Turkey*, 1940), 32–33; *L'uomo dalla croce* (*The Man with a Cross*, 1943), 32; *La vispa Teresa* (*Lively Teresa*, 1940), 32–33. See also *India: Matri Bhumi* (Rossellini, 1959); *Voyage to Italy* (Rossellini, 1954)

Rouch, Jean, 30–31, 35–37, 88; *Au Pays des mages noirs* (1947), 35; *Jaguar* (1971), 35–36; *Moi un noir* (1958), 35, 36

Il ruscello di Ripasottile (*The Brook of Ripasottile*) (Rossellini, 1940), 32–33

Russell, Catherine, 30

Said, Edward, 9, 11–13, 17, 20n31, 26–27, 98, 112, 117

Salazkina, Masha, 5

Salgari, Emilio, 50

INDEX

Salut le cubain (Varda, 1963), 85
Sand, George, 34
San Diego Film, 61
Sartre, Jean-Paul, 1, 3, 68–69, 71
Savage, Archie, 94
Schifano, Mario, 153
Scola, Ettore, 2
Seeking Chung Kuo (Liu and Zhu, 2019), 162n94
Sembène, Ousmane, 65n54
semiotic counter-strategies, 73–76
Sen, Amartya, 48
Senghor, Leopold, 107n82
Senso (Visconti, 1954), 33
Servire il popolo (newspaper), 149–50, 152, 153
Sette canne, un vestito (*Seven Weeds, One Suit*) (Antonioni, 1949), 138–39
Shadoud, Suhail, 99, 100
Shahani, Kumar, 60
Shanghai New Wind (Ushiyama, 1978), 160n73
The Shanghai Wenhui Daily (newspaper), 124
Shklovsky, Victor, 106n73
shockumentaries, 10–11
sineciosi, 95
sinistra extraparlamentare (extraparliamentary Left), 71
Sironi, Mario, 139
Sissako, Abderrahmane, 16, 98
Situationist International, 80
société du spectacle, 80
Socrates (Rossellini, 1971), 59
solidarity: Italian intelligentsia and, 1–11, 70–71; Pasolini and, 68–73, 79–80, 88–96; political and travel cinema and, 1–11, 101–2
Sopralluoghi in Palestina per il Vangelo secondo Matteo (*Location Scouting in Palestine*) (Pasolini, 1964), 15, 75, 82, 99–100

Sorace, Christian, 136
sound: in *Chung Kuo, Cina* (Antonioni, 1972), 155; in *Images de Chine* (*Images of China*) (Carrière, 1974), 119; in *India: Matri Bhumi* (Rossellini, 1959), 36, 41, 43–44, 48; in *J'ai fait un beau voyage* (Rossellini, 1959), 57; in Pasolini's films, 94; in *Stendalì* (Mangini, 1960), 72
Soviet Union, 70, 135–36
Spagnulo, Pino, 153
Spell Reel (César, 2017), 16
Spivak, Gayatri, 86–87
Srivastava, Neelam, 3, 4, 18, 71
Steimatsky, Noa, 138, 139, 146
Stendalì (Mangini, 1960), 72
Stoler, Ann Laura, 4
Stromboli (Rossellini, 1950), 14, 25, 31, 35, 42, 47–48
Stuart, Mel: *China: The Roots of Madness* (1967), 135
Sucksdorff, Arne: *Indian Village* (1951), 28; *The Wind and the River* (1953), 28
Sud e magia (De Martino), 72
Sukhdev, S.: *A Village Smiles* (1974), 66n74
Sun Yu: *The Life of Wu Xun* (1950), 124

Il tacchino prepotente (*The Bullying Turkey*) (Rossellini, 1940), 32–33
Tagore, Rabindranath, 38, 56, 81
Taking Tiger Mountain by Strategy (Xie, 1970), 159n49
Tannous, Karam, 99
Tattoli, Elda, 163n122
television: Antonioni and. See *Chung Kuo, Cina* (Antonioni, 1972); Astruc on, 34; Rossellini and, 30–31, 48–59, 61. See also *L'India vista da Rossellini* (1959); *J'ai fait un beau voyage* (1959)

Tel Quel (journal), 115
tempi morti (dead-time scenes, waiting scenes), 42
Il tempo (newspaper), 81
temporality, 26, 27, 99, 110
Teorema (1968), 85
Thapa, N. S.: *Bhakra Nangal* (1958), 45
thick description, 36
The Third Eye (Rony), 13
Third World. *See* solidarity
three prominences, 124–25, 161n83
Thunderbirds in China (Les Rose, 1974), 157n27
Tiananmen Square massacre (1989), 110
Tian Yongchang, 140
Der Tiger von Eschnapur (*The Tiger of Eschnapur*) (Lang, 1958), 28–29
Time and the Other (Fabian), 26
Todorov, Tzvetan, 9
Toerist in China (*Tourists in China*) (Kiers, 1972), 119
Togliatti, Palmiro, 103n8
Tonti, Aldo, 43–44, 48
Torri, Bruno, 7
Tout va bien (Dziga Vertov Group, 1972), 150
Tovoli, Luciano, 140, 144
Tranchant, François, 26
transitional figures, 2–3
travel and travel cinema, 8–11. *See also* specific directors and films
"Traveling Theory" (Said), 9, 112
Trento, Giovanna, 71, 103n10
Tricontinental (Cuban journal), 6
Tricontinental Conference (Cuba, 1966), 3
Trinh T. Minh-ha, 10, 96
Tropici (*Tropics*) (Amico, 1968), 94–95
Truffaut, François, 33, 34, 36

UCG (Union Générale Cinématographique), 38

L'ultimo imperatore (*The Last Emperor*) (Bertolucci, 1987), 109
Ultimo tango a Parigi (*Last Tango in Paris*) (Bertolucci, 1972), 94–95, 129
uncanny, 11–13, 24–25
Under Her Spell (Padgaonkar), 38, 59–60, 65n59
UNESCO (United Nations Educational, Scientific and Cultural Organization), 77, 78
"Die Unheimlich" (Freud), 12
unhomeliness, 12
Unione dei Comunisti Italiani, 149–53
L'uomo dalla croce (*The Man with a Cross*) (Rossellini, 1943), 32
"L'uomo di Bandung" (Bandung Man) (Pasolini), 22n61
useful cinema, 155
Ushiyama, Junichi: *Shanghai New Wind* (1978), 160n73
Utopian Ruins (Li), 113

Vaidya, Prem, 38
Valet, Gérard: *Chine* (with Roanne, 1971), 121, 145–46
Varda, Agnès, 10, 37, 84; *Black Panthers* (1968), 85; *Loin du Vietnam* (*Far from Vietnam*) (with Ivens et al., 1967), 85; *Salut le cubain* (1963), 85
"Varshavianka" (song), 95
Vautier, René, 10; *Avoir 20 ans dans les Aurès* (*To Be Twenty in the Aures*, 1972), 85; *Peuple en marche* (1963), 85
Vautrin, Jean (Jean Herman), 37–38, 66n76
Vazquez-Arroyo, Antonio, 84
Le Vent d'est (Dziga Vertov Group, 1969), 150
Verdi, Giuseppe, 137
Vérité, Jean-Marie, 26

INDEX

Videocartolina dalla Cina (*Videopostcard from China*) (Bertolucci, 1985), 109–11, 145

Viénet, Rene: *Chinois, encore un effort pour être révolutionnaires* (*Peking Duck Soup*) (with Ji, 1977), 150

Vie nuove (weekly), 50

A Village Smiles (Sukhdev, 1974), 66n74

Visconti, Luchino: *Ossessione* (*Obsession*, 1943), 32; *Senso* (1954), 33

Les visiteurs du soir (*The Devil's Envoy*) (Carné, 1942), 137–38

La vispa Teresa (*Lively Teresa*) (Rossellini, 1940), 32–33

visual ethnography, 30–31, 35–37, 72, 88. *See also* ethnographic cinema

Vitti, Monica, 127

Viva il primo maggio rosso proletario (*Long Live the Red and Proletarian May First*) (Bellocchio, 1969), 150, 151, 152–53

Vladimir et Rosa (*Vladimir and Rosa*) (Dziga Vertov Group, 1971), 150

Voyage to Italy (Rossellini, 1954): dissection of love and relationships in, 14, 25; *L'India vista da Rossellini* (1959) and, 52; Kittu and, 65n59; Naples in, 58; neorealism and, 31; reception of, 33–34; *The River* (Renoir, 1956) and, 29

Voynich, Ethel, 148–49

waiting, 42

Waiting for Pasolini (Aoula-Syad, 2007), 16, 98, 100–102

Wasson, Haidee, 155

Watt, Harry: *Where No Vultures Fly* (1951), 46–47

Waugh, Tom, 120, 132, 144, 159n53

Weerasethakul, Apichatpong, 42

Weill, Claudia: *The Other Half of the Sky: A China Memoir* (with MacLaine, 1975), 119–21, 132–33

Welt Spiegel Kino (*World Mirror Cinema*) (Deutsch, 2005), 129

Wertmüller, Lina, 2

Wham! (pop band), 110

Where No Vultures Fly (Watt, 1951), 46–47

Willemont, Jacques: *La reprise du travail aux usines Wonder* (*The Return to Work at the Wonder Factory*) (with Bonneau, 1968), 152

The Wind and the River (Sucksdorff, 1953), 28

"Wo ai Beijing Tiananmen" ("I Love Beijing Tiananmen") (song), 122–23, 129, 132, 155

Wondrous Difference (Griffiths), 13

World Cinema, 5, 7, 101–2

World Heritage Sites, 78

Xiao Jiwei, 130

Xie Tieli: *Taking Tiger Mountain by Strategy* (1970), 159n49

Yellow Earth (Zhang, 1984), 110

Yemen, 76–81

Zaina, Haissam, 99

Zavattini, Cesare, 64n43

Zhang Yimou: *Yellow Earth* (1984), 110

Zhou Enlai, 113, 123

Zhu Qiansheng, 111–12

Zhu Yun: *Seeking Chung Kuo* (2019), 162n94

Zika, Damouré, 35

zones of contact, 8–9

Luca Caminati is Professor of Film and Moving Image Studies at Concordia University, Montreal. He is author of three monographs in Italian and editor (with James Leo Cahill) of *Cinema of Exploration: Essays on an Adventurous Film Practice*.

For Indiana University Press
Tony Brewer, Artist and Book Designer
Allison Chaplin, Acquisitions Editor
Sophia Hebert, Assistant Acquisitions Editor
Samantha Heffner, Marketing and Publicity Manager
Brenna Hosman, Production Coordinator
Katie Huggins, Production Manager
Nancy Lightfoot, Project Editor and Manager
Dan Pyle, Online Publishing Manager
Pamela Rude, Senior Artist and Book Designer